PREFACE

This book is a collection of essays, all but one of which have appeared previously. While none of the pieces is reprinted verbatim, most of them appear here with only minor changes. To improve continuity and readability, I have, wherever possible, eliminated redundancies; and to insure uniformity of style, I have recast the references in a format more appropriate for this edition. Two selections, "Involuntary Mental Hospitalization: A Crime Against Humanity" and "Mental Health Services in the School," were first published in much shorter versions and appear here for the first time in their original, full-length form; a third, "Psychiatry, the State, and the University," has not been published before.

I thank the editors and publishers of the journals and books in which these pieces first appeared for opening their pages to me and for granting permission for this republication; my colleagues, Dr. Seth Many and Dr. Shirley Rubert, for wise suggestions concerning the Introduction; Mrs. Andrea Bottstein of the Doubleday Anchor staff for assistance with the selection and editing of the essays for publication in book form; and my secretary, Mrs. Margaret Bassett, for her customarily devoted help in connection with every phase of this work.

Thomas S. Szasz

Syracuse, New York
February 1, 1969

IDEOLOGY AND INSANITY

ESSAYS ON THE
PSYCHIATRIC DEHUMANIZATION OF MAN

THOMAS S. SZASZ, M.D.

MARION BOYARS

LONDON

NEW YORK

First published in 1973 by
Calder and Boyars Ltd
Reprinted in 1983 by
MARION BOYARS Ltd
18 Brewer Street, London W1R 4AS

Distributed in Australia and New Zealand by
Thomas C. Lothian Pty
8-12 Tattersalls Lane
Melbourne, Victoria 3000

© Thomas S. Szasz 1970, 1973, 1983

British Library Cataloguing in Publication Data
Szasz, Thomas
  Ideology and insanity.
  1. Psychiatry
  I. Title
  616.89   RC454

ISBN 0 7145 1054 8 paper

IDEOLOGY AND INSANITY

Grateful acknowledgment is made to the following sources for permission to use the articles that appear in this volume in adapted form:

"The Myth of Mental Illness." Adapted from "The Myth of Mental Illness," *The American Psychologist*, 15:113–18 (Feb.), 1960; copyright © 1960 by the American Psychological Association; reprinted by permission.

"The Mental Health Ethic." From *Ethics and Society*, edited by Richard T. DeGeorge. Copyright © 1966 by Kansas University Endowment Association; reprinted by permission of Doubleday & Company, Inc.

"The Rhetoric of Rejection." Adapted from "The Uses of Naming and the Origin of the Myth of Mental Illness," *The American Psychologist*, 16:59–65 (Feb.), 1961; copyright © 1961 by the American Psychological Association; reprinted by permission.

"Mental Health as Ideology." Adapted from "Psychiatry as Ideology," in Hawton, H., ed., *The Rationalist Annual for the Year 1965* (London: The Pemberton Publishing Co. Ltd., 1965), pp. 43–52; copyright © 1965 by The Pemberton Publishing Co. Ltd.; reprinted by permission.

"What Psychiatry Can and Cannot Do." Adapted from "What Psychiatry Can and Cannot Do," copyright © 1964, by Harper's Magazine, Inc.; reprinted from the February 1964 issue of *Harper's Magazine* by permission of the author.

"Bootlegging Humanistic Values Through Psychiatry." Adapted from "Bootlegging Humanistic Values Through Psychiatry," *The Antioch Review*, 22:341–49 (Fall), 1962; copyright © 1962 by The Antioch Press; reprinted by permission.

"The Insanity Plea and the Insanity Verdict." Adapted from "The Insanity Plea and the Insanity Verdict," *Temple Law Quarterly*, 40:271–82 (Spring–Summer), 1967; copyright © 1967 by Temple University; reprinted by permission.

"Involuntary Mental Hospitalization: A Crime Against Humanity." Adapted from "Science and Public Policy: The Crime of Involuntary Mental Hospitalization," *Medical Opinion and Review*, 4:24–35 (May), 1968; reprinted by permission.

"Mental Health Services in the School." Adapted from "The Psychiatrist: A Policeman in the Schools," *This Magazine is About Schools*, October 1967, pp. 114–34; copyright © 1967 by *This Magazine is About Schools;* reprinted by permission.

"Psychiatric Classification as a Strategy of Personal Constraint." Adapted from "The Psychiatric Classification of Behavior: A Strategy of Personal Constraint," in Leonard D. Eron, ed., *The Classification of Behavior Disorders* (Chicago: Aldine Publishing Co., 1966), pp. 123–70; copyright © 1966 by Leonard D. Eron; reprinted by permission.

"Whither Psychiatry?" Adapted from "Whither Psychiatry?" *Social Research*, 33:439–62 (Autumn), 1966; copyright © 1966 by The New School for Social Research; reprinted by permission.

CONTENTS

1 · INTRODUCTION

Among the many foolish things Rousseau said, one of the most foolish, and most famous, is: "Man is born free, and yet everywhere he is in chains." This high-flown phrase obscures the nature of freedom. For if freedom is the ability to make uncoerced choices, then man is born in chains. And the challenge of life is liberation.

A person's ability to make uncoerced choices is contingent on his internal and external conditions. His internal conditions, that is, his character, personality, or "mind"—comprising his aspirations and desires as well as his aversions and self-discipline—propel him toward, and restrain him from, various actions. His external conditions, that is, his biological makeup and his physical and social environment—comprising the capabilities of his body, and the climate, culture, laws, and technology of his society—stimulate him to act in some ways, and inhibit him from acting in others. These conditions shape and define the extent and quality of a person's options. In general, the more control man gains over his internal and external conditions, the more free he becomes; whereas, if he fails to gain such control, he remains enslaved, or, if, having gained it, he loses it, he becomes enslaved.

There is, however, an important limitation to man's freedom—namely, the freedom of other men. The external conditions man seeks to control include other people and social institutions, forming a complex net of mutual interactions and interdependencies. Often, a person can enlarge his range of uncoerced choices only by reducing that of his fellow man. This is true even if man aspires only to self-control and leaves others in peace: his self-discipline will render it more difficult, if not impossible, for others to control and dominate him. Worse still, if man aspires to control his fellows, *his* freedom entails *their* slavery. The limitless maximization of uncoerced choices for all is clearly impossible. Thus it is that individual liberty has always been, and is likely to remain, a hard-won prize, requiring a delicate balance between self-assertion sufficient to safeguard personal autonomy, and self-control sufficient to protect the autonomy of others.

Man is born in chains, the innocent and helpless victim of internal passions and external controls that shape and possess him. Personal development, then, is a process of individual liberation, in which self-control and self-direction supplant internal anarchy and external constraint. Hence, the prerequisites of individual liberty are not only freedom from arbitrary political and interpersonal control, mastery of the technical complexities of sophisticated artifacts, and self-assertion and self-confidence sufficient for the development and display of one's creative potentialities, but also, and more important still, self-discipline.

The dialectical interplay of the opposing tendencies or themes of freedom and slavery, liberation and oppression, competence and incompetence, responsibility and license, order and chaos, so essential to the growth, life, and death of the individual, is transformed, in psychiatry and allied fields, into the opposing tendencies or themes of "maturity" and "immaturity," "independence" and "dependence," "mental health" and "mental illness," and "sanity" and "insanity." I believe all these psychiatric terms are inadequate and unsatisfactory, for each neglects, or deflects attention from, the essentially *moral* and *political* character of human development and social existence. The language of psychiatry thus de-ethicizes and depoliticizes human relations and personal conduct. In much of my work I have sought to undo this by restoring ethics and politics to their rightful places in matters of so-called mental health and mental illness. In short, I have tried to re-ethicize and repoliticize the language of psychiatry.

Although the essays assembled in this volume were written over a period of about ten years, each is concerned with some aspect of the same problem—namely, the relation between ideology and insanity, as reflected in the theory and practice of psychiatry. The results of this inquiry have, I believe, a two-fold significance: they define the moral dilemmas of the contemporary mental health professional, and, at the same time, illuminate the fundamental political problem of our age, or, perhaps, of the human condition itself.

My approach to psychiatry as essentially a moral and political enterprise led me to reappraise numerous situations in which this perspective appeared most promising of new insights —such as education, law, the control of conception and of drug abuse, politics, and, of course, pyschiatry itself. In each instance, I tried to show that, on the one hand, by seeking relief from the burden of his moral responsibilities, man mystifies and technicizes his problems in living; and that, on the other hand, the demand for "help" thus generated is now met by a behavioral technology ready and willing to free man of his moral burdens by treating him as a sick patient. This human need and the professional-technical response to it form a self-sustaining cycle, resembling what the nuclear physicist calls a breeder reaction; once initiated and having reached a "critical" stage, the process feeds on itself, transforming more and more human problems and situations into specialized technical "problems" to be "solved" by so-called mental health professionals.

This process, which began in the seventeenth century and progressed apace in the eighteenth, went "critical"—becoming explosive—in the second half of the nineteenth century. Since that time, psychiatry (together with its sister disciplines, psychoanalysis and psychology) has laid claims to progressively larger areas of personal conduct and social relations.

II

The conquest of human existence, or of the life process, by the mental health professions started with the identification and classification of so-called mental illnesses, and has culminated in our day with the claim that all of life is a "psychiatric problem" for behavioral science to "solve." According to psychiatry's most prominent spokesmen, this process is now complete. For example, Howard P. Rome, senior consultant in psychiatry at the Mayo Clinic and former president of the American Psychiatric Association, confidently asserts, "Actually, no less than the entire world is a proper catchment area for present-day psychiatry, and psychiatry need not be appalled by the magnitude of this task."[1]

Like all invasions, the invasion of man's journey through life by psychiatry began at the borderlands of his existence and then extended gradually into the interior. The first to succumb were what we have come to regard as the "obvious" or "severe" cases of mental illness"—that is, so-called conversion hysteria and the psychoses—which, although now unquestioningly accepted as psychiatric maladies, belonged formerly to literature, mythology, and religion.

This psychiatric take-over was supported and spurred by the logic, the imagery, and the rhetoric of science, and especially medicine. Thus, who could object to the claim that the person who acted as if he were sick but really wasn't should be called a "hysteric," and should be declared a fit subject for the ministrations of neuropsychiatric physicians? Was this not simply an advance of medical science, similar to its advances in bacteriology or surgery? Likewise, who could object if other "deranged persons"—for example, those who withdrew from the challenge of real life into their self-created dramatic productions, or who, dissatisfied with their real identities, asserted false ones—were claimed for psychiatry as "schizophrenics" and "paranoids"?

After the turn of the century, and especially following each of the two world wars, the pace of this psychiatric conquest increased rapidly. The result is that, today, particularly in the affluent West, all of the difficulties and problems of living are considered psychiatric diseases, and everyone (but the diagnosticians) is considered mentally ill. Indeed, it is no exaggeration to say that life itself is now viewed as an illness that begins with conception and ends with death, requiring, at every step along the way, the skillful assistance of physicians and, especially, mental health professionals.

[1] Rome, H. P.: "Psychiatry and foreign affairs: The expanding competence of psychiatry." *Amer. J. Psychiatry*, 125:725–30 (Dec.), 1968, p. 729.

The discerning reader may detect a faint note of familiarity here. Modern psychiatric ideology is an adaptation—to a scientific age—of the traditional ideology of Christian theology. Instead of being born into sin, man is born into sickness. Instead of life being a vale of tears, it is a vale of diseases. And, as in his journey from the cradle to the grave man was formerly guided by the priest, so now he is guided by the physician. In short, whereas in the Age of Faith the ideology was Christian, the technology clerical, and the expert priestly; in the Age of Madness the ideology is medical, the technology clinical, and the expert psychiatric.

Actually, this medicalization and psychiatrization—and, more generally, this technicization—of personal, social, and political affairs is, as has often been remarked, a pervasive characteristic of the modern, bureaucratic age. What I have sought to capture here, in a few sentences—and, at greater length, in the essays that make up this volume—is but one feature, albeit an important one, of this modern, scientific-technological ideology, namely, the ideology of sanity and insanity, of mental health and mental illness.

As I suggested earlier, this ideology is but an old trap in new trappings. Rulers have always conspired against their subjects and sought to keep them in bondage; and, to achieve their aims, they have always relied on force and fraud. Indeed, when the justificatory rhetoric with which the oppressor conceals and misrepresents his true aims and methods is most effective—as had been the case formerly with tyranny justified by theology, and is the case now with tyranny justified by therapy—the oppressor succeeds not only in subduing his victim but also in robbing him of a vocabulary for articulating his victimization, thus making him a captive deprived of all means of escape.

The ideology of insanity has achieved precisely this result in our day. It has succeeded in depriving vast numbers of people —sometimes it seems very nearly everyone—of a vocabulary of their own in which to frame their predicament without paying homage to a psychiatric perspective that diminishes man as a person and oppresses him as a citizen.

III

Like all ideologies, the ideology of insanity—communicated through the scientistic jargon of psychiatric "diagnoses," "prognoses," and "treatments," and embodied in the bureaucratic system of institutional psychiatry and its concentration camps called "mental hospitals"—finds its characteristic expression in what it opposes: commitment to an officially forbidden image or definition of "reality." The people we call "mad" have, for better or worse, taken a stand on the really significant issues of everyday life. In doing so they may be right or wrong, wise or stupid, saintly or sinful—but at least they are not neutral. The madman does not murmur timidly that he does not know who he is, as the "neurotic" might; instead, he asserts confidently that he is the Saviour or the discoverer of a formula for world peace. Similarly, the madwoman does not accept with resignation the insignificant identity of a domestic slave, as her "normal" counterpart might; instead, she proclaims proudly that she is the Holy Virgin or the victim of a dastardly plot against her by her husband.

How does the psychiatrist confront the so-called mental patient or those incriminated as mentally ill? How does he respond to their claims, and to the claims of those who, because of their relationship to the patient, have an interest in his condition? Ostensibly, the psychiatrist behaves as the medical scientist he claims to be is supposed to behave—by remaining "dispassionate" and "neutral" with respect to the "mental diseases" he "diagnoses" and tries to "cure." But what if these "diseases" are, as I claim, largely human conflicts and the products of such conflicts? How can an expert help his fellow man in conflict and remain aloof from the conflict? The answer is that he can't. Thus, while ostensibly acting as neutral scientists, psychiatrists are actually the partisan advocates of one party to a conflict and the opponents of another. As a rule, when the psychiatrist is faced with minor ethical and social conflicts, such as "neurotic patients" often present, he actually supports the patient's self-defined interests (and opposes the interests of those with whom the patient is in conflict); whereas, when the psychiatrist is faced with major ethical and social conflicts, such as "psychotic patients" often present, he actually opposes the patient's self-defined interests (and supports the interests of those with whom the patient is in conflict). However—and this is the point I wish to emphasize here—in both instances psychiatrists habitually conceal and mystify their partisanship behind a cloak of therapeutic neutrality, never admitting to being either the patient's ally or his adversary. Instead of friend or foe, the psychiatrist claims to be doctor and scientist. Instead of defining his intervention as helping or harming, liberating or oppressing the "patient," the psychiatrist insists on defining it as "diagnosing" and "treating mental illness." Precisely herein, I submit, lie the contemporary psychiatrist's moral failure and technical incompetence.

The following statements, chosen almost at random from contemporary psychiatric sources, illustrate the deliberate demoralization and technicization of ethical problems, thus justifying their psychiatric "management." "Since the psychiatrist, *from a scientific point of view,* must regard all behavior—criminal and law-abiding, healthy and sick—as determined," writes Edward J. Sachar, Associate Professor of Psychiatry at the Albert Einstein College of Medicine in New York City, "he finds the issue of moral condemnation of the individual to be inappropriate. . . . Just as the functions of the sick body and the healthy body proceed in accordance with the laws of physiology, so sick and healthy minds function in accordance with the laws of psychology. . . . [T]he finding that someone is criminally responsible means to the psychiatrist that the criminal *must* change his behavior before he can resume his position in society. This injunction is dictated *not by morality* but, so to speak, *by reality*" (italics added).[2]

Similarly, experiments carried out at Clinton Prison, in Dannemora, New York, by Ernest G. Poser, an associate professor

[2] Sachar, E. J.: "Behavioral science and the criminal law." *Scientific American,* 209:39–45 (Nov.), 1963, p. 41.

in the departments of Psychology and Psychiatry at McGill University in Montreal, supported by a grant from Governor Rockefeller's Committee on Criminal Offenders, are described as promising to ". . . help us reach a point some day where the decision whether a person will be put behind bars will be based on the chances of his committing another crime, and *not his guilt or innocence*" (italics added).[3]

Karl Menninger, the dean of American psychiatrists, has preached this gospel for more than forty years. In his latest book, revealingly titled *The Crime of Punishment*, he writes: "The word *justice* irritates scientists. No surgeon expects to be asked if an operation for cancer is just or not. . . . Behavioral scientists regard it as equally absurd to invoke the question of justice in deciding what to do with a woman who cannot resist her propensity to shoplift, or with a man who cannot repress an impulse to assault somebody."[4]

Crime is thus no longer a problem of law and morals, but is instead a problem of medicine and therapeutics. This transformation of the ethical into the technical—of crime into illness, law into medicine, penology into psychiatry, and punishment into therapy—is, moreover, enthusiastically embraced by many physicians, social scientists, and lay persons. For example, in a review of *The Crime of Punishment* in *The New York Times*, Roger Jellinek declares, "As Dr. Menninger proves so searingly, criminals are surely ill, not evil."[5]

"Criminals are surely ill . . . ," say the "behavioral scientists" and their followers. Punishers are criminals, adds Menninger. We are thus asked to believe that the illegal acts of criminals are the symptoms of mental illness, and the legal acts of law enforcers are crimes. If so, the punishers are themselves criminals, and hence they too are "ill, not evil." Here we catch the

[3] Burnham, D.: "Convicts treated by drug therapy." *The New York Times*, December 8, 1968, p. 17.

[4] Menninger, K.: *The Crime of Punishment* (New York: Viking, 1968), p. 17.

[5] Jellinek, R. M.: "Revenger's tragedy." *The New York Times*, December 27, 1968, p. 31.

ideologist of insanity at his favorite activity—the manufacture of madness.[6]

"Criminals are surely ill. . . ." Think of it! And remember that anyone convicted of law breaking is, by definition, a criminal: not only the hired killer, but also the physician who performs an illegal abortion; not only the armed robber, but also the businessman who cheats on his income tax; not only the arsonist and the thief, but also the gambler and the manufacturer, seller, and often the consumer of prohibited drugs (alcohol during Prohibition, marijuana now). Criminals all! Not evil; and certainly not good; just mentally sick—every one of them without exception. But remember: it must always be *them*—never *us!*

In short, then, whereas the so-called madman is one who characteristically *commits* himself, the psychiatrist is one who characteristically remains *uncommitted*. Then, claiming a false neutrality toward the issues at hand, he *excludes* the madman and his troublesome claims from society. (Interestingly, the procedure by which this exclusion is accomplished is also called "commitment.")

IV

Because psychiatrists avoid taking a forthright and responsible stand on the problems they deal with, the major intellectual and moral predicaments of psychiatry remain unacknowledged and unexamined. These may be stated succinctly in the form of a series of questions posing fundamental choices about the nature, scope, methods, and values of psychiatry.

1. Is the scope of psychiatry the study and treatment of medical conditions, or the study and influencing of social performances? In other words, are psychiatry's objects of inquiry diseases or roles, happenings or actions?

2. Is the aim of psychiatry the study of human behavior, or the control of human (mis)behavior? In other words, is the goal

[6] Szasz, T. S.: *The Manufacture of Madness: A Comparative Study of the Inquisition and the Mental Health Movement* (New York: Harper & Row, to be published in 1970).

of psychiatry the advancement of knowledge, or the regulation of (mis)conduct?

3. Is the method of psychiatry the exchange of communications, or the administration of diagnostic tests and curative treatments? In other words, what does psychiatric practice actually consist of—listening and talking, or prescribing drugs, operating on the brain, and imprisoning persons labeled as "mentally ill"?

4. Finally, is the guiding value of psychiatry individualism or collectivism? In other words, does psychiatry aspire to be the servant of the individual or of the state?

Contemporary psychiatry is characterized by systematically hedging on all these questions. Almost any journal article or book by an accepted psychiatric authority illustrates this assertion. Two brief examples should suffice here.

In the article cited earlier, Sachar explicitly rejects the view that the psychiatrist is a party to a conflict. He writes: "For whose sake does the psychiatrist attempt to change the criminal? For the criminal's sake or for society's? For the sake of both, he would argue, just as the physician, confronted with a case of smallpox, thinks immediately of saving the patient as well as protecting the community."[7]

In an essay devoted to the defense of the idea that "mental illness" is a disease, Roy R. Grinker, Sr., the director of the Institute for Psychosomatic and Psychiatric Research and Training of Michael Reese Hospital and Medical Center in Chicago, writes: "The truly medical model is one in which psychotherapy is only a part. The total field in terms of therapy includes . . . the choice of therapeutic environment, such as home, clinic, or hospital; the choice of therapy, such as drugs, shock, and psychotherapy. . . ."[8] Grinker speaks of "choice" and yet remains discreetly, and strategically, silent about all the questions I have listed above. He does not say *who* chooses the "therapeutic environment" or the "therapy"—the patient, the patient's relatives,

[7] Sachar, op. cit., pp. 41–42.

[8] Grinker, R. R., Sr.: "Emerging concepts of mental illness and models of treatment: The medical point of view." *Amer. J. Psychiatry,* 125:865–69 (Jan.), 1969, p. 866.

the psychiatrist, the judge, the legislator. Nor does he say *what happens* when the "patient" chooses not to be a patient at all, or when the psychiatrist recommends mental hospitalization and the patient refuses to comply.

These omissions are not fortuitous. On the contrary, they constitute, as I shall try to show in the essays that follow, the very essence of present-day "scientific" psychiatry. The mandate of the contemporary psychiatrist—that is, of the professionally loyal "dynamic" or "progressive" psychiatrist—is precisely to obscure, and indeed to deny, the ethical dilemmas of life, and to transform these into medicalized and technicalized problems susceptible to "professional" solutions.

In short, I shall try to show that the claims and practices of modern psychiatry dehumanize man by denying—on the basis of spurious scientific reasoning—the existence, or even the possibility, of personal responsibility. But the concept of personal responsibility is central to the concept of man as moral agent. Without it, individual freedom, Western man's most cherished value, becomes a "denial of reality," a veritable "psychotic delusion" to endow man with a grandeur he does not in fact possess. Clearly, then, psychiatry is not simply a "medical healing art"— the phrase behind which, with false modesty, many of its practitioners now like to hide their actual practices; instead, it is an ideology and a technology for the radical remaking of man.

2 · THE MYTH OF MENTAL ILLNESS

At the core of virtually all contemporary psychiatric theories and practices lies the concept of mental illness. A critical examination of this concept is therefore indispensable for understanding the ideas, institutions, and interventions of psychiatrists.

My aim in this essay is to ask if there is such a thing as mental illness, and to argue that there is not. Of course, mental illness is not a thing or physical object; hence it can exist only in the same sort of way as do other theoretical concepts. Yet, to those who believe in them, familiar theories are likely to appear, sooner or later, as "objective truths" or "facts." During certain historical periods, explanatory concepts such as deities, witches, and instincts appeared not only as theories but as *self-evident causes* of a vast number of events. Today mental illness is widely regarded in a similar fashion, that is, as the cause of innumerable diverse happenings.

As an antidote to the complacent use of the notion of mental illness—as a self-evident phenomenon, theory, or cause—let us ask: What is meant when it is asserted that someone is mentally ill? In this essay I shall describe the main uses of the concept of mental illness, and I shall argue that this notion has outlived whatever cognitive usefulness it might have had and that it now functions as a myth.

II

The notion of mental illness derives its main support from such phenomena as syphilis of the brain or delirious conditions —intoxications, for instance—in which persons may manifest certain disorders of thinking and behavior. Correctly speaking, however, these are diseases of the brain, not of the mind. According to one school of thought, *all* so-called mental illness is of this type. The assumption is made that some neurological defect, perhaps a very subtle one, will ultimately be found to explain all the disorders of thinking and behavior. Many contemporary physicians, psychiatrists, and other scientists hold this view, which implies that people's troubles cannot be caused by conflicting personal needs, opinions, social aspirations, values, and so forth. These difficulties—which I think we may simply call *problems in living*—are thus attributed to physicochemical processes that in due time will be discovered (and no doubt corrected) by medical research.

Mental illnesses are thus regarded as basically similar to other diseases. The only difference, in this view, between mental and bodily disease is that the former, affecting the brain, manifests itself by means of mental symptoms; whereas the latter, affecting other organ systems—for example, the skin, liver, and so on—manifests itself by means of symptoms referable to those parts of the body.

In my opinion, this view is based on two fundamental errors. In the first place, a disease of the brain, analogous to a disease of the skin or bone, is a neurological defect, not a problem in living. For example, a *defect* in a person's visual field may be explained by correlating it with certain lesions in the nervous system. On the other hand, a person's *belief*—whether it be in Christianity, in Communism, or in the idea that his internal organs are rotting and that his body is already dead—cannot be explained by a defect or disease of the nervous system. Explanations of this sort of occurrence—assuming that one is interested in the belief itself and does not regard it simply as a symptom or expression of something else that is more interesting —must be sought along different lines.

The second error is epistemological. It consists of interpreting communications about ourselves and the world around us as symptoms of neurological functioning. This is an error not in observation or reasoning, but rather in the organization and expression of knowledge. In the present case, the error lies in making a dualism between mental and physical symptoms, a dualism that is a habit of speech and not the result of known observations. Let us see if this is so.

In medical practice, when we speak of physical disturbances we mean either signs (for example, fever) or symptoms (for example, pain). We speak of mental symptoms, on the other hand, when we refer to a patient's communications about himself, others, and the world about him. The patient might assert that he is Napoleon or that he is being persecuted by the Communists. These would be considered mental symptoms only if the observer believed that the patient was *not* Napoleon or that he was *not* being persecuted by the Communists. This makes it apparent that the statement "X is a mental symptom" involves rendering a judgment that entails a covert comparison between the patient's ideas, concepts, or beliefs and those of the observer and the society in which they live. The notion of mental symptom is therefore inextricably tied to the social, and particularly the ethical, context in which it is made, just as the notion of bodily symptom is tied to an anatomical and genetic context.[1]

To sum up: For those who regard mental symptoms as signs of brain disease, the concept of mental illness is unnecessary and misleading. If they mean that people so labeled suffer from diseases of the brain, it would seem better, for the sake of clarity, to say that and not something else.

III

The term "mental illness" is also widely used to describe something quite different from a disease of the brain. Many people today take it for granted that living is an arduous affair. Its hardship for modern man derives, moreover, not so much from a struggle for biological survival as from the stresses and strains inherent in the social intercourse of complex human personalities. In this context, the notion of mental illness is used to identify or describe some feature of an individual's so-called personality. Mental illness—as a deformity of the personality, so to speak—is then regarded as the cause of human disharmony. It

[1] See Szasz, T. S.: *Pain and Pleasure: A Study of Bodily Feelings* (New York: Basic Books, 1957), especially pp. 70–81; "The problem of psychiatric nosology." *Amer. J. Psychiatry*, 114:405–13 (Nov.), 1957.

is implicit in this view that social intercourse between people is regarded as something inherently harmonious, its disturbance being due solely to the presence of "mental illness" in many people. Clearly, this is faulty reasoning, for it makes the abstraction "mental illness" into a cause of, even though this abstraction was originally created to serve only as a shorthand expression for, certain types of human behavior. It now becomes necessary to ask: What kinds of behavior are regarded as indicative of mental illness, and by whom?

The concept of illness, whether bodily or mental, implies deviation from some clearly defined norm. In the case of physical illness, the norm is the structural and functional integrity of the human body. Thus, although the desirability of physical health, as such, is an ethical value, what health is can be stated in anatomical and physiological terms. What is the norm, deviation from which is regarded as mental illness? This question cannot be easily answered. But whatever this norm may be, we can be certain of only one thing: namely, that it must be stated in terms of psychosocial, ethical, and legal concepts. For example, notions such as "excessive repression" and "acting out an unconsious impulse" illustrate the use of psychological concepts for judging so-called mental health and illness. The idea that chronic hostility, vengefulness, or divorce are indicative of mental illness is an illustration of the use of ethical norms (that is, the desirability of love, kindness, and a stable marriage relationship). Finally, the widespread psychiatric opinion that only a mentally ill person would commit homicide illustrates the use of a legal concept as a norm of mental health. In short, when one speaks of mental illness, the norm from which deviation is measured is a *psychosocial and ethical* standard. Yet, the remedy is sought in terms of *medical* measures that—it is hoped and assumed—are free from wide differences of ethical value. The definition of the disorder and the terms in which its remedy are sought are therefore at serious odds with one another. The practical significance of this covert conflict between the alleged nature of the defect and the actual remedy can hardly be exaggerated.

Having identified the norms used for measuring deviations in cases of mental illness, we shall now turn to the question, Who defines the norms and hence the deviation? Two basic answers may be offered: First, it may be the person himself—that is, the patient—who decides that he deviates from a norm; for example, an artist may believe that he suffers from a work inhibition; and he may implement this conclusion by seeking help *for himself* from a psychotherapist. Second, it may be someone other than the "patient" who decides that the latter is deviant—for example, relatives, physicians, legal authorities, society generally; a psychiatrist may then be hired by persons other than the "patient" to do something *to him* in order to correct the deviation.

These considerations underscore the importance of asking the question, Whose agent is the psychiatrist? and of giving a candid answer to it. The psychiatrist (or non-medical mental health worker) may be the agent of the patient, the relatives, the school, the military services, a business organization, a court of law, and so forth. In speaking of the psychiatrist as the agent of these persons or organizations, it is not implied that his moral values, or his ideas and aims concerning the proper nature of remedial action, must coincide exactly with those of his employer. For example, a patient in individual psychotherapy may believe that his salvation lies in a new marriage; his psychotherapist need not share this hypothesis. As the patient's agent, however, he must not resort to social or legal force to prevent the patient from putting his beliefs into action. If his *contract* is with the patient, the psychiatrist (psychotherapist) may disagree with him or stop his treatment, but he cannot engage others to obstruct the patient's aspirations.[2] Similarly, if a psychiatrist is retained by a court to determine the sanity of an offender, he need not fully share the legal authorities' values and intentions in regard to the criminal, nor the means deemed appropriate for dealing with him; such a psychiatrist cannot testify, however, that the accused is not insane, but that the legislators are—for

[2] See Szasz, T. S.: *The Ethics of Psychoanalysis: The Theory and Method of Autonomous Psychotherapy* (New York: Basic Books, 1965).

passing the law that decrees the offender's actions illegal.[3] This sort of opinion could be voiced, of course—but not in a courtroom, and not by a psychiatrist who is there to assist the court in performing its daily work.

To recapitulate: In contemporary social usage, the finding of mental illness is made by establishing a deviance in behavior from certain psychosocial, ethical, or legal norms. The judgment may be made, as in medicine, by the patient, the physician (psychiatrist), or others. Remedial action, finally, tends to be sought in a therapeutic—or covertly medical—framework. This creates a situation in which it is claimed that psychosocial, ethical, and legal deviations can be corrected by medical action. Since medical interventions are designed to remedy only medical problems, it is logically absurd to expect that they will help solve problems whose very existence have been defined and established on non-medical grounds.

IV

Anything that people *do*—in contrast to things that *happen* to them[4]—takes place in a context of value. Hence, no human activity is devoid of moral implications. When the values underlying certain activities are widely shared, those who participate in their pursuit often lose sight of them altogether. The discipline of medicine—both as a pure science (for example, research) and as an applied science or technology (for example, therapy)—contains many ethical considerations and judgments. Unfortunately, these are often denied, minimized, or obscured, for the ideal of the medical profession as well as of the people whom it serves is to have an ostensibly value-free system of medical care. This sentimental notion is expressed by such things as the doctor's willingness to treat patients regardless of their religious or political beliefs. But such claims only serve to

[3] See Szasz, T. S.: *Law, Liberty, and Psychiatry: An Inquiry into the Social Uses of Mental Health Practices* (New York: Macmillan, 1963).

[4] Peters, R. S.: *The Concept of Motivation* (London: Routledge & Kegan Paul, 1958), especially pp. 12–15.

obscure the fact that ethical considerations encompass a vast range of human affairs. Making medical practice neutral with respect to some specific issues of moral value (such as race or sex) need not mean, and indeed does not mean, that it can be kept free from others (such as control over pregnancy or regulation of sex relations). Thus, birth control, abortion, homosexuality, suicide, and euthanasia continue to pose major problems in medical ethics.

Psychiatry is much more intimately related to problems of ethics than is medicine in general. I use the word "psychiatry" here to refer to the contemporary discipline concerned with problems in living, and not with diseases of the brain, which belong to neurology. Difficulties in human relations can be analyzed, interpreted, and given meaning only within specific social and ethical contexts. Accordingly, the psychiatrist's socio-ethical orientations will influence his ideas on what is wrong with the patient, on what deserves comment or interpretation, in what directions change might be desirable, and so forth. Even in medicine proper, these factors play a role, as illustrated by the divergent orientations that physicians, depending on their religious affiliations, have toward such things as birth control and therapeutic abortion. Can anyone really believe that a psychotherapist's ideas on religion, politics, and related issues play no role in his practical work? If, on the other hand, they do matter, what are we to infer from it? Does it not seem reasonable that perhaps we ought to have different psychiatric therapies—each recognized for the ethical positions that it embodies—for, say, Catholics and Jews, religious persons and atheists, democrats and Communists, white supremacists and Negroes, and so on? Indeed, if we look at the way psychiatry is actually practiced today, especially in the United States, we find that the psychiatric interventions people seek and receive depend more on their socioeconomic status and moral beliefs than on the "mental illnesses" from which they ostensibly suffer.[5] This fact should occasion no greater surprise than that practicing Catho-

[5] Hollingshead, A. B. and Redlich, F. C.: *Social Class and Mental Illness* (New York: Wiley, 1958).

lics rarely frequent birth-control clinics, or that Christian Scientists rarely consult psychoanalysts.

V

The position outlined above, according to which contemporary psychotherapists deal with problems in living, not with mental illnesses and their cures, stands in sharp opposition to the currently prevalent position, according to which psychiatrists treat mental diseases, which are just as "real" and "objective" as bodily diseases. I submit that the holders of the latter view have no evidence whatever to justify their claim, which is actually a kind of psychiatric propaganda: their aim is to create in the popular mind a confident belief that mental illness is some sort of disease entity, like an infection or a malignancy. If this were true, one could *catch* or *get* a mental illness, one might *have* or *harbor* it, one might *transmit* it to others, and finally one could *get rid* of it. Not only is there not a shred of evidence to support this idea, but, on the contrary, all the evidence is the other way and supports the view that what people now call mental illnesses are, for the most part, *communications* expressing unacceptable ideas, often framed in an unusual idiom.

This is not the place to consider in detail the similarities and differences between bodily and mental illnesses. It should suffice to emphasize that whereas the term "bodily illness" refers to physicochemical occurrences that are not affected by being made public, the term "mental illness" refers to sociopsychological events that are crucially affected by being made public. The psychiatrist thus cannot, and does not, stand apart from the person he observes, as the pathologist can and often does. The psychiatrist is committed to some picture of what he considers reality, and to what he thinks society considers reality, and he observes and judges the patient's behavior in the light of these beliefs. The very notion of "mental symptom" or "mental illness" thus implies a covert comparison, and often conflict, between observer and observed, psychiatrist and patient. Though obvious, this fact needs to be re-emphasized, if one wishes, as I do here, to counter the prevailing tendency to deny the moral aspects of psychiatry and to substitute for them allegedly value-free medical concepts and interventions.

Psychotherapy is thus widely practiced as though it entailed nothing other than restoring the patient from a state of mental sickness to one of mental health. While it is generally accepted that mental illness has something to do with man's social or interpersonal relations, it is paradoxically maintained that problems of values—that is, of ethics—do not arise in this process. Freud himself went so far as to assert: "I consider ethics to be taken for granted. Actually I have never done a mean thing."[6] This is an astounding thing to say, especially for someone who had studied man as a social being as deeply as Freud had. I mention it here to show how the notion of "illness"—in the case of psychoanalysis, "psychopathology," or "mental illness"—was used by Freud, and by most of his followers, as a means of classifying certain types of human behavior as falling within the scope of medicine, and hence, by fiat, outside that of ethics. Nevertheless, the stubborn fact remains that, in a sense, much of psychotherapy revolves around nothing other than the elucidation and weighing of goals and values—many of which may be mutually contradictory—and the means whereby they might best be harmonized, realized, or relinquished.

Because the range of human values and of the methods by which they may be attained is so vast, and because many such ends and means are persistently unacknowledged, conflicts among values are the main source of conflicts in human relations. Indeed, to say that human relations at all levels—from mother to child, through husband and wife, to nation and nation—are fraught with stress, strain, and disharmony is, once again, to make the obvious explicit. Yet, what may be obvious may be also poorly understood. This, I think, is the case here. For it seems to me that in our scientific theories of behavior we have failed to accept the simple fact that human relations are inherently fraught with difficulties, and to make them even relatively harmonious requires much patience and hard work. I sub-

[6] Quoted in Jones, E.: *The Life and Work of Sigmund Freud* (New York: Basic Books, 1957), Vol. III, p. 247.

mit that the idea of mental illness is now being put to work to obscure certain difficulties that at present may be inherent—not that they need to be unmodifiable—in the social intercourse of persons. If this is true, the concept functions as a disguise: instead of calling attention to conflicting human needs, aspirations, and values, the concept of mental illness provides an amoral and impersonal "thing"—an "illness"—as an explanation for problems in living. We may recall in this connection that not so long ago it was devils and witches that were held responsible for man's problems in living. The belief in mental illness, as something other than man's trouble in getting along with his fellow man, is the proper heir to the belief in demonology and witchcraft. Mental illness thus exists or is "real" in exactly the same sense in which witches existed or were "real."

VI

While I maintain that mental illnesses do not exist, I obviously do not imply or mean that the social and psychological occurrences to which this label is attached also do not exist. Like the personal and social troubles that people had in the Middle Ages, contemporary human problems are real enough. It is the labels we give them that concern me, and, having labeled them, what we do about them. The demonologic concept of problems in living gave rise to therapy along theological lines. Today, a belief in mental illness implies—nay, requires—therapy along medical or psychotherapeutic lines.

I do not here propose to offer a new conception of "psychiatric illness" or a new form of "therapy." My aim is more modest and yet also more ambitious. It is to suggest that the phenomena now called mental illnesses be looked at afresh and more simply, that they be removed from the category of illnesses, and that they be regarded as the expressions of man's struggle with *the problem of how he should live*. This problem is obviously a vast one, its enormity reflecting not only man's inability to cope with his environment, but even more his increasing self-reflectiveness.

By problems in living, then, I refer to that explosive chain reaction that began with man's fall from divine grace by partaking of the fruit of the tree of knowledge. Man's awareness of himself and of the world about him seems to be a steadily expanding one, bringing in its wake an ever larger *burden of understanding.*[7] This burden is to be expected and must not be misinterpreted. Our only rational means for easing it is more understanding, and appropriate action based on such understanding. The main alternative lies in acting as though the burden were not what in fact we perceive it to be, and taking refuge in an outmoded theological view of man. In such a view, man does not fashion his life and much of his world about him, but merely lives out his fate in a world created by superior beings. This may logically lead to pleading non-responsibility in the face of seemingly unfathomable problems and insurmountable difficulties. Yet, if man fails to take increasing responsibility for his actions, individually as well as collectively, it seems unlikely that some higher power or being would assume this task and carry this burden for him. Moreover, this seems hardly a propitious time in human history for obscuring the issue of man's responsibility for his actions by hiding it behind the skirt of an all-explaining conception of mental illness.

VII

I have tried to show that the notion of mental illness has outlived whatever usefulness it may have had and that it now functions as a myth. As such, it is a true heir to religious myths in general, and to the belief in witchcraft in particular. It was the function of these belief-systems to act as social tranquilizers, fostering hope that mastery of certain problems may be achieved by means of substitutive, symbolic-magical, operations. The concept of mental illness thus serves mainly to obscure the everyday fact that life for most people is a continuous struggle, not for biological survival, but for a "place in the sun," "peace of mind,"

[7] In this connection, see Langer, S. K.: *Philosophy in a New Key* [1942] (New York: Mentor Books, 1953), especially Chap. 5 and 10.

or some other meaning or value. Once the needs of preserving the ~~body, and~~ perhaps of the race, are satisfied, man faces the problem of personal significance: What should he do with himself? For what should he live? Sustained adherence to the myth of mental illness allows people to avoid facing this problem, believing that mental health, conceived as the absence of mental illness, automatically insures the making of right and safe choices in the conduct of life. But the facts are all the other way. It is the making of wise choices in life that people regard, retrospectively, as evidence of good mental health!

When I assert that mental illness is a myth, I am not saying that personal unhappiness and socially deviant behavior do not exist; what I am saying is that we categorize them as diseases at our own peril.

The expression "mental illness" is a metaphor that we have come to mistake for a fact. We call people physically ill when their body-functioning violates certain anatomical and physiological norms; similarly, we call people mentally ill when their personal conduct violates certain ethical, political, and social norms. This explains why many historical figures, from Jesus to Castro, and from Job to Hitler, have been diagnosed as suffering from this or that psychiatric malady.

Finally, the myth of mental illness encourages us to believe in its logical corollary: that social intercourse would be harmonious, satisfying, and the secure basis of a good life were it not for the disrupting influences of mental illness, or psychopathology. However, universal human happiness, in this form at least, is but another example of a wishful fantasy. I believe that human happiness, or well-being, is possible—not just for a select few, but on a scale hitherto unimaginable. But this can be achieved only if many men, not just a few, are willing and able to confront frankly, and tackle courageously, their ethical, personal, and social conflicts. This means having the courage and integrity to forego waging battles on false fronts, finding solutions for substitute problems—for instance, fighting the battle of stomach acid and chronic fatigue instead of facing up to a marital conflict.

Our adversaries are not demons, witches, fate, or mental illness. We have no enemy that we can fight, exorcise, or dispel by "cure." What we do have are problems in living—whether these be biologic, economic, political, or sociopsychological. In this essay I was concerned only with problems belonging in the last-mentioned category, and within this group mainly with those pertaining to moral values. The field to which modern psychiatry addresses itself is vast, and I made no effort to encompass it all. My argument was limited to the proposition that mental illness is a myth, whose function it is to disguise and thus render more palatable the bitter pill of moral conflicts in human relations.

3 · THE MENTAL HEALTH ETHIC

Let us begin with some definitions. According to *Webster's Third New International Dictionary* (unabridged), ethics is "the discipline dealing with what is good and bad or right and wrong or with moral duty and obligation . . ."; it is also "a group of moral principles or set of values . . ." and "the principles of conduct governing an individual or a profession: standards of behavior. . . ."

Ethics is thus a distinctly human affair. There are "principles of conduct" governing individuals and groups, but there are no such principles governing the behavior of animals, machines, or stars. Indeed, the word "conduct" implies this: only persons *conduct* themselves; animals *behave*, machines *function*, and stars *move*.

Is it too much to say, then, that any human behavior that constitutes conduct—which, in other words, is a product of choice or potential choice, and not simply of a reflex—is, *ipso facto*, moral conduct? In all such conduct, considerations of good and bad, or right and wrong, play a role. Logically, its study belongs in the domain of ethics. The ethicist is a behavioral scientist par excellence.

If we examine the definition and practice of psychiatry, however, we find that in many ways it is a covert redefinition of the nature and scope of ethics. According to Webster's, psychiatry is "a branch of medicine that deals with the science and practice of treating mental, emotional, or behavioral disorders esp. as originating in endogenous causes or resulting from faulty interpersonal relationships"; further, it is "a treatise or text on or theory of the etiology, recognition, treatment, or prevention of mental, emotional, or behavioral disorder or the application of psychiatric principles to any area of human activity (social psychiatry)"; thirdly, it is "the psychiatric service in a general hospital (this patient should be referred to psychiatry)."

The nominal aim of psychiatry is the study and treatment of mental disorders. But what are mental disorders? To accept the existence of a class of phenomena called "mental diseases," rather than to inquire into the conditions under which some persons may designate others as "mentally ill," is the decisive step in the embracing of the mental health ethic.[1] If we take the dictionary definition of this discipline seriously, the study of a large part of human behavior is subtly transferred from ethics to psychiatry. For while the ethicist is supposedly concerned only with normal (moral) behavior, and the psychiatrist only with abnormal (emotionally disordered) behavior, the very distinction between the two rests on ethical grounds. In other words, the assertion that a person is mentally ill involves rendering a moral judgment about him. Moreover, because of the social consequences of such a judgment, both the "mental patient" and those who treat him as one become actors in a morality play, albeit one written in a medical-psychiatric jargon.

Having removed mentally disordered behavior from the purview of the ethicist, the psychiatrist has had to justify his reclassification. He has done so by redefining the quality or nature of the behavior he studies: whereas the ethicist studies moral behavior, the psychiatrist studies biological or mechanical behavior. In Webster's words, the psychiatrist's concern is with behavior "originating in endogenous causes or resulting from faulty interpersonal relationships." We should fasten our attention here on the words "causes" and "resulting." With these words, the transition from ethics to physiology, and hence to medicine and psychiatry, is securely completed.

Ethics is meaningful only in a context of self-governing individuals or groups exercising more or less free, uncoerced choices. Conduct resulting from such choices is said to have reasons and meanings, but no causes. This is the well-known polarity between determinism and voluntarism, causality and free will, natural science and moral science.

Defining psychiatry in the above way leads not only to a re-

[1] See Szasz, T. S.: *The Myth of Mental Illness: Foundations of a Theory of Personal Conduct* (New York: Hoeber-Harper, 1961).

apportionment of disciplines taught in universities, but also promotes a point of view about the nature of some types of human behavior, and about man in general.

By assigning "endogenous causes" to human behavior, such behavior is classified as *happening* rather than as *action*. Diabetes mellitus is a disease caused by an endogenous lack of enzymes necessary to metabolize carbohydrates. In this frame of reference, the endogenous cause of a depression must be either a metabolic defect (that is, an antecedent chemical event) or a defect in "interpersonal relationships" (that is, an antecedent historical event). Future events or expectations are excluded as possible "causes" of a feeling of depression. But is this reasonable? Consider the millionaire who finds himself financially ruined because of business reverses. How shall we explain his "depression" (if we so want to label his feeling of dejection)? By regarding it as the result of the events mentioned, and perhaps of others in his childhood? Or as the expression of his view of himself and of his powers in the world, present and future? To choose the former is to redefine ethical conduct as psychiatric malady.

The healing arts—especially medicine, religion, and psychiatry—operate within society, not outside it. Indeed, they are an important part of society. It is not surprising, therefore, that these institutions reflect and promote the primary moral values of the community. Moreover, today, as in the past, one or another of these institutions is used to mold society by supporting certain values and opposing others. What is the role of psychiatry in promoting a covert system of ethics in contemporary American society? What are the moral values it espouses and imposes on society? I shall try to suggest some answers by examining the position of certain representative psychiatric works and by making explicit the nature of the mental health ethic. And I shall try to show that in the dialogue between the two major ideologies of our day—individualism and collectivism—the mental health ethic comes down squarely on the side of collectivism.

II

Men desire freedom and fear it. Karl R. Popper speaks of the "enemies of the open society,"[2] and Erich Fromm of those who "escape from freedom."[3] Craving liberty and self-determination, men desire to stand alone as individuals, but, fearing loneliness and responsibility, they wish also to unite with their fellow men as members of a group.

Theoretically, individualism and collectivism are antagonistic principles: for the former, the supreme values are personal autonomy and individual liberty, for the latter, solidarity with the group and collective security. Practically, the antagonism is only partial: man needs to be both—alone, as a solitary individual, and with his fellow man as a member of a group. Thoreau at Walden Pond and the man in the gray flannel suit in his bureaucratic organization are two ends of a spectrum: most men seek to steer a course between these extremes. Individualism and collectivism may thus be pictured as the two shores of a fast-moving river, between which we—as moral men —must navigate. The careful, the timid, and perhaps the "wise" will take the middle course: like the practical politician, such a person will seek accommodation to "social reality" by affirming and denying both individualism and collectivism.

Although, in general, an ethical system that values individualism will be hostile to one that values collectivism, and vice versa, an important difference between the two must be noted: In an individualistic society, men are not prevented by force from forming voluntary associations, nor are they punished for assuming submissive roles in groups. In contrast, in a collectivistic society, men are forced to participate in certain organizational activities, and are punished for pursuing a solitary and independent existence. The reason for this difference is simple: as a social ethic, individualism seeks to minimize coercion and fosters

[2] Popper, K. R.: *The Open Society and Its Enemies* (Princeton, N.J.: Princeton University Press, 1950).

[3] Fromm, E.: *Escape from Freedom* (New York: Rinehart, 1941).

the development of a pluralistic society; whereas collectivism regards coercion as a necessary means for achieving desired ends and fosters the development of a singularistic society.

The collectivist ethic is exemplified in the Soviet Union, as in the case of Iosif Brodsky. A twenty-four-year-old Jewish poet, Brodsky was brought to trial in Leningrad for "pursuing a parasitic way of life." The charge stems from "a Soviet legal concept that was enacted into law in 1961 to permit the exiling of city residents not performing 'socially useful labor.' "[4]

Brodsky had two hearings, the first on February 18 and the second on March 13, 1964. The transcript of the trial was smuggled out of Russia and its translation published in *The New Leader*.[5] In the first hearing Brodsky was vaguely accused of being a poet and of not doing more "productive" work. At its conclusion, the judge ordered Brodsky to be sent "for an official psychiatric examination during which it will be determined whether Brodsky is suffering from some sort of psychological illness or not and whether this illness will prevent Brodsky from being sent to a distant locality for forced labor. Taking into consideration that from the history of his illness it is apparent that Brodsky has evaded hospitalization, it is hereby ordered that division No. 18 of the militia be in charge of bringing him to the official psychiatric examination."[6]

This point of view is characteristic of the collectivist ethic. It is also indistinguishable from that of contemporary American institutional psychiatry. In both systems, a person who has harmed no one but is considered "deviant" is defined as mentally ill; he is ordered to submit to psychiatric examination; if he resists, this is viewed as a further sign of his mental abnormality.[7]

Brodsky was found guilty and sent "to a distant locality for

[4] Quoted in *The New York Times*, August 31, 1964, p. 8.

[5] "The trial of Iosif Brodsky: A transcript." *The New Leader*, 47: 6–17 (August 31), 1964.

[6] Ibid., p. 14.

[7] For a comparison of Soviet criminal law and American mental hygiene law, see Szasz, T. S.: *Law, Liberty, and Psychiatry: An Inquiry into the Social Uses of Mental Health Practices* (New York: Macmillan, 1963), pp. 218–21.

a period of five years of enforced labor."[8] His sentence, it should be noted, was at once therapeutic, in that it sought to promote Brodsky's "personal well-being," and penal, in that it sought to punish him for the harm he had inflicted on the community. This, too, is the classic collectivist thesis: what is good for the community is good for the individual. Since the individual is denied any existence apart from the group, this equation of the one with the many is quite logical.

Another Russian man of letters, Valeriy Tarsis, who had published a book in England describing the predicament of writers and intellectuals under the Khrushchev regime, was incarcerated in a mental hospital in Moscow. It may be recalled that the American poet Ezra Pound had been dealt with in the same way: he was incarcerated in a mental hospital in Washington, D.C.[9] In his autobiographical novel, *Ward 7*, Tarsis gives the impression that involuntary mental hospitalization is a widely used Soviet technique for repressing social deviance.[10]

It seems clear that the enemy of the Soviet state is not the capitalist entrepreneur, but the lonely worker—not the Rockefellers, but the Thoreaus. In the religion of collectivism, heresy is individualism: the outcast par excellence is the person who refuses to be a member of the team.

I shall argue that the main thrust of contemporary American psychiatry—as exemplified by so-called community psychiatry—is toward the creation of a collectivist society, with all this implies for economic policy, personal liberty, and social conformity.

III

If by "community psychiatry" we mean mental health care provided by the community through public funds—rather than by the individual or by voluntary groups through private funds—then community psychiatry is as old as American psychiatry.

[8] "The trial of Iosif Brodsky," op. cit., p. 14.

[9] See Szasz, *Law, Liberty, and Psychiatry, supra*, Chap. 17.

[10] Tarsis, V.: *Ward 7: An Autobiographical Novel*, transl. by Katya Brown (London and Glasgow: Collins and Harvill, 1965).

(In most other countries, too, psychiatry began as a community enterprise and never ceased to function in that role.)

Fresh as the term "community psychiatry" is, many psychiatrists freely admit that it is just another slogan in the profession's unremitting campaign to sell itself to the public. At the fourth annual meeting of the Association of Medical Superintendents of Mental Hospitals, the main topic was community psychiatry —"What it is and what it isn't."[11]

"What is community psychiatry?" asked the director of an eastern state hospital. His answer: "I went to two European congresses this summer and I don't know what is meant by the term. . . . When people talk about it, it is rarely clear what it is."[12] To a psychiatrist in a midwestern state, "Community psychiatry . . . means that we collaborate within the framework of existing medical and psychiatric facilities."[13] This view was supported by a psychiatrist from an eastern state hospital who asserted, "In Pennsylvania, the state hospitals are already serving the communities in which they are located. . . . They have been carrying out community psychiatry."[14] Such is the path of progress in psychiatry.

What I found particularly disturbing in this report was that, although many who attended the meeting were uncertain about what community psychiatry is or might be, all declared their firm intention to play a leading role in it. Said a psychiatrist from a midwestern state hospital: "What community psychiatry is, whatever it becomes, we'd better have a part in it. We'd better assume leadership or we will get the part relegated to us. We should be functioning as community mental hospitals. If we sit back and say we are not community mental health centers, we will have a great many people telling us what to do."[15] The president of the medical superintendents' organization then called upon the members to "assume a role of leader-

[11] "Roche Report: Community psychiatry and mental hospitals." *Frontiers of Hospital Psychiatry*, 1:1–2 & 9 (November 15), 1964.
[12] Ibid., p. 2.
[13] Ibid.
[14] Ibid.
[15] Ibid., p. 9.

ship." There was general agreement on this: "Unless we participate and take a dominant part, we will be relegated to the bottom of the heap,"[16] warned a psychiatrist from a midwestern state hospital.

If this is community psychiatry, what is new about it? Why is it praised and recommended as if it were some novel medical advance that promises to revolutionize the "treatment" of the "mentally ill"? To answer these questions would require an historical study of our subject, which I shall not attempt here.[17] Let it suffice to note the specific forces that launched community psychiatry as a discrete movement or discipline. These forces are of two kinds—one political, the other psychiatric.

The social policies of modern interventionist liberalism, launched by Franklin D. Roosevelt in this country, received powerful reinforcement during the presidency of John F. Kennedy. President Kennedy's Message to Congress on "Mental Illness and Mental Retardation" on February 5, 1963, reflects this spirit. Although the care of the hospitalized mentally ill has been traditionally a welfare-state operation—carried out through the facilities of the various state departments of mental hygiene and the Veterans Administration—he advocated an even broader program, supported by public funds. Said the President: "I propose a national mental health program to assist in the inauguration of a wholly new emphasis and approach to care for the mentally ill. . . . Government at every level—federal, state, and local—private foundations and individual citizens must face up to their responsibilities in this area."[18]

Gerald Caplan, whose book Robert Felix called the "Bible . . . of the community mental health worker," hailed this message as "the first official pronouncement on this topic by the head

16 Ibid.
17 For further discussion, see Szasz, T. S.: "Whither psychiatry?" This volume, pp. 218–45.
18 Kennedy, J. F.: Message from the President of the United States Relative to Mental Illness and Mental Retardation, February 5, 1963; 88th Cong., First Sess., House of Representatives, Document No. 58; reprinted in Amer. J. Psychiatry, 120:729–37 (Feb.), 1964, p. 730.

of a government in this or any other country."[19] Henceforward, he added, "the prevention, treatment, and rehabilitation of the mentally ill and the mentally retarded are to be considered a community responsibility and not a private problem to be dealt with by individuals and their families in consultation with their medical advisers."[20]

Without clearly defining what community psychiatry is, or what it can or will do, the enterprise is proclaimed good merely because it is a team effort, involving the community and the government, and not a personal effort, involving individuals and their voluntary associations. We are told that the promotion of "community mental health" is so complex a problem that it requires the intervention of the government—but that the individual citizen is responsible for its success.

Community psychiatry is barely off the drawing boards; its nature and achievements are but high-flown phrases and utopian promises. Indeed, perhaps the only thing clear about it is its hostility to the psychiatrist in private practice who ministers to the individual patient: he is depicted as one engaged in a nefarious activity. His role has more than a slight similarity to that of Brodsky, the parasite-poet of Leningrad. Michael Gorman, for example, quotes approvingly Henry Brosin's reflections about the social role of the psychiatrist: "There is no question that the challenge of the role of psychiatry is with us all the time. The interesting thing is what we will be like in the future. Not the stereotypes and strawmen of the old AMA private entrepreneurs."[21]

I have cited the views of some of the propagandists of community psychiatry. But what about the work itself? Its main goal seems to be the dissemination of a collectivistic mental health ethic as a kind of secular religion. I shall support this view by quotations from the leading textbook of community

[19] Caplan, G.: *Principles of Preventive Psychiatry* (New York: Basic Books, 1964), p. 3.

[20] Ibid.

[21] Quoted in Gorman, M.: "Psychiatry and public policy." *Amer. J. Psychiatry*, 122:55–60 (Jan.), 1965, p. 56.

psychiatry, *Principles of Preventive Psychiatry*, by Gerald Caplan.

What Caplan describes is a system of bureaucratic psychiatry in which more and more psychiatrists do less and less actual work with so-called patients. The community psychiatrist's principal role is to be a "mental health consultant"; this means that he talks to people, who talk to other people, and finally someone talks to, or has some sort of contact with, someone who is considered actually or potentially "mentally ill." This scheme works in conformity with Parkinson's Law:[22] the expert at the top of the pyramid is so important and so busy that he needs a huge army of subordinates to help him, and his subordinates need a huge army of second-order subordinates, and so on. In a society faced with large-scale unemployment due to automation and great technological advances, the prospect of a "preventive" mental health industry, ready and able to absorb a vast amount of manpower, should be politically attractive indeed. It is. Let us now look more closely at the actual work of the community psychiatrist.

According to Caplan, a main task of the community psychiatrist is to provide more and better "sociocultural supplies" to people. It is not clear what these supplies are. For example, "the mental health specialist" is described as someone who "offers consultation to legislators and administrators and collaborates with other citizens in influencing governmental agencies to change laws and regulations."[23] In plain English, a lobbyist for the mental health bureaucracy.

The community psychiatrist also helps "the legislators and welfare authorities improve the moral atmosphere in the homes where [illegitimate] children are being brought up and to influence their mothers to marry and provide them with stable fathers."[24] Although Caplan mentions the community psychiatrist's concern with the effects of divorce upon children, there

---

[22] Parkinson, C. N.: *Parkinson's Law and Other Studies in Administration* [1957] (Boston: Houghton Mifflin Co., 1962).

[23] Caplan, op. cit., p. 56.

[24] Ibid., p. 59.

is no comment about advising women who want help in securing divorces, abortions, or contraceptives.

Another function of the mental health specialist is to review "the conditions of life of his target group in the population and then influence[s] those who help to determine these conditions so that their laws, regulations, and policies . . . are modified in an appropriate direction."[25] Caplan emphasizes that he is not advocating government by psychiatrists; he is aware that the psychiatrist may thus become the agent or spokesman of certain political or social groups. He disposes of the problem by declaring that every psychiatrist must make this decision for himself, and that his book is not addressed to those who wish to provide services for special-interest groups, but rather to "those who direct their efforts primarily to the reduction of mental disorder in our communities."[26] But he admits that the distinction between psychiatrists who exploit their professional knowledge in the service of an organization and "those who work in the organization in order to achieve the goals of their profession" is not that simple in practice. For example, commenting on the role of consulting psychiatrists in the Peace Corps, he blandly observes that their success "is not unassociated with the fact that they were able to wholeheartedly accept the major goals of that organization, and their enthusiasm was quickly perceived by its leaders."[27]

On the psychiatrist's proper role in the medical clinics of his community (specifically in relation to his function in a well-baby clinic, seeing a mother who has a "disturbed" relationship with her child), Caplan writes: "If the preventive psychiatrist can convince the medical authorities in the clinics that his operations are a logical extension of traditional medical practice, his role will be sanctioned by all concerned, including himself. All that remains for him to do is to work out the technical details."[28]

25 Ibid., pp. 62–63.
26 Ibid., p. 65.
27 Ibid.
28 Ibid., p. 79.

But this is precisely what I regard as the central question: Is so-called mental health work "a logical extension of traditional medical practice," either preventive or curative? I say it is not a logical but a rhetorical extension of it.[29] In other words, the practice of mental health education and community psychiatry is not medical practice, but moral suasion and political coercion.

IV

As was pointed out earlier, mental health and illness are but new words for describing moral values. More generally, the semantics of the mental health movement is but a new vocabulary for promoting a particular kind of secular ethic.

This view may be supported in several ways. Here I shall try to do so by citing the opinions expressed by the Scientific Committee of the World Federation for Mental Health in the monograph, *Mental Health and Value Systems*, edited by Kenneth Soddy.

In the first chapter, the authors candidly acknowledge "that mental health is associated with principles dependent upon the prevailing religion or ideology of the community concerned."[30]

There then follows a review of the various concepts of mental health proposed by different workers. For example, in Soddy's opinion, "A healthy person's response to life is without strain; his ambitions are within the scope of practical realization. . . ."[31] While in the opinion of a colleague whose view he cites, mental health "demands good interpersonal relations with oneself, with others, and with God"[32]—a definition that neatly places all atheists in the class of the mentally sick.

[29] See Szasz, *The Myth of Mental Illness, supra;* also "The myth of mental illness." This volume, pp. 12–24, and "The rhetoric of rejection." This volume, pp. 49–68.

[30] Soddy, K., ed.: *Cross-Cultural Studies in Mental Health: Identity, Mental Health, and Value Systems* (Chicago: Quadrangle, 1962), p. 70.

[31] Ibid., p. 72.

[32] Ibid., p. 73.

The authors consider the vexing problem of the relation between social adaptation and mental health. They succeed admirably in evading the problem that they claim to be tackling: "[M]ental health and social adaptation are not identical. . . . [This] can be illustrated by the fact that few people would regard a person who had become better adjusted as a result of leaving home and moving into a different society as having thereby become mentally healthy. . . . In the past, and still today in some societies, adaptation to society has tended to be highly valued . . . as a sign of mental health; and failure to adapt has been even more strongly regarded as a sign of mental ill-health. . . . There are occasions and situations in which, from the point of view of mental health, rebellion and non-conformity may be far more important than social adaptation."[33] But no criteria are given for distinguishing, "from the point of view of mental health," the situations to which we ought to conform from those against which we ought to rebel.

There is much more of this kind of sanctimonious foolishness. Thus we are told, "While it is unlikely that agreement could be reached on the proposition that all 'bad' people are mentally unhealthy, it might be possible to agree that no 'bad' person could be said to have the highest possible level of mental health, and that many 'bad' people are mentally unhealthy."[34] The problems of who is to decide who the "bad" people are, and by what criteria they are to decide, are glossed over. This evasion of the reality of conflicting ethics in the world as it exists is the most outstanding feature of this study. Perhaps one of the aims of propounding a fuzzy, yet comprehensive, mental health ethic is to maintain this denial. Indeed, the true goal of the community psychiatrist seems to be to replace a clear political vocabulary with an obscure psychiatric semantic, and a pluralistic system of moral values with a singularistic mental health ethic. Here is an example of the way this is accomplished:

"Our view is that the assumption of an attitude of superiority by one social group towards another is not conducive to the

[33] Ibid., pp. 75–76.
[34] Ibid., p. 82.

mental health of either group."[35] Some simplistic comments about the Negro problem in America then follow. No doubt, the sentiment here expressed is admirable. But the real problems of psychiatry are bound up not with abstract groups but with concrete individuals. Yet nothing is said about actual relations between people—for example, between adults and children, doctors and patients, experts and clients; and how, in these various situations, the attainment of a relationship that is both egalitarian and functional requires the utmost skill and effort of all concerned (and may, in some cases, be impossible to realize).

Self-revealing as the mental health ethicist is when he discusses mental health and illness, his moral stance is even clearer when he discusses psychiatric treatment. Indeed, the promoter of mental health now emerges as a social engineer on the grand scale: he will be satisfied with nothing less than gaining license to export his own ideology to a world market.

The authors begin their discussion of the promotion of mental health by noting the "resistances" against it: "The principles underlying success in attempts to alter cultural conditions *in the interest of mental health,* and the hazards of such attempts, are very important considerations for practical mental health work. . . . The introduction of change in a community may be subject to conditions not unlike those which obtain in the case of *the child . . .*" (italics added).[36] We recognize here the familiar medical-psychiatric model of human relations: the client is like the ignorant child who must be "protected," if need be autocratically and without his consent, by the expert, who is like the omnicompetent parent.

The mental health worker who subscribes to this point of view and engages in this kind of work adopts a condescending attitude toward his (unwilling) clients: he regards them, at best, as stupid children in need of education, and, at worst, as evil criminals in need of correction. All too often he seeks to impose value change through fraud and force, rather than

35 Ibid., p. 106.
36 Ibid., p. 173.

through truth and example. In brief, he does not practice what he preaches. The egalitarian-loving attitude toward one's fellow man, which the mental health worker is so eager to export to the "psychiatrically underdeveloped" areas of the world, seems to be in rather short supply everywhere. Or are we to overlook the relations in the United States between white and black, or psychiatrist and involuntary patient?

The authors are not wholly oblivious of these difficulties. But they seem to think it sufficient to acknowledge their awareness of such problems. For example, after commenting on the similarities between Chinese brainwashing and involuntary psychiatric treatment, they write:

"The term brain-washing has . . . been applied with unfortunate connotations to psychotherapeutic practice *by those who are hostile to it*. We consider that the lesson of this needs to be taken to heart by all who are responsible for securing psychiatric treatment of non-volitional patients. The use of compulsion or deceit will almost certainly *appear, to those who are unfriendly to or frightened of* the aims of psychotherapy, to be wicked" (italics added).[37]

The "benevolent" despot, whether political or psychiatric, does not like to have his benevolence questioned. If it is, he resorts to the classic tactic of the oppressor: he tries to silence his critic, and, if this fails, he tries to degrade him. The psychiatrist accomplishes this by calling those who disagree with him "hostile" or "mentally ill." Here we are told that if a person admits to the similarities between brain-washing and involuntary psychiatric treatment he is, *ipso facto, hostile* to psychotherapy.

The statement about "the lesson . . . to be taken to heart by all who are *responsible* for securing psychiatric treatment of non-volitional patients" [italics added] requires special comment. The language used implies that involuntary mental patients exist in nature—whereas, in fact, they are created, largely by psychiatrists. Thus, after raising the vexing problem of involuntary psychiatric treatment, the authors fail to deal with it in

37 Ibid., p. 186.

a clear and forthright manner; instead, they impugn the emotional health and moral intentions of those who would dare to look at the problem critically.

This antagonism to a critical examination of his doctrines and methods may be necessary for the mental health worker, just as it is for the missionary or the politician: the aim of each is to conquer souls or minds, not to understand human problems. Let us not forget the dangers of trying to understand another person: the effort invites disproof of one's views and questioning of one's beliefs. The thoughtful person who is content to teach by the example of his own conduct must always be ready to acknowledge error and to change his ways. But this is not what the mental health worker wants: he does not want to change his ways, but those of others.

In an analysis of the mental hygiene movement written nearly thirty years ago, Kingsley Davis has suggested this and more. Commenting on the "family clinic," Davis observed that such agencies offer not medical treatment but moral manipulation: "Before one can cure such patients, one must alter their purpose; in short, one must operate, not on their anatomy, but on their system of values."[38] The trouble is, of course, that people usually do not want to *alter* their goals—they want to *attain* them. As a result, "Only those clients whose ends correspond to socially sanctioned values may be expected to come voluntarily to such a clinic. Other troubled persons, whose wishes are opposed to accepted values, will stay away; they can be brought in only through force or fraud."[39] Nor does Davis shirk from stating what many know but few dare articulate—namely, that " . . . many clients are lured to family clinics by misrepresentation."[40] Similarly, many more are lured to state mental hospitals and community-sponsored clinics. Community psychiatry thus emerges, in my opinion at least, as a fresh attempt to revitalize and expand the old mental hygiene industry.

[38] Davis, K.: "The application of science to personal relations: A critique of the family clinic idea." *Amer. Sociological Rev.*, 1:236–47 (April), 1936, p. 238.

[39] Ibid., p. 241.

[40] Ibid.

First, there is a new advertising campaign: mental health education is an effort to lure unsuspecting persons into becoming clients of the community mental health services. Then, having created a demand—or, in this case, perhaps merely the appearance of one—the industry expands: this takes the form of steadily increasing expenditures for existing mental hospitals and clinics and for creating new, more highly automated factories, called "community mental health centers."

Before concluding this review of the ethics of mental health work, I want to comment briefly on the values advocated by the authors of *Mental Health and Value Systems*.

They promote change as such; its direction is often left unspecified. "The success of mental health promotion depends partly upon the creation of a climate favorable to change and a belief that change is desirable and possible."[41] They also emphasize the need to scrutinize certain "unproven assumptions"; none of these, however, pertains to the nature of mental health work. Instead, they list as unproven assumptions such ideas as " . . . the mother is always the best person to have charge of her own child."[42]

I believe that we ought to object to all this on basic logical and moral grounds: if moral values are to be discussed and promoted, they ought to be considered for what they are—moral values, not health values. Why? Because moral values are, and must be, the legitimate concern of everyone and fall under the special competence of no particular group; whereas health values (and especially their technical implementation) are, and must be, the concern mainly of experts on health, especially physicians.

V

Regardless of what we call it, mental health today is a big business. This is true in every modern society, whatever its political structure. It is impossible, therefore, to comprehend

41 Soddy, op. cit., p. 209.
42 Ibid., p. 208.

the struggle between individualistic and collectivistic values in psychiatry without a clear understanding of the social organization of mental health care.

Surprising as it may seem, in the United States 98 per cent of the care for the hospitalized mentally ill is provided by federal, state, and county governments.[43] The situation in Great Britain is similar. In the Soviet Union the figure is, of course, 100 per cent.

To be sure, this is not the whole picture for the United States or Great Britain. Private practice is still what the term implies: private. Yet this does not mean that psychiatric inpatient care is paid for by public funds, and psychiatric outpatient care by private funds. Outpatient services are financed both privately and publicly. Including all types of care, it has been estimated that "about 65% of all the treatment of mental patients goes on in tax supported services, and 35% in private and voluntary services."[44]

The implications of the vast and expanding involvement of the government in mental health care have, I think, been insufficiently appreciated. Moreover, whatever problems stem from government control of mental hospital care, these difficulties are connected with a logically antecedent problem: What is the aim of the care provided? It does not help to say that it is to transform the mentally sick into the mentally healthy. We have seen that the terms "mental health" and "mental sickness" designate ethical values and social performances. The mental hospital system thus serves, however covertly, to promote certain values and performances, and to suppress others. Which values are promoted and which suppressed depends, of course, on the nature of the society sponsoring the "health" care.

Again, these points are not new. Similar views have been voiced by others. Davis observed that the prospective clients of family clinics "are told in one way or another, through lectures, newspaper publicity, or discreet announcement, that the clinic

[43] Blain, D.: "Action in mental health: Opportunities and responsibilities of the private sector of society." *Amer. J. Psychiatry*, 121: 422–27 (Nov.), 1964, p. 425.
[44] Ibid.

exists for the purpose of helping individuals out of their troubles; whereas it really exists for the purpose of helping the established social order. Once lured to the clinic, the individual may suffer further deception in the form of propaganda to the effect that his own best interest lies in doing the thing he apparently does not want to do, as if a man's 'best interest' could be judged by anything else than his own desires."[45]

Because of the involuntary character of this kind of clinic or hospital, it follows, according to Davis (and I agree with him), that the service "must find support through subsidy (philanthropic or governmental) rather than through profit from fees. Furthermore, since its purpose is identified with the community at large rather than the person it serves, and since it requires the use of force or misrepresentation to carry out this purpose, it must function as an arm of the law and government. We do not permit the use of force and fraud to individuals in their private capacity. . . . In order, therefore, to settle familial conflicts by enforcing social dictates, a family clinic must in the long run be clothed with the power or at least the mantle of some state-authorized institution for the exercise of systematic deception, such as the church."[46]

Could the community support a clinic devoted to promoting the best interests of the client, rather than of the community? Davis considered this possibility, and concluded that it could not. For, if this kind of clinic is to exist, then, "like the other kind, [it] must use force and deception—not on the client, but on the community. It must lobby in legislative halls, employ political weapons, and above all deny publicly its true purpose."[47] (We have seen organized American psychoanalysis do just this.)[48]

Davis is clear about the basic alternatives that psychiatry

[45] Davis, op. cit., pp. 241–42.
[46] Ibid., pp. 242–43.
[47] Ibid., p. 243.
[48] See Szasz, T. S.: "Psychoanalysis and taxation: A contribution to the rhetoric of the disease concept in psychiatry." *Amer. J. Psychotherapy,* 18:635–43 (Oct.), 1964; "A note on psychiatric rhetoric." *Amer. J. Psychiatry,* 121:1192–93 (June), 1965.

must face, but that it refuses to face: "The individualistic clinic would accept the standard of its client. The other kind of clinic would accept the standard of society. In practice only the latter is acceptable, because the state is clothed with the power to use force and fraud."[49] Insofar as family clinics or other kinds of mental health facilities try to render services of both kinds, "they are trying to ride two horses headed in opposite directions."[50]

Comparison of the care provided by mental hospitals in Russia and America supports the contention that the values and performances that psychiatry promotes or suppresses are related to the society sponsoring the psychiatric service. The proportion of physicians and hospital beds to population is about the same in both countries. However, this similarity is misleading. In the Soviet Union, there are about 200,000 psychiatric hospital beds; in the United States, about 750,000. Accordingly, "11.2% of all hospital beds in the Soviet Union [are] allocated to psychiatric patients, compared with 46.4% in the USA."[51]

This difference is best accounted for by certain social and psychiatric policies that encourage mental hospitalization in America, but discourage it in Russia. Moreover, the Soviets' main emphasis in psychiatric care is enforced work, whereas ours is enforced idleness; they compel psychiatric patients to produce, whereas we compel them to consume. It seems improbable that these "therapeutic" emphases should be unrelated to the chronic labor shortage in Russia, and the chronic surplus here.

In Russia, "work therapy" differs from plain work in that the former is carried out under the auspices of a psychiatric institution, the latter under the auspices of a factory or farm. Furthermore, as we saw in the case of Iosif Brodsky, the Russian criminal is sentenced to work—not to idleness (or make-work), like his American counterpart. All this stems from two basic

[49] Davis, op. cit., p. 244.
[50] Ibid., p. 245.
[51] Wortis, J. and Freundlich, D.: "Psychiatric work therapy in the Soviet Union." *Amer. J. Psychiatry*, 121:123–25 (Aug.), 1964, p. 123.

sources: first, from the Soviet sociopolitical theory that holds that "productive work" is necessary and good for both society and the individual; second, from the Soviet socioeconomic fact that in a system of mammoth bureaucracies (lacking adequate checks and balances) more and more people are needed to do less and less work. Thus, the Soviets have a chronic labor shortage.

Consistent with these conditions, the Russians try to keep people at their jobs, rather than put them in mental hospitals. If a person is no longer tolerated at his job, he is made to work in "psychiatric outpatient clinics . . . where patients [can] spend the entire day at work. . . ."[52] In the 1930s, during the heyday of Stalinism, there developed an "uncritical infatuation with work therapy," as a result of which "the hospitals came to resemble industrial plants."[53]

It is evident that the distinction, in Russia, between work therapy and plain work is of the same kind as the distinction, in the United States, between confinement in a hospital for the criminally insane and imprisonment in jail. Many of the Soviet hospital shops, we learn, "settle down to operate like regular factory units, keeping their mildly disabled but productive patients there for interminable periods, paying them regular wages while they travel daily back and forth to their homes as if they had permanent jobs. . . . Instances have been reported where the sheltered workshops have been exploited by their managers for private gain. . . ."[54]

In the United States, the government does not usually own or control the means of production. The manufacture of goods and the provision of (most) services is in the hands of private individuals or groups. If the government should have persons under its care produce goods or provide services, it would create a problem of competition with private enterprise. This problem first arose in connection with prisons and now faces us in connection with mental health facilities. The stockholders of General Motors Corporation (or its employees) would be less

52 Ibid.
53 Ibid., p. 124.
54 Ibid., p. 127.

than happy if the United States Government were to have the inmates of federal prisons manufacture automobiles. Thus, prisoners in America are reduced to making license plates, and mental patients, to mopping floors or working in the kitchen or back ward of the hospital.

The point I wish to make is simple: unlike in Russia, the major socioeconomic problem in the United States is an over-abundance, not a scarcity, of consumer goods; likewise, we have an excess, not a shortage, of productive manpower. The result is our well-known chronic unemployment, which rarely dips below 5 per cent of the labor force (without including many elderly persons capable of working). Accordingly, in American mental hospitals, meaningful and productive work is discouraged and, if need be, prevented by force. Instead of defining forced labor as therapy—as do the Soviets—we define forced idleness as therapy. The only work permitted (or encouraged) is labor necessary to maintain the hospital plant and services, and, even in this category, only such work as is considered non-competitive with private enterprise.

As I suggested some time ago,[55] in the United States mental hospitalization serves a twofold socioeconomic function. First, by defining people in mental hospitals as unfit for work (and often preventing them from working even after their discharge), the mental health care system serves to diminish our national pool of unemployment; large numbers of people are classified as mentally ill rather than as socially incompetent or unemployed. Second, by creating a vast organization of psychiatric hospitals and affiliated institutions, the mental health care system helps to provide employment; indeed, the number of psychiatric and parapsychiatric jobs thus created is staggering. As a result, major cutbacks in the expenditures of the mental health bureaucracy threaten the same kind of economic dis-location as do cutbacks in the expenditures of the defense establishment and are, perhaps, equally "unthinkable."

[55] Szasz, T. S.: "Review of *The Economics of Mental Illness*, by Rashi Fein (New York: Basic Books, 1958)." *AMA Archives of General Psychiatry*, 1:116–18 (July), 1959.

It seems to me, therefore, that contrary to the oft-repeated propaganda about the high cost of mental illness, we have a subtle economic stake in perpetuating, and even increasing, such "illness." Faced as we are with overproduction and underemployment, we can evidently afford the "cost" of caring for hundreds of thousands of "mental patients" and their dependents. But can we afford the "cost" of not caring for them, and thus adding to the ranks of the unemployed not only the so-called mentally ill, but also the people who now "treat" them and do "research" on them?

Whatever the ostensible aims of community psychiatry may be, its actual operations are likely to be influenced by socio-economic and political considerations and facts such as I have discussed here.

VI

Psychiatry is a moral and social enterprise. The psychiatrist deals with problems of human conduct. He is, therefore, drawn into situations of conflict—often between the individual and the group. If we wish to understand psychiatry, we cannot avert our eyes from this dilemma: we must know whose side the psychiatrist takes—the individual's or the group's.

Proponents of the mental health ideology describe the problem in different terms. By not emphasizing conflicts between people, they avoid enlisting themselves explicitly as the agents of either the individual or the group. As they prefer to see it, instead of promoting the interests of one or another party or moral value, they promote "mental health."

Considerations such as these have led me to conclude that the concept of mental illness is a betrayal of common sense and of an ethical view of man. To be sure, whenever we speak of a concept of man, our initial problem is one of definition and philosophy: What do we mean by man? Following in the tradition of individualism and rationalism, I hold that a human being is a person to the extent that he makes free, uncoerced choices. Anything that increases his freedom, increases his manhood; anything that decreases his freedom, decreases his manhood.

Progressive freedom, independence, and responsibility lead to being a man; progressive enslavement, dependence, and irresponsibility, to being a thing. Today it is inescapably clear that, regardless of its origins and aims, the concept of mental illness serves to enslave man. It does so by permitting—indeed commanding—one man to impose his will on another.

We have seen that the purveyors of mental health care, especially when such care is provided by the government, are actually the purveyors of the moral and socioeconomic interests of the state. This is hardly surprising. What other interests could they represent? Surely not those of the so-called patient, whose interests are often antagonistic to those of the state. In this way, psychiatry—now proudly called "community psychiatry"—becomes largely a means for controlling the individual. In a mass society, this is best accomplished by recognizing his existence only as a member of a group, never as an individual.

The danger is clear, and has been remarked on by others. In America, when the ideology of totalitarianism is promoted as fascism or communism, it is coldly rejected. However, when the same ideology is promoted under the guise of mental health care, it is warmly embraced. It thus seems possible that where fascism and communism have failed to collectivize American society, the mental health ethic may yet succeed.

4 · THE RHETORIC OF REJECTION

In a previous paper[1] I sought to clarify the concept of mental illness by offering a logical analysis of it. In the physical sciences, where language is used mainly descriptively—that is, to communicate how things *are*—such an analysis often suffices to dispel obscurities. However, in the social or human sciences, where language is used not only descriptively but also promotively—that is, to communicate not only how things are but also how they *ought to be*—this often does not suffice, and must therefore be supplemented by an analysis of the historical, moral, and tactical aspects of the concept in question. The aim of this essay, then, is to further clarify the concept of mental illness by examining its historical antecedents, moral implications, and strategic functions.

II

Language has three main functions: to transmit information, to induce mood, and to promote action.[2] It should be emphasized that conceptual clarity is required only for the cognitive, or information-transmitting, use of language. Lack of clarity may be no handicap when language is used to influence people; indeed, it is often an advantage.

The social sciences—psychiatry among them—are devoted to the study of how people influence one another. The promotive use of language is, therefore, a significant aspect of the observations the social sciences seek to describe and explain. A major difficulty in this enterprise is that the social sciences have no specialized idiom of their own. They use everyday language,

[1] Szasz, T. S.: "The myth of mental illness." This volume, pp. 12–24.
[2] Reichenbach, H.: *Elements of Symbolic Logic* (New York: Macmillan, 1947), pp. 1–20.

which is often imprecise and which lends itself readily to promotive usage. Thus, psychiatric and sociological descriptions frequently offer promotive statements in the guise of cognitive assertions. In other words, while allegedly describing conduct, psychiatrists often prescribe it. Calling a person mentally sick is an example: it asserts, or implies, that his behavior is unacceptable and that he should conduct himself in other, more acceptable ways. When social science functions in this fashion, its own formulations present a barrier against the recognition of the very phenomena it seeks to elucidate and comprehend. (Of course, insofar as language is a public rather than a private affair, it is inherently promotive of *something;* for example, scientific explanation promotes intersubjective understanding. My concern in this essay, however, is not with this kind of promotive use of language, but rather with the kind that leads to and justifies social action, and especially social action utilizing the coercive powers of the state.)

Whether it is helpful or harmful for a person to be called and considered "sick" cannot be decided *a priori,* nor can it be deduced from one's own, private concept of "illness"; it depends, instead, on how the person so identified and those about him react to this labeling. Actually, whether it is therapeutic or punitive to be called "sick" (or "mentally sick") depends largely on the social context in which the person so diagnosed lives. Penetrating insight into this fact—namely, that the word "illness" is the name of certain moves in a linguistic and social game, and not necessarily the name of an abnormal biological condition or disease—may be found in Samuel Butler's *Erewhon.*[3] In this remarkable book Butler describes an imaginary civilization that punishes illness as ours punishes crime, and that treats crime as ours treats illness.

For our present purposes it is enough to recall that during the second half of the nineteenth century—when modern neurology and psychiatry originated—the rules of the game of living made it advantageous for a disabled person to be called

[3] Butler, S.: *Erewhon* [1872] (Harmondsworth, Eng.: Penguin, 1954).

sick. Confronted with such people—regardless of why they were or acted disabled—physicians had therefore two choices: they could classify or rename as "sick" all who were disabled in any way, so as to improve their lot; or they could examine and extend the rules of the medical game (that is, the humane treatment accorded the sick) to other disadvantaged, incapacitated, or unfortunate members of society. Invariably, physicians adopted the first course. It was, in every way, the expedient alternative.

Specifically, the decisions that faced the pioneer neuropsychiatrists—Charcot, Janet, Bernheim, Kraepelin, Freud, and others—was how to label persons acting disabled *and* displaying certain kinds of neuromuscular and sensory "symptoms." Should they be called malingerers, hysterics, physically or mentally ill patients, or something else? Before Charcot, all those without demonstrable physical illness were usually diagnosed as malingerers. Thus, one of Charcot's alleged discoveries was not a discovery at all. Rather, it was a reclassification and relabeling of malingerers as hysterics.[4] It is this process of relabeling that will occupy our attention in this essay.

III

Naming or labeling persons—that is, the taxonomic approach applied to people—is a tactic full of hidden pitfalls. This is illustrated by the invidious labeling and persecution of Jews, the attempts to counteract this discrimination by means of strategic reclassification, and the consequences of such reclassification.

In Freud's day, to be Jewish was like being ill, and to be Christian was like being healthy. Hence, Jews wishing to improve their status had two choices: One was to rename and re-

---

[4] In this connection, see Freud, S.: "Charcot" [1893], in *The Standard Edition of the Complete Psychological Works of Sigmund Freud* (London: Hogarth, 1962), Vol. III, pp. 7–23; Guillain, G.: *J.-M. Charcot, 1825–1893: His Life—His Work* (New York: Hoeber, 1959), Szasz, T. S.: *The Myth of Mental Illness: Foundations of a Theory of Personal Conduct* (New York: Hoeber-Harper, 1961), especially pp. 21–26.

classify themselves; Jews could assume German names and could embrace the Christian religion. Another was to escape from the constricting and unsatisfactory social game; Jews could leave their European homelands and move to the United States, Canada, Palestine, or elsewhere.

The first option, religious conversion, constitutes a socially accepted form of deception. People agree to call something by a new name for purely strategic reasons—in this case, to secure a better life for the renamed. This is exactly what was involved in the renaming of malingerers as hysterics: their "conversion" secured for them the rights and privileges of the sick, just as the conversion of German and Austro-Hungarian Jews secured for them the rights and privileges of full-fledged citizens.[5]

It is important to note that this kind of renaming involves only the instrumental use of language. The proposition implicit in the language games of traditional anti-Semitism and traditional medicine—namely, that Jews are inferior to Christians and that "malingerers" are inferior to "patients"—remained unexamined and unaltered. Efforts to remedy social injustices by means of such acts of reclassification and renaming must be contrasted with efforts to remedy them by criticizing and changing the discriminatory rules. For example, the declaration that all Jews should be converted to Christianity so that they can be treated equally with Christians must be contrasted with the declaration that all men should be equal before the law, regardless of race, religion, or disability.

The second option, migration, means leaving the field of traditional (past) action, and seeking a new (future) field, in the expectation that the fresh game-rules will be more favorable for the immigrant. As the Jew could protect himself from religious persecution by removing himself from Europe and migrating to America, so the malingerer could be protected from social persecution by removing him from the field of criminality (or quasi criminality) and transferring him to that of medicine (or quasi medicine, that is, psychiatry).

[5] Szasz, T. S.: "Malingering: Diagnosis or social condemnation?" *AMA Arch. Neurol. & Psychiatry,* 76:432–43 (Oct.), 1956.

Although the analogy between the persecution of Jews and malingerers, and the attempts to combat each, is a close one, there is an important difference between these two phenomena, to which we must attend: It is that while Jews could remove themselves from Europe and migrate to America on their own effort, malingerers could move from the area of criminality to that of medicine only with the active assistance and formal approval of the medical profession. This difference brings us back to the social ramifications of the classificatory act.

IV

Classification is a social act. The classification of individuals or groups entails the participation of at least three different types of persons: classifier, classified, and a public called upon to accept or reject a particular classification.

An individual may classify himself or others, and, in turn, may be classified by others. In each case, the categorization proposed by the classifier may be accepted or rejected by others. To have one's classification of self or others accepted requires, in general, having a measure of power over others; this power may be intellectual (scientific) or political (coercive). Again, the workings of this process may be illustrated by means of our examples.

Psychiatrists are both the agents of classification (that is, they classify), and the objects of classification by others (that is, they are classified). It should be recalled that not only did psychiatrists traditionally classify certain persons as madmen or lunatics, but that, in turn, they themselves were classified, by other physicians and the public at large, as "not real doctors," or medical jailers. In Freud's day, this was true for Jews also: they could classify themselves (as God's chosen people) and others (as God's stepchildren), and could, in turn, be classified by others (as second-class citizens). Hitler changed this, by casting the Jews into a role similar to that of mental patients. This was achieved by depriving the Jews of their roles as classifiers, and by converting them into objects classified by Nazis. What has always characterized madmen or mental patients—

and this is my reason for pointing this out here—is that they have been robbed of their rights and powers to classify themselves or others, and have been treated solely as the objects of classification by society, and especially by alienists, psychiatrists, and psychoanalysts.

We have noted that a person caught in a social situation (or game) in which he is handicapped or harmed has the option to convert or to migrate. To this we may now add the option to change the game. These three basic choices may be summarized as follows. 1. Conversion: the handicapped person changes to a more favorable role, but the game remains the same (for example, Jew becoming Christian, alienist becoming psychoanalyst). 2. Migration: the handicapped person abandons the existing game and seeks out one more favorable for him (for example, European Jew moving to America). 3. Social change: the handicapped person (usually in concert with others similarly situated or in sympathy with him) changes the rules of the ongoing social game so that they will be more favorable for him (for example, Jew gaining acceptance as Jew rather than as new Christian, psychoanalyst gaining acceptance as psychotherapist rather than as psychoanalytic physician). Of these options, conversion is the easiest to effect, migration is the next most difficult, and bringing about social change resulting in a genuine increase in the acceptance of human (that is, religious, professional, personal, etc.) differences is the hardest of all.

Conversion requires only the adoption of the behavioral repertoire of those who are the new role-models. Migration, on the other hand, requires leaving one's homeland and acquiring citizenship in a new country. For the alienist, this meant abandoning his role as physician and adopting a new professional identity. In part, this is just what Freud and the early psychoanalysts did: they abandoned traditional medical and psychiatric practice and created a new profession, psychoanalysis. This role-change was, however, never adequately acknowledged or asserted. On the contrary, the new game was built on the model of the old. As the Pilgrims created a "New England," so the psychoanalysts created a "new therapy." The method of resolving the problem—whether of the relation between Christian and Jew, or between physicians ("real doctors") and psychoanalysts ("fake doctors")—confirms the justification for the discrimination and hence renders a more radical and effective solution of it impossible.

To achieve a more profound solution of this kind of problem, it is necessary to proceed by a different route. This requires, first, the acceptance of the previously rejected person, group, or activity (Jews, psychiatrists), and, second, the repudiation of the rules legitimizing the discrimination. For psychiatry, psychoanalysis, medicine, and the intellectual community, this would have meant recognizing the important differences between psychoanalytic concepts and methods and the theories and practices of other professions and sciences. For psychoanalysts, it would have meant that instead of aspiring to share in the power and prestige of the medical profession, they would have had to content themselves with whatever role modern Western societies might assign to students of human behavior and to secular healers of the soul. In short, psychiatrists and psychoanalysts would have had to proceed by emphasizing the differences, rather than the similarities, between psychotherapy and medical practices; instead of defining their aims in terms of mental illness and treatment, they would have had to define them in terms of increasing our knowledge about man as a social being, and of helping certain persons by means of special methods of influencing people (psychoanalysis, suggestion, etc.).

Mutatis mutandis, the same considerations apply to anti-Semitism. Instead of seeking the solution of the "Jewish problem" in conversion, Jews could have sought it in the recognition and acceptance of the Jew as Jew. The justification for this strategy might have been put thus: Although Jews differ from Gentiles in certain ways—for example, in their religion, and sometimes their physical appearance—they may nevertheless be considered citizens of Germany and Austria-Hungary because they belong to its social fabric. Such an argument implies a rejection of the legitimacy of discrimination not only against Jews but also against other native minorities, such as Czechs, Rumanians, Serbs, and so forth. But doing so would have brought the Jews into fresh conflict with their Christian country-men. This is why the strategy of critically repudiating religious, racial, national, sexual, and other discriminations and persecutions was shunned in the battle against European anti-Semitism as well as in the fight against the stigma of insanity; and why it has continued to be shunned in all situations in which the reformer's aim is not to enlarge cognitive horizons and thus gradually improve the human condition, but to appeal to emotions and thus speedily remedy a specific social wrong.

v

The mistreatment of Jews by Christians, and of malingerers by physicians, rests on, or at least is made possible by, the names used to label such persons and groups. I propose to call this language of social discrimination *the rhetoric of rejection*. Whenever people propose to *exclude* others from their midst, they attach stigmatizing labels to them. There are many such labels in addition to Jew and malingerer; child, foreigner, enemy, criminal, Negro, and mentally ill are currently some of the most important ones.

Like all methods of persuasion, the rhetoric of rejection invites its opposite: *the rhetoric of acceptance*. Whenever people propose to *include* others in their midst, they shun and even prohibit the use of certain stigmatizing labels, especially in certain situations, such as in courts of law, newspapers, and so forth.

A rhetoric of rejection, opposed by a rhetoric of acceptance that it has generated and that, in turn, generates a fresh rhetoric of rejection, and so on, thus form a dialectic justifying excluding some people from the group and then reincluding them in it. This process is again reflected in both the history of European anti-Semitism and the history of the rejection of the insane.

As I noted, the relabeling of malingerers as hysterics left unexamined and unaltered the underlying rules of the medical game characteristic of, and legitimized by, late nineteenth-century European culture. These rules—which governed the behavior not only of physicians and patients, but also of judges, legislators, and the general public—were, as is so often the case, actually of two kinds: professed and practiced. The professed rules were that patients (that is, sick persons) were helpless and deserved the care and devotion of physicians and society generally, and that malingerers (that is, persons who only feigned being sick) were malefactors who deserved punishment by physicians and scorn by society. The rules actually followed, however, were that only "good patients" (typically, those suffering from bodily diseases that could be diagnosed and cured) deserved care and devotion, whereas others (typically, those suffering from incurable bodily illnesses or "mental diseases") deserved no more than a right to survive as society's outcasts.

In this context, the conversion of malingerers to hysterics could, of course, achieve no more than the removal of some persons from among the stigmatized and their inclusion among the less stigmatized or non-stigmatized. Similarly, the conversion of Jews to Christianity could achieve no more than the inclusion of converted Jews in the general population. In neither case was the process of stigmatization illuminated, criticized, and repudiated.

Such tactical evasions of a real confrontation with the phenomenon of social stigmatization and rejection appear to invite countermoves designed to "close the loophole," re-eject the members newly included in the group, and re-establish the original dynamic of stigmatization. For each step of conversion there is thus a corresponding step of reconversion or deconversion.

In the history of psychiatry, the process of reconversion took the following form: Soon after psychiatrically stigmatized disabilities such as "malingering" or "insanity" were renamed as "mental" or "emotional illnesses," the new labels began to be treated exactly as the terms they displaced had been treated formerly. People bearing the names of mental illnesses, like Jews with certain distinguishing German names, thus reacquired their former ill repute. And so it has come to pass that the label "mental illness" (and its variants) has acquired the same meanings and social functions as those possessed by previously abandoned terms of psychiatric denigration. To be sure, in the context of some psychiatric and psychoanalytic writings, certain words like "hysteria" or "schizophrenia" may have some descriptive value. My point here is not to deny this, but to emphasize that, as generally used, psychiatric diagnostic terms do not describe identifiable disease entities, but instead degrade and demean the person to whom they are attached.[6]

Although this characteristic of the language of psychiatry has until now not been clearly identified, I believe it has been widely recognized. How else can we explain the periodic renaming of the "diseases" from which "mental patients" suffered, and the institutions in which they were "treated"? In the relatively short, three-hundred-year history of psychiatry, the condition now called mental illness has been labeled and relabeled as madness, lunacy, insanity, idiocy, dementia, dementia praecox, neurasthenia, psychopathy, mania, schizophrenia, neurosis, psychoneurosis, psychosis, ego failure, ego dyscontrol, emotional illness, emotional disorder, psychological illness, psychological disorder, psychiatric illness, psychiatric disorder, immaturity, social failure, social maladaptation, behavior disorder, and so forth. Similarly, the institution for the confinement of such "patients" has been called madhouse, lunatic asylum, insane asylum, state hospital, state mental hospital, mental hospital, psychopathic hospital, psychiatric hospital, psychiatric institute, psychiatric institute for research and training, psychiatric center, and community mental health center. Since each of these terms is intended to identify and at the same time to conceal a bad person (that is, one who is mad, or does mad things), or a bad place (that is, an institution where such persons are incarcerated), no single term can fulfill these contradictory functions, except temporarily. With persistent usage—often after only a decade or two—the pejorative meaning of the term becomes increasingly apparent and its value as semantic camouflage diminishes and disappears. New psychiatric terms for

[6] For further discussion, see Szasz, T. S.: "The moral dilemma of psychiatry." *Amer. J. Psychiatry*, 121:521–28 (Dec.), 1964; and "Psychiatric classification as a strategy of personal constraint." This volume, pp. 190–217.

"mental illness" and "mental hospital" are then coined, giving the public—and usually the medical and psychiatric professions as well—the impression that an important new psychiatric discovery has been made. When the fresh terms become familiar, they, in turn, are discarded and a new crop of therapeutic-sounding words is introduced. This process has been repeated several times during the past century, most recently in the early 1960s, when mental hospitals were renamed as "community mental health centers."

VI

In the history of European anti-Semitism, the cycles in the conversion and reconversion, naming and renaming, of Jews exhibit a similar pattern. German and other Central European Jews, having acquired German, Czech, Hungarian, and other national surnames and often having embraced Christianity, were included in the political makeup of their respective homelands only to be excluded from it by the legal structure of Hitlerism. The Nazis thus removed converted Jews from the class of non-persecutables, and returned them to the class of persecutables, to which they had formerly belonged. This process was undone once more in postwar Europe.

In contemporary West Germany, moreover, we are witnessing a curious blending of the two rhetorical modes I have described. The rhetoric of rejection couched in the vocabulary of race (stigmatization as a Jew), and that couched in the vocabulary of medicine (stigmatization as mentally ill), are no longer merely two similar languages, with easy translation from one to another; instead, there is a confluence of the two languages, with a merging of their respective vocabularies.

In an article entitled "The Sickness of Germany," appearing in *Hadassah Magazine* (the publication of the Women's Zionist Organization of America), the author, Leo Katcher, reports an interview with Maon Gid, a Jew born in Poland but now living in Munich. When asked what the 30,000 Jews now living in Germany had in common, Gid replies: "We call ourselves

Jews and we are all sick. Ours is the sickness of being a Jew in Germany."[7]

These tragic victims of the Nazis do not stop at rejecting themselves in the idiom of medicine and psychiatry; they also reject their persecutors in the same idiom. The result is a paroxysm of medicalized abjuration of self and others. Says Gid: "My head aches. My body aches. My soul—if I have a soul—aches. That is the penalty of being a Jew here. But I have one revenge. The Germans also are sick. The Jews are the sickness of Germany."[8]

The total depravity of Nazi Germany has thus given way to the total sinfulness of post-Nazi Germany, but—what irony! —this claim is framed, as was the Nazi justification for the extermination of European Jewry, in the language of medicine, of sickness.

Why, asks Katcher, do these people, and especially those who have no roots in Germany, stay there? Because, says Gid, "I am as sick as all the others. . . . It is the sickness of being a Jew in this country. A crazy man is one who invents his own world, is he not? Well, that is what we are doing. . . . You will find out for yourself. . . . But don't stay here too long. If you do, you will catch it. It happens to every Jew."[9]

Evidently Katcher did "catch" the disease. For, perhaps to quiet his lingering doubts about the adequacy of attributing all this turmoil and unhappiness to illness, he concludes his article with this sentence: "All the time I was in Germany, I remembered, when I talked with the sick people, that I had not experienced it."[10]

Thus have the Jews in Germany been transformed, first, from Jewish aliens into patriotic Germans; then, from patriotic Germans into Jewish vermin; and now, from God's chosen people to His incurable, insane patients.

---

[7] Katcher, Leo: "The sick Jews of Germany." *Hadassah Magazine,* 50:13, 27 (Nov.), 1968, p. 13.

[8] Ibid., p. 27.

[9] Ibid.

[10] Ibid.

VII

My thesis that terms like "neurosis," "psychosis," "mental ill-ness"—indeed, the whole gamut of psychiatric diagnostic labels—function mainly as counters in a pseudomedical rhetoric of re-jection may be readily documented by examining their actual usage. As an example, I shall quote some passages from Ernest Jones's biography of Freud. This will show that even the most brilliant and outstanding men in psychoanalysis use psychiatric labeling as a medicalized and technicized disguise for personal condemnation. In other hands, this pejorative use of psychiatric diagnoses is even more frequent and flagrant.

As we know, the psychoanalytic movement was racked by periodic "dissensions" and "secessions." When Jung and Adler left the Freudian circle, Jones was hurt, but he accepted their defection without impugning their mental health. However, Rank's and Ferenczi's deviations were too much for him; he interpreted their struggle for independence as a symptom of their "underlying" mental illness.

By 1923, writes Jones, "The evil spirit of dissension arose, and . . . the Committee, so important to Freud's peace of mind, looked like disintegrating."[11] The Committee to which Jones refers here consisted of the pioneer psychoanalysts Karl Abraham, Sándor Ferenczi, Ernest Jones, Otto Rank, Hans Sachs, and Max Eitingon. It was a secret circle—a group en-trusted by Freud with safeguarding the fortunes of psycho-analysis, and especially with protecting it from hostile outsiders and treasonous insiders. When the Committee was founded, it was Jones's hope ". . . that the six of us were suitably endowed for that purpose. It turned out, alas, that only four of us were. Two of the members, Rank and Ferenczi, were not able to hold out to the end. Rank in a dramatic fashion presently to be described, and Ferenczi more gradually toward the end of his life, developed *psychotic manifestations that revealed them-*

11 Jones, E.: *The Life and Work of Sigmund Freud,* 3 vols. (New York: Basic Books, 1953, 1955, 1957), Vol. III, p. 45.

selves in, among other ways, *a turning away from Freud and his doctrines.* The seeds of a *destructive psychosis,* invisible for so long, at last germinated" (italics added).[12] Jones, at least, is candid: He frankly states that he considers "turning away from Freud and his doctrines" a "psychotic manifestation." Surely, this criterion speaks for itself.

It is not surprising, then, that Jones consistently interprets Rank's and Ferenczi's attempts to break away from Freud's domination not as legitimate efforts to gain personal and professional independence, but as symptoms of mental illness. "It was only after a lapse of a few years that the true sources of the trouble [in the Committee] became manifest: namely, in the failing mental integration of Rank and Ferenczi."[13]

Let us see just what it is that Jones offers as evidence to support his diagnoses of Rank and Ferenczi. In 1924, while traveling to the United States, Rank—so Jones tells us—got only as far as Paris, ". . . and was seized there with a severe attack of depression; his last one had been five years before." Jones then cites Freud's letter to Joan Riviere in which Freud writes: "You will have heard that there has been a disagreeable intermezzo with Dr. Rank, but still it was only a passing feature. *He has come back to us completely . . .*" (italics added). Finally, Jones refers to Freud's ". . . knowledge that Rank suffered from cyclothymia . . . ,"[14] as if cyclothymia (which Jones himself renders as "manic-depressive psychosis" in a footnote) were an illness just like any other.

Though long close friends with Freud, in the end Ferenczi, too, fared no better. Jones quotes the following from a letter Freud wrote to Marie Bonaparte in 1932: "Ferenczi is a bitter drop in the cup. His wise wife has told me I should think of him as a *sick child!* You are right: psychical and intellectual decay is far worse than the unavoidable bodily one" (italics added).[15]

[12] Ibid.
[13] Ibid., p. 46.
[14] Ibid., pp. 72–73.
[15] Ibid., p. 174.

But if Ferenczi suffered from a "decay," why was this a "bitter drop" for Freud? The choice of words is significant here: "bitter drop" instead of "heartache" or "sorrow."

Actually, we know two things for certain about Ferenczi's last years: first, that he suffered from pernicious anemia, the disease that finally killed him; and second, that he was developing a psychotherapeutic technique that differed from Freud's and that Freud viewed with (I think justifiable) displeasure. But do these circumstances warrant Jones's unqualified assertion that, during the last months of his life, Ferenczi's ". . . disease [pernicious anemia] . . . undoubtedly exacerbated his latent *psychotic trends*" (italics added)?[16] What "psychotic trends?" The fact is that in March 1933, only two months before his death (in May 1933) and immediately after the Reichstag fire in Berlin, which signaled Hitler's ascension to total power, Ferenczi wrote to Freud urging him to flee with his family from Austria while the time was ripe. This was Freud's reply to Ferenczi's suggestion: "As to the immediate reason for your writing, the *flight motif*, I am glad to be able to tell you that I am not thinking of leaving Vienna. I am not mobile enough, and am too dependent on my treatment . . . ; furthermore, I do not want to leave my possessions here. *Probably, however, I should stay even if I were in full health and youth.* . . . It is not certain that the Hitler regime will master Austria too. That is possible, it is true, but *everybody believes* it will not attain the crudeness of brutality here that it has in Germany. There is no personal danger for me . . ." (italics added).[17]

How ironic! When it came to infantile sexuality, the meaning of dreams, or the "scientific" value of psychoanalysis, Freud was justly contemptuous of what "everybody believed"; but in replying to a letter from his "deluded" erstwhile friend, he cites what "everybody believes" as the ultimate test of "reality." Long before Freud, traditional wisdom has cautioned us that emotion and prejudice cloud our judgment. Freud greatly amplified this

16 Ibid., p. 176.
17 Ibid., pp. 177–78.

warning and supported it with impressive evidence about the influence of man's "unconscious" mind on his beliefs and actions. But this warning was too mild: emotion and prejudice do not merely *cloud* our judgment; they often *shape* it.

Thus, Ferenczi's good judgment with respect to the vital issue of the danger of Nazism in 1933 fails to make a favorable impression on Jones: He dismisses Ferenczi's astute advice to Freud with the condescending remark, ". . . with our hindsight one must admit there was some method in his madness."[18] With *our* hindsight, I would submit that this is an obscene remark, signifying the intellectual and moral bankruptcy of psychoanalytic nosology.

Even in Jones's hands, then, psychoanalytic character assassination can be pretty crude. Where Ferenczi's judgment is poor, it is a symptom of his "psychotic trends"; where it is good, it is "the method in his madness."

VIII

Not only do psychodiagnosticians declare, with wanton capriciousness, who is psychotic, but also who is normal. We thus find Freud, Jones, and other psychoanalysts labeling as "mentally ill" those whom they wish to condemn, and as "mentally healthy" those whom they wish to commend. How Freud's personal prejudice *in favor* of a psychiatrist shaped his diagnostic judgment of him is dramatically illustrated by the Frink episode.

H. W. Frink was a New York psychiatrist who behaved in a socially disordered manner before his analysis with Freud and "passed through a psychotic phase during it."[19] Thus, although by "common-sense" criteria Frink was far more abnormal than Rank or Ferenczi, Freud considered him to be in excellent mental health. "This year [1923]"—writes Jones—"brought Freud a keen personal *disappointment,* second only to that con-

18 Ibid., p. 177.
19 Ibid., p. 106.

cerning Rank. Frink of New York had resumed his analysis in Vienna in April, 1922, continuing until February, 1923, and Freud had formed the very highest opinion of him. He was, so Freud maintained, by far the ablest American he had come across, the only one from whose gifts he expected something. Frink had passed through a *psychotic phase* during his analysis —he had indeed to have a male nurse with him for a time— but Freud considered he had quite overcome it, and he counted on his being the leading analyst in America. Unfortunately, on returning to New York Frink behaved very arrogantly to the other analysts, particularly Brill, telling everyone how out of date they were. Frink's second marriage, which had caused so much scandal and on which high hopes of happiness had been set, had proved a failure, and his wife was suing for divorce. That, together with the quarrels just mentioned, must have precipitated another attack. Frink wrote to me in November, 1923, that for reasons of ill health he had to give up his work for the Journal and also his private practice. In the following summer he was a patient in the Phipps Psychiatric Institute, and *he never recovered his sanity*. He died in the Chapel Hill Mental Hospital in North Carolina some ten years later" (italics added).[20]

Why the recurrence of Frink's "illness" should have surprised Freud is puzzling, especially in view of the fact that Freud and the early Freudians regarded "psychoses" as incurable mental diseases. But, then, Frink could not have been *really* "psychotic" so long as he was the "ablest American . . . [from whose mental] gifts [Freud] expected something." For Freud, that *expectation* was enough to render Frink sane, just as his *disappointment* in Rank and Ferenczi was enough to render them insane.

The Frink affair exemplifies the typical problems that arose in the later course of psychoanalytic education and that are rampant today. Training analysts are prone to see evidence of mental health in the candidates they like and consider worthy disciples; whereas the candidates they dislike or with whom they

20 Ibid., pp. 105–6.

disagree are likely to be found mentally sick and to require prolonged and repeated analyses.[21]

The criteria governing admission to psychoanalytic institutes are pertinent in this connection. Eisendorfer, for many years the chairman of the New York Psychoanalytic Institute's committee on the selection of candidates, states, "Such factors as overt psychopathology, perversions, homosexuality, and antisocial psychopathic acting out automatically eliminate the candidate."[22] Then, only one paragraph later, he observes, "A not uncommon characteristic of a considerable number of candidates (about ten percent) is a façade of normality. . . . A dogged determination to present himself as being normal, more often than not, serves as a veneer to conceal chronic pathology."[23] Apparently Eisendorfer does not regard these two requirements—namely, presenting no overt psychopathology on the one hand, and presenting no façade of normality on the other—as contradictory.

Eisendorfer states that candidates diagnosed as having "perversions" or "overt psychopathology" are automatically excluded from acceptance. But he does not say what definition of perversion or psychopathology is used. This makes for a convenient arrangement for the admissions committee, but gives no clue to the actual practices employed. Eisendorfer's statements thus illustrate that psychoanalytic training organizations use the notion of psychopathology, and the process of psychiatric diagnostic labeling, to promote their particular ends, rather than to communicate verifiable observations.

It is clear, then, that in practically all situations (except that of a fully confidential and private psychotherapeutic relationship), psychiatric diagnoses do not function in the same way as medical diagnoses: whereas the latter identify diseases to enable physicians to treat the afflicted patients, the former identify

[21] Szasz, T. S.: "Three problems in contemporary psychoanalytic training." *AMA Arch. Gen. Psychiatry*, 3:82–94 (July), 1960.
[22] Eisendorfer, A.: "The selection of candidates applying for psychoanalytic training." *Psychoanalyt. Quart.*, 28:374–78, p. 376.
[23] Ibid., p. 377.

stigmatized individuals to enable other individuals or groups to mistreat the victims.

IX

Renaming and reclassification play a fundamental role in the development, the theory, and the practice of psychiatry. Social deviance, renamed as "mental illness," became the subject matter of psychiatry; social outcasts and other incompetent, troubled, oppressed, and persecuted individuals, renamed "neurotics" and "psychotics," became the "patients" whom psychiatric "physicians" were expected to "treat"; and the doctors who assumed the task of verbally or physically controlling troublesome individuals, renamed "psychiatrists," became the scientifically accredited experts in the diagnosis and treatment of "mental diseases." Nearly all of this is humbug.

This does not mean that psychiatrists and psychoanalysts possess no special knowledge and skills. They do. But their competence pertains to personal conduct and social control, not to bodily illness and medical treatment. In short, my point is not that psychiatry and psychoanalysis are disciplines devoid of a theory and a technology useful to some people in certain circumstances, but that they have acquired their social power and prestige largely through a deceptive association with the principles and practice of medicine.

I believe that in order to place psychiatry on a solid scientific foundation it is now necessary to recast its theories and practices in a moral and psychosocial framework and idiom. This would emphasize the differences, rather than the similarities, between social man and biological man. It would also result in abandoning the persistent attempts to convert psychiatrists and psychologists to physicians and physicists. In turn, these people themselves would no longer need to aspire to these roles.[24]

[24] In this connection, see Szasz, T. S.: "Psychiatry, psychotherapy, and psychology." *AMA Arch. Gen. Psychiatry, 1*:455–63 (Nov.), 1959; "Psychoanalysis and Medicine," in Levitt, M., ed., *Readings in Psychoanalytic Psychology* (New York: Appleton-Century-Crofts, 1959), pp. 355–74.

We know that an individual can secure his personal integrity only by a forthright recognition of his historical origins and an accurate assessment of his unique characteristics and potentialities. The same holds true for a profession or a science. Psychiatry cannot attain professional integrity by imitating medicine, or scientific integrity by imitating physics. It can attain such integrity—and hence respect as a profession and recognition as a science—only by a courageous confrontation with its historical origins and an honest appraisal of its authentic characteristics and potentialities.

5 · MENTAL HEALTH AS IDEOLOGY

It has been persuasively argued, especially by Professor Daniel Bell,[1] that since the end of the Second World War political ideas have lost their power to influence American society. Bell has called this phenomenon "the end of ideology." If by ideology we mean political ideology, then this view is substantially correct. In the United States, political doctrines—whether they be democratic, socialist, or communist; liberal, conservative, or any other kind—have little consistent effect on the everyday behavior of people.

However, inasmuch as ideology has been defined as "the conversion of ideas into social levers,"[2] we cannot conclude that, because political ideology is dead, we have come to the end of all ideologies. Indeed, we do not have to look far to find another kind of ideology—namely, psychiatry, or the ideology of mental health and illness. Though originally only a professional ideology, its scope and effect now extend to virtually all aspects of society.

What is the evidence for this view? And, if true, how did it happen? To answer these questions, let us begin with a glimpse at the historical background of the subject.

II

Before Freud, psychiatry was a poorly defined branch of medicine that had no significant influence on the culture of its day. Freud changed all this. He developed a method of inquiry, staked out a subject matter, and named them "psychoanalysis." This discipline leaned heavily on both the natural sciences (*Naturwissenschaften*) and the spiritual sciences (*Geisteswissen-*

[1] Bell, D.: *The End of Ideology* (Glencoe, Ill.: The Free Press, 1960).
[2] Ibid., p. 370.

schaften). It transformed psychiatry, especially in the United States, from a purely medical enterprise into a psychological and social one. In the process, psychiatry became a popular ideology, with "mental health and illness" its key symbols.

Freud did not intend to create a psychiatric ideology. He saw himself as a student of depth psychology—that is, of the unconscious. This is too abstruse a basis for an ideology. Although Freud occasionally used psychiatric diagnostic terms, he rejected, as scientifically unworthy, the problems posed by the notions of mental health and sickness. As we shall see, the very issues that Freud avoided have become the cornerstone of modern psychiatric ideology. But first, let me illustrate Freud's pertinent views.

One of the best sources for Freud's ideas on mental health and illness is Joseph Wortis' book, *Fragments of an Analysis with Freud.* The young Wortis was evidently much troubled by this problem and, in his analysis, sought answers from Freud:

> "Unusual conduct isn't necessarily neurotic," said Freud. "Many people take it for granted, too," I [Wortis] said, "that homosexuals are neurotic, though they might be perfectly capable of leading happy and quiet lives if society would tolerate them."
>
> "No psychoanalyst has ever claimed that homosexuals cannot be perfectly decent people," said Freud. "Psychoanalysis does not undertake to judge people in any case."[3]

Later, Freud added that psychoanalysts should treat only those homosexuals who want to change.

Time and again Wortis raised the question of mental health and illness, only to provoke increasingly emphatic dismissals of the problem from Freud:

> "We disregard such problems," said Freud. "I don't understand how you can concern yourself with such purely conventional problems (*rein konventionelle Probleme*),

[3] Wortis, J.: *Fragments of an Analysis with Freud* (New York: Simon and Schuster, 1954), p. 55.

what is a neurosis and what is not a neurosis, what is pathological or not pathological—all mere words—fights about words. . . . Your business is to learn something about yourself."[4]

A few weeks later Wortis brought up the issue of mental health again. This time he drew Freud out still further:

"Healthiness is a purely conventional practical concept," he [Freud] said, "and has no real scientific meaning. It simply means that a person gets on well; it doesn't mean that the person is particularly worthy. There are 'healthy' people who are not worth anything, and on the other hand 'unhealthy,' neurotic people who are very worthy (*wertvoll*) individuals indeed."

"Does this 'healthiness' correspond to the state of a person after a successful analysis?" I asked.

"It does in a way," he said. "Analysis enriches the individual but he loses some of his Ego, his *Ich*. It may not always be worth while." (I am not sure I recorded this last statement correctly.)[5]

It is clear, then, that in his consulting room Freud tried not to use psychiatric diagnoses as derogatory epithets. In his writings, however, he did use such diagnoses as a means of invidious labeling—his earnest protestations to the contrary notwithstanding.[6]

The impact of psychoanalysis on American psychiatry produced a pervasive pseudomedical ideology. I can only speculate on the probable causes of this development: the traditional American social ethic, which is a combination of pragmatic rationalism and Protestant puritanism; a medical profession

[4] Ibid., p. 57.
[5] Ibid., pp. 79–80.
[6] See, for example, Freud, S.: "Leonardo da Vinci and a memory of his childhood" [1910], in *The Standard Edition of the Complete Psychological Works of Sigmund Freud*, Vol. XI, pp. 57–137 (London: Hogarth Press, 1957), especially pp. 63 and 131; also, Freud, S. and Bullitt, W. C.: *Thomas Woodrow Wilson: A Psychological Study* (Boston: Houghton Mifflin Co., 1967).

that has high status economically as well as socially; a psychiatry that is ambivalent rather than simply hostile toward psychoanalysis; and a "melting pot" culture, devoid of stable ethical standards, that seeks secular-scientific and middle-class values. But whatever the causes, the result was obvious. "We must grudgingly admit," wrote Erik Erikson, "that even as we were trying to devise, with scientific determinism, a therapy for the few, we were led to promote an ethical disease among the many."[7] The "ethical disease" to which Erikson refers is part and parcel of what I call the psychiatric ideology.

III

It is often asserted that there is grave peril in trying to scrutinize the ideology of the group to which one belongs. Speaking of the ideology of the democratic West in contrast to that of Communist Russia and China, Erikson commented: ". . . our own ideology, as it must, forbids us ever to question and analyze the structure of what we hold to be true, since only thus can we maintain the fiction that we chose to believe what in fact we had no choice but to believe, short of ostracism or insanity."[8]

Hazardous as the scrutiny of religious and political ideologies may be, I believe, perhaps naively, that the scrutiny of a professional ideology—which has no foreign enemies like Communists or capitalists to which it can point—is slightly less dangerous. In any case, it is what I have been attempting to do for some time.

What then, is the contemporary American mental health ideology? The answer is: It is the traditional psychiatric ideology, refurbished with some new words, simplified for general consumption, and endorsed by the healing professions, the legislators, the courts, the churches, and so forth—thus establishing a sort of general consensus that emerges as plain common sense.

As God and the devil were the key symbols in the ideology of medieval theology, so are mental health and illness the key

[7] Erikson, E. H.: *Young Man Luther: A Study in Psychoanalysis and History* (New York: Norton, 1958), p. 19.
[8] Ibid., p. 135.

symbols of the contemporary psychiatric ideology. The dichotomy of good and evil is now replaced by that of mental health and illness. We thus have such typical antinomies as: the mental health movement versus the anti-mental health movement; psychiatric healers who wish to help versus mental patients who refuse to be treated; people who are criminals because they are sick versus those who offend because they choose to be bad; and so forth. More specifically, the ideology of mental health and illness not only serves to explain all manner of riddles, but also points the way to their solution.[9]

To see how the ideology of psychiatry serves modern man, let us first note how the ideology of Christianity served Luther. "When during a wedding somebody dropped the ring"—wrote Erikson—"he [Luther] loudly told the devil to stay out of the ceremony. When he was disturbed, he would often be satisfied with recognizing that it was the devil's work, and with a contemptuous air go to sleep. Every age has its interpretations which seem to take care of inner interference with our plans and with our self-esteem."[10]

Of course, today we "know" that these symptoms of Luther's, and many others that we are told he had, signify that he was mentally sick. If so, he was in good company. Psychiatrists have pronounced Jesus of Nazareth mentally ill, too.[11]

IV

I should now like to illustrate the actual day-to-day working of the psychiatric ideology: in particular, its wide influence, and the relative poverty of significant skepticism about the explanations and cures it offers.

Not so many years ago, the newspapers offered advice to the lovelorn. But no more. Today, they offer advice to the mentally

[9] For further discussion and documentation, see Szasz, T. S.: *Law, Liberty, and Psychiatry: An Inquiry into the Social Uses of Mental Health Practices* (New York: Macmillan, 1963).

[10] Erikson, op. cit., p. 249.

[11] See Schweitzer, A.: *The Psychiatric Study of Jesus* [1913], transl. by Charles R. Joy (Boston: Beacon Press, 1948).

sick, or, more often, to persons who are troubled by friends and relatives who are mentally sick but who do not know that they are sick. Here are some typical examples:

DEAR ANN LANDERS: Can you save this marriage? My wife has become friendly with a woman whose reputation isn't worth a plugged nickel. She has gone through three or four husbands. I am not sure which.

This woman got my wife interested in mixed-league bowling. At least three nights a week they are out until 2 a.m.—sometimes later. Last month they went to Toledo on an overnight bowling trip. Next week they plan to go to Columbus.

I phoned the woman yesterday and told her to leave my wife alone. She read me off in pretty salty language, and said my wife is old enough to choose her own friends.

We have two children who are beginning to wonder what's going on. The house is always a mess and I've had to cook dinner for myself and the kids more times than I care to admit. Please give me some advice.
THE SPARE.

DEAR SPARE: The woman is right when she says your wife is old enough to choose her own friends. And if THIS is her choice she doesn't deserve the respectability of home, husband, and children.

Tell her she can go with you to a marriage counselor or a clergyman and discuss the problem. Something is wrong or she wouldn't be running around.[12]

Nearly every day, Ann Landers not only finds mental illness but recommends psychiatric (or parapsychiatric) help as the cure. A woman writes that her husband "likes to break rules." "If there is a sign that says, 'No smoking,'"—writes the wife—"he lights up at once. 'Keep off the Grass' is an invitation. I have seen him step right over and stomp on the newly seeded lawn just for the devil of it." The writer ends the letter by pleading: "Please tell me why he is like this and what I can do

[12] *The Syracuse Herald-Journal*, March 27, 1963, p. 35.

about it" and signs it "Married to a Nut." Ann Landers' diagnosis: "The 'Nut' has emotional problems which go back many years. . . . He needs professional help."[13]

In short, the columnist defines behavior that is annoying, improper, or unusual as due to mental illness, and recommends psychiatric (or similar "professional") treatment for it. This secular gospel is eagerly believed by the faithful, hungering for a properly "scientific" ideology: "I'm absolutely, positively normal, and I just want to stay that way," exclaims Miss Melissa Babish, aged 16, after being named the new Miss Teenage America.[14]

Moreover, spreading the faith in mental health is now considered an appropriate, indeed a commendable, activity for all groups. Thus, not only the psychiatric and allied professions, the newspapers and other news media, but the courts and legislators as well are imbued with and purvey the ideology of mental health and illness. For example, when, in 1954, the United States Court of Appeals for the District of Columbia handed down the Durham decision—ruling that ". . . an accused is not criminally responsible if his unlawful act was the product of mental disease or defect"[15]—the court decreed, by fiat, that every psychiatrist could do what Freud said he could not do, namely, decide who is mentally ill and who is not.

The point, of course, is not that this is an exceptionally difficult determination to make, but rather that it is unclear what is to be determined, for mental illness remains undefined. The courts refuse to define it. The psychiatrists and psychologists say they cannot define it—or else define it so broadly that everyone qualifies for the diagnosis. Despite this, jurists expect to place some men in the class of the mentally healthy and others in the class of the mentally sick; and psychiatrists and psychologists accept these categories and eagerly supply professional opinions that transform them into social realities.

[13] Ibid., April 23, 1963, p. 11.
[14] The Syracuse Herald-American, December 8, 1968, p. 11.
[15] Durham v. United States, 214 F. 2d 862 (D. C. Cir.), 1954; for further discussion, see Szasz, T. S.: "The insanity plea and the insanity verdict." This volume, pp. 98–112.

In the framework of the medieval Christian ideology, one could never be sure that the devil was not lurking about: he could be anywhere, influence anyone's actions. Just so with mental sickness. In the framework of the modern psychiatric ideology, one can never be sure that a person is *not* mentally sick. This uncertainty is the inevitable consequence of the lack of a clear and verifiable definition of mental illness.

If there could be a precise definition of mental illness, it is possible that no psychiatrist or psychologist would be required to diagnose it; perhaps any intelligent person could do so. However, because mental illness is undefined, the person with the social responsibility for making this determination is asked, in effect, not to ascertain facts, but to create a definition and to exercise social control.

Illustrations are hardly necessary; examples are all around us. Consider, for instance, the case of Miss Suzanne Clift, whose cold-blooded killing of her lover (in 1962) received much publicity. She admitted, and indeed no one disputed, that she had committed the act. Disposition of the case: The judge placed her on probation for ten years "with the stipulation that she voluntarily commit herself to the Massachusetts Mental Health Center for treatment."[16] To question the meaning of the adjective "voluntarily," or of the sort of disorder for which she will be "treated," is to appear either foolish or presumptuous.

In the framework of the psychiatric ideology, the questions are adequately answered. Miss Clift is a "mental patient"; hence, she does not know her own will, nor can she control it properly. Thus, she will seek treatment voluntarily, because the word "voluntarily" here means not "of her own accord," but "beneficial to her." To balk at these answers is considered presumptuous. Why? Not merely because such skepticism calls into question the judgment of experts in a particular case, but because it undermines a professionally and socially accepted point of view.

The current social dialogue between judges (and legislators) on the one hand and psychiatrists (and psychologists) on the

16 *Parade*, March 31, 1963, p. 3.

other may be paraphrased as follows. The jurists declare: "There are two kinds of criminals, one mentally healthy, the other mentally sick. Only you, psychiatrists (and psychologists), can determine who belongs in which group. You must help us and society by discharging this important professional obligation." The psychiatrists reply: "Of course, we shall try to fulfill this important social responsibility to the best of our abilities."

The psychiatric ideology offers significant rewards to the mental health experts willing to play this game. Indeed, why should the true believers in the ideology scrutinize the game, or, worse, refuse to play it? The faithful would have nothing to gain and much to lose: By rocking the boat, in which they themselves are precariously balanced passengers, they would only heighten the risk of being tossed into the raging seas of conceptual anomie and economic insecurity.

v

Every ideology presents the individual with a painful choice: What should be his attitude toward it? Should he be a loyal ideologist or a critical thinker?

The mental health professional who chooses to be a loyal member of his profession will thus embrace the ideology of mental health: he will teach it, apply it, refine it, distribute it as widely as possible, and, above all, defend it against those who assail it. Whereas the professional who chooses to be a critical thinker will scrutinize the ideology: he will analyze it; examine it historically, logically, and sociologically; criticize it, and hence undermine it as an ideology.

These two positions have always been inimical to each other. The reasons for this are fundamental to both ideology and science, and were stated succinctly in a recent address by Professor Daniel Bell. "A community of science"—he wrote—"has its own norms, its standards of research, common principles of verification, and, basically, a commitment to knowledge which cannot be warped by parochial loyalties. To this extent, there is an inherent conflict between science and ideology, to the detriment of ideology."[17]

However, this conflict could also work to the detriment of science. In the mental health professions, I think it has.

At the beginning of this century, Freud laid the foundations, within psychiatry, of a humane study of man. To Freud and his early colleagues this was not a study of man as object, whose worth is gauged by his social usefulness, and whose conduct is manipulated by his fellow man for the alleged good of society. On the contrary, it was a study of man as subject, a sentient being whose self-concept was never to be subordinated to his social image, and whose conduct was to be governed, not by benevolent therapists, but by his own ego.

This was a high-spirited program of scientific-humanistic exploration. The program and its great initial success rested, in large part, on three admonitions. Although Freud never enunciated them clearly, they deserve to be stated now: 1. The mental health or illness of a person is a matter of convention; 2. questions of mental health and illness do not merit serious scientific attention; and, in any case, 3. psychoanalysts ought to treat only those persons who want to be treated.

I have stated these admonitions so boldly to show that they are now honored in the breach. Although psychoanalysis began as a critique of the psychiatric ideology, it was soon absorbed into it, and now furnishes, especially in the United States, its principal justificatory imagery and rhetoric. Hence it is that rejecting (1) the validity of the concepts of mental health and illness, (2) the policy of restricting the practice of psychotherapy and psychoanalysis to physicians, and (3) the legitimacy of subjecting people to involuntary mental hospitalization and "treatment," have become the hallmarks of psychiatric heresy.

[17] Bell, D.: "The post-industrial society." Background paper for the forum discussion on "The Impact of Technological and Social Change" (Boston: mimeographed, 1962), pp. 34–35.

6 · WHAT PSYCHIATRY CAN

AND CANNOT DO

Psychiatry today is in the curious position of being viewed simultaneously with too much reverence and with undue contempt. Indeed, thoughtful Americans can be roughly divided between those who dismiss all forms of psychiatric practice as worthless or harmful, and those who regard it as a panacea for crime, unhappiness, political fanaticism, promiscuity, juvenile delinquency, and virtually every other moral, personal, and social ill of our time.

The adherents of this exaggerated faith are, I believe, the larger and certainly the more influential group in shaping contemporary social policy. It is they who beat the drums for large-scale mental health programs and who use the prestige of a massive psychiatric establishment as a shield of illusion, concealing some ugly realities we would rather not face. Thus when we read in the paper that the alcoholic, the rapist, or the vandal needs or will be given "psychiatric care," we are reassured that the problem is being solved or, in any event, effectively dealt with, and we dismiss it from our minds.

I contend that we have no right to this easy absolution from responsibility. In saying this I do not, as a practicing psychiatrist, intend to belittle the help that my profession can give to some troubled individuals. We have made significant progress since the pre-Freudian era, when psychiatry was a purely custodial enterprise.

However, our refusal to recognize the differences between medicine and psychiatry—that is, between deviations from biological norms, which we usually call "illness," and deviations from psychological or social norms, which we often call "mental illness"—has made it possible to popularize the simplistic clichés of current mental health propaganda. One of these, for instance, is the deceptive slogan "Mental illness is like any other illness." This is not true; psychiatric and medical problems are fundamentally dissimilar. In curing a disease like syphilis or pneumonia, the physician benefits both the patient and society. Can the psychiatrist who cures a "neurosis" make the same claim? Often he cannot, for in "mental illness" we find the individual in conflict with those about him—his family, his friends, his employer, perhaps his whole society. Do we expect psychiatry to help the individual—or society? If the interests of the two conflict, as they often do, the psychiatrist can help one only by harming the other.

II

Let us, for example, examine the case of a man I will call Victor Clauson. He is a junior executive with a promising future, a wife who loves him, and two healthy children. Nevertheless he is anxious and unhappy. He is bored with his job, which he believes saps his initiative and destroys his integrity; he is also dissatisfied with his wife, and convinced he never loved her. Feeling like a slave to his company, his wife, and his children, Clauson realizes that he has lost control over the conduct of his life.

Is this man "sick"? And, if so, what can be done about it? At least half a dozen alternatives are open to him: He could throw himself into his present work or change jobs or have an affair or get a divorce. Or he could develop a psychosomatic symptom such as headaches and consult a doctor. Or he could seek help from a psychotherapist. Which of these alternatives is the right one for him? The answer is not easy.

For, in fact, hard work, an affair, a divorce, a new job may all "help" him; and so may psychotherapy. But "treatment" cannot change his external, social situation; only he can do that. What psychoanalysis (and some other therapies) can offer him is a better knowledge of himself, which may enable him to make new and better choices in the conduct of his life.

Is Clauson "mentally sick"? If we so label him, what then is he to be cured of? Unhappiness? Indecision? The consequences of earlier, unwise decisions?

In my opinion, these are problems in living, not diseases. And by and large it is such problems that are brought to the psychiatrist's office. To ameliorate them he offers not treatment or cure but psychological counseling. To be of any avail, this process requires a consenting, co-operative client. There is, indeed, no way to "help" an individual who does not want to be a psychiatric patient. When treatment is imposed on a person, inevitably he sees it as serving not his own best interests, but the interests of those who brought him to the psychiatrist (and who often pay him).

Take the case of an elderly widow I will call Mrs. Rachel Abelson. Her husband was a successful businessman who died five years ago, bequeathing part of his estate of four million dollars to his children and grandchildren, part to charities, and one third to his wife. Mrs. Abelson has always been a frugal woman, whose life revolved around her husband. After he died, however, she changed. She began to give her money away—to her widowed sister, to charities, and finally to distant relatives abroad.

After a few years, Mrs. Abelson's children remonstrated, urging her to treat herself better, instead of wasting her money on people who had long managed by themselves. But Mrs. Abelson persisted in doing what she felt was "the right thing." Her children were wealthy; she enjoyed helping others.

Finally, the Abelson children consulted the family attorney. He was equally dismayed by the prospect that Mrs. Abelson might [in this fashion] dissipate all the funds she controlled. Like the children, he reasoned that if Mr. Abelson had wanted to help his third cousin's poverty-stricken daughters in Rumania, he could have done so himself; but he never did. Convinced that they ought to carry out the essence of their father's intention and keep the money in the family, the Abelson children petitioned to have their mother declared mentally incompetent to manage her affairs. This was done. Thereafter Mrs. Abelson became inconsolable. Her bitter accusations and the painful scenes that resulted only convinced her children that she really was mentally abnormal. When she refused to enter a private sanitarium voluntarily, she was committed by court order. She died two years later, and her will—leaving most of her assets to distant relatives—was easily broken on psychiatric grounds.

Like thousands of other involuntary mental patients, Mrs. Abelson was given psychiatric care in the hope of changing behavior offensive to others. Indeed, what was Mrs. Abelson's illness? Spending her money unwisely? Disinheriting her sons? In effect, recourse to psychiatry provided Mrs. Abelson's children with a socially acceptable solution for their dilemma, not hers. To an appalling degree, state mental hospitals perform a like function for the less affluent members of our society.

Out of all too many comparable cases, I will cite that of a man we may call Tim Kelleher, who worked steadily as a truck driver for forty years, supporting a wife and nine children. In his early sixties Kelleher found jobs getting scarcer. Now in his late seventies, he has not worked for over a decade. Since his wife died a few years ago, he has lived with one or another of his children.

For two years his daughter Kathleen, mother of four, has been caring for him. Because the old man has grown progressively senile and burdensome, Kathleen's husband wants to shift the responsibility to the other children, but they all feel they've done their share.

Mr. Kelleher's future depends on what his family decides to do with him. One of them may still be willing to take care of him, but, if not, he will be committed to a state mental hospital. His case will be diagnosed as a "senile psychosis" or something similar. More than a third of the patients now in our mental hospitals are such "geriatric" cases. This is how psychiatry meets a purely socioeconomic need.

If Mr. Kelleher or one of his children were even moderately wealthy, they could hire a companion or nurse to care for him at home, or they could place him in a private nursing home. There would be no need to label him a "mental patient" and confine him to a building he will never again leave, and where he will doubtless die within a year.

But, for the poor, the mental hospital is often the only way.

Such is the plight of Mrs. Anna Tarranti (this is not her real name). At thirty-two—but looking ten years older—she has just been delivered of her seventh child. Her husband is a construction worker, sporadically employed, and a heavy drinker. After each of the last three babies was born, Mrs. Tarranti was so "depressed" that she had to stay in the hospital an extra week or more. Now she complains of exhaustion, cannot eat or sleep, and does not want to see her baby. At the same time she feels guilty for not being a good mother, and says she ought to die.

The fact is that Mrs. Tarranti is overwhelmed. She has more children than she wants, a husband who earns only a marginal living, and religious beliefs that virtually prohibit birth control. What should she do? She knows that if she goes home, she'll soon be pregnant again, a prospect she cannot endure. She would like to stay in the hospital, but the obstetrical ward is too busy to keep her long without a bona fide obstetrical illness.

Again psychiatry comes to the rescue. Mrs. Tarranti's condition is diagnosed as a "post-partum depression" and she is committed to the state hospital. As in the case of Mr. Kelleher, society has found no more decent solution to a human problem than confinement in a mental hospital.

In effect, psychiatry has accepted the job of warehousing society's undesirables. Such, alas, has long been its role. More than a hundred and fifty years ago, the great French psychiatrist Philippe Pinel observed, "Public asylums for maniacs have been regarded as places of confinement for such of its members as have become dangerous to the peace of society."[1]

III

Nor have we any right to comfort ourselves with the belief that in our enlightened age confinement in a mental institution is really the same as any other kind of hospitalization. For even though we show more compassion and understanding toward the insane than some of our forebears, the fact is that the person

[1] Pinel, P.: *A Treatise on Insanity* [1801, 1809], transl. by D. D. Davis, facsimile of the London 1806 edition (New York: Hafner Publishing Co., 1962), pp. 3–4.

diagnosed as mentally ill is stigmatized—particularly if he has been confined in a public mental hospital. These stigmata cannot be removed by mental health "education," for the root of the matter is our intolerance of certain kinds of behavior.

Most people who are considered mentally sick (especially those confined involuntarily) are so defined by their relatives, friends, employers, or perhaps the police—not by themselves. These people have upset the social order—by disregarding the conventions of polite society or by violating laws—so we label them "mentally ill" and punish them by commitment to a mental institution.

The patient knows that he is deprived of freedom because he has annoyed others, not because he is sick. And in the mental hospital he learns that until he alters his behavior he will be segregated from society. But even if he changes and is permitted to leave, his record of confinement goes with him. And the practical consequences are more those of a prison than a hospital record. The psychological and social damage thus incurred often far outweighs the benefits of any psychiatric therapy.

Consider, for example, the case of a young nurse I will call Emily Silverman, who works in a general hospital in a small city. Unmarried and lonely, she worries about the future. Will she find a husband? Will she have to go on supporting herself in a job that has become drudgery? She feels depressed, sleeps poorly, loses weight. Finally, she consults an internist at the hospital and is referred to a psychiatrist. He diagnoses her trouble as a case of "depression" and prescribes "anti-depressant" drugs. Emily takes the pills and visits the psychiatrist weekly, but she remains depressed and begins to think about suicide. This alarms the psychiatrist, who recommends hospitalization. Since there is no private mental hospital in the city, Emily seeks admission to the state hospital nearby. There, after a few months, she realizes that the "treatment" the hospital offers cannot help solve her problems. She then "recovers" and is discharged.

From now on, Emily is no longer just a nurse; she is a nurse with a "record" of confinement in a state mental hospital. When she tries to return to her job, she will probably find it filled and that there are no openings. Indeed, as an ex-mental patient she may find it impossible to obtain any employment in nursing. This is a heavy price to pay for ignorance, yet no one warned her of the hazards involved before she decided to enter the hospital for her "depression."

Because the therapeutic potentialities of psychiatry are consistently exaggerated and its punitive functions minimized or even denied, a distorted relationship between psychiatry and the law has evolved in our time.

Years ago some people accused of serious crimes pleaded "insanity." Today they are often charged with it. Instead of receiving a brief jail sentence, a defendant may be branded "insane" and incarcerated for life in a psychiatric institution.[2]

This is what happened, for example, to a filling-station operator I will call Joe Skulski. When he was told to move his business to make way for a new shopping center, he stubbornly resisted eviction. Finally the police were summoned. Joe greeted them with a warning shot in the air. He was taken into custody and denied bail, because the police considered his protest peculiar and thought he must be crazy. The district attorney requested a pretrial psychiatric examination of the accused. Mr. Skulski was examined, pronounced mentally unfit to stand trial, and confined in the state hospital for the criminally insane. Through it all, he pleaded for the right to be tried for his offense. Now in the mental hospital, he will spend years of fruitless effort to prove that he is sane enough to stand trial. If he had been convicted, his prison sentence would have been shorter than the term he has already served in the hospital.

IV

This is not to say that our public mental hospitals serve no socially useful purpose. They do, in fact, perform two essential —and very different—functions. On the one hand, they help patients recover from personal difficulties by providing them with

[2] Szasz, T. S.: *Psychiatric Justice* (New York: Macmillan, 1965).

room, board, and a medically approved escape from everyday responsibilities. On the other hand, they help families, and society, care for those who annoy or burden them unduly. It is important that we sort out these very different services, for unfortunately their goals are not the same. To relieve people annoyed by the eccentricities, failings, or outright meanness of so-called mentally disturbed persons requires that something be done *to* mental patients, not *for* them. The aim here is to safeguard the sensibilities not of the patient, but of those he upsets. This is a moral and social, not a medical, problem. How, for example, do you weigh the right of Mr. Kelleher to spend his declining years in freedom and dignity rather than as a psychiatric prisoner, against the right of his children to lead a "life of their own" unburdened by a senile father? Or the right of Mrs. Tarranti to repudiate overwhelming responsibilities, against her husband's and children's need for the services of a full-time wife and mother? Or the right of Mrs. Abelson to give away her money to poor relatives, against her children's claim on their father's fortune?

Granting that there can often be no happy resolution to such conflicts, there is no reason to feel that we are as yet on the right road. For one thing, we still tolerate appalling inequities between our treatment of the rich and the poor. Though it may be no more than a dimly grasped ideal, both medicine and law strive to treat all people equally. In psychiatry, however, we not only fail to approximate this goal in our practice; we do not even value it as an ideal.

We regard the rich and influential psychiatric patient as a self-governing, responsible client—free to decide whether or not to be a patient. But we look upon the poor and the aged patient as a ward of the state—too ignorant or too "mentally sick" to know what is best for him. The paternalistic psychiatrist, as an agent of the family or the state, assumes "responsibility" for him, defines him as a "patient" against his will, and subjects him to "treatment" deemed best for him, with or without his consent.

Do we really need more of this kind of psychiatry?

Among the vast numbers of "tranquilizing" functions[1] performed by psychiatrists in present-day American society, there is one to which I should like to call special attention. I call it "bootlegging humanism."

Although humanism is a rather vague term, it is not altogether a useless one. To most of us, it means that personal autonomy, dignity, liberty, and responsibility are considered positive values. Further, humanism implies the approbation of such traits as gentleness, understanding, and mercifulness. Conversely, the humanist ethic regards inequality before the law, social oppression, harsh punishments, and viciousness of all sorts as bad and condemnable.

Bootlegging is a good American slang term for the illegal supply of a product—as in bootlegging liquor. For bootlegging to occur, two conditions must be met: first, there must be a powerful need that men will seek to satisfy; second, gratification of the need must be legally prohibited. If these conditions obtain, satisfaction of the need by illegal means will be stimulated and most likely will flourish.

We tend to associate bootlegging with the illegal satisfaction of morally reprehensible desires, such as the need for liquor and narcotics. This is misleading. It often happens that the satisfaction of lofty aspirations and needs is prohibited by law. Let us remember that laws can degrade and stultify human dignity and welfare as easily as they can uplift them. We then speak of bad, stupid, or unreasonable laws. When laws frustrate the satisfaction of certain important human aspirations, the stage is set to gratify the pent-up desires illegally, that is, by boot-

[1] See Szasz, T. S.: "The myth of mental illness." This volume, pp. 12–24.

legging. During the Nazi era, for example, many Germans, Dutchmen, and especially Danes, hid Jews, or helped to smuggle them abroad, in violation of the law. We—and I am speaking collectively here, meaning "we," American psychiatrists—are engaged in a somewhat similar smuggling operation. I shall describe this smuggling operation by using therapeutic abortion on psychiatric grounds as an illustrative example.

II

Like most prohibitive laws, those regulating abortion do not absolutely forbid this practice. Rather, abortion is considered illegal unless certain conditions obtain. The conditions that allow a woman to have an abortion—much like the excusing conditions that permit killing someone—vary from state to state. Mental illness is usually one such condition. In other words, in some states, if psychiatrists certify that a woman is mentally ill or is likely to become so if allowed to carry a pregnancy to term, she is permitted to have a legal, or so-called therapeutic, abortion.

Wherever therapeutic abortions are performed in appreciable numbers, more are performed on psychiatric grounds than on any other. At the Mount Sinai Hospital in New York, for example, thirty-nine per cent of all therapeutic abortions performed between 1952 and 1957 were justified on psychiatric grounds. In contrast, only eleven per cent of the abortions were performed because of cardiorenal disease, and only ten per cent because of malignancy.[2] In the first nine months following the enactment of a "liberalized" abortion law in Colorado in 1967, 109 therapeutic abortions were performed at the Denver General Hospital, ninety per cent for "psychiatric reasons."[3] When a similar law was enacted in California in 1968, the incidence of "mental illness" during pregnancy rose even more precipitously:

[2] "Therapeutic abortion." MD, The Medical Newsmagazine, December 1958, p. 61.

[3] "Colorado abortions rise following law revision." Psychiatric News, 3:10 (July), 1968.

in the first six months of the year, 1,777 pregnant women in that state were found to require a therapeutic abortion to "safe-guard [their] mental health"; during the same period, only 115 therapeutic abortions were performed to "preserve [the woman's] physical health."[4]

At present, there continues to be widespread interest among members of the medical and psychiatric professions in measures aimed at "liberalizing" abortion laws. Such liberalization, it seems to me, may be sought in one of two ways.

One way is to advocate an ever increasing number of medical, eugenic, psychiatric, and social considerations as "therapeutic indications" for abortion, thus making more abortions legal. This has the advantage, if it be an advantage, of providing the op-portunity, at least for some persons, to have abortions if they so desire. At the same time, it leaves the ethical premises that un-derlie our attitudes and laws about abortion unexamined and unchanged.

This type of social action also has some important disadvan-tages. Perhaps the most important one is that it places a pre-mium on being sick or disabled. If a woman is healthy and pregnant, she must bear her child whether she likes it or not. If, however, she can get herself defined as sick, she may avail herself of a legal abortion. So far as psychiatry is concerned, the obvious difficulty with this arrangement is that while one can-not readily acquire, say, rheumatic heart disease simply because it might be advantageous to be sick, one can, in such circum-stances, develop mental illness. Providing certain privileges for people afflicted with so-called mental illness—for example, ex-empting them from the military draft, or excusing them from the consequences of certain misbehaviors, or permitting them to have abortions, and thus, by comparison, penalizing those who are mentally healthy—is a rather risky enterprise. Is it desirable that one be "mentally ill" to enjoy freedom from being coerced by the physiological consequences of the sexual act?

Another fundamental disadvantage of current medical-

[4] "5,000 legal abortions done in California in 9 months." *Hospital Tribune*, November 18, 1968, p. 3.

psychiatric efforts to liberalize abortion is that they increase rather than diminish the covert ethical conflict between medical and self-willed abortion. Implicit in all such reforms is the thesis that it is all right for medical and psychiatric experts to decide whether or not a woman should bear a child she does not want, but it is not all right for her to do so. In other words, abortion justified on medical and psychiatric grounds, as opposed to self-willed abortion, makes medical and psychiatric experts, rather than adult, self-reliant citizens, responsible for determining whether the physiological chain reaction initiated with the sexual act and culminating in delivery should be interrupted or not.

An alternative course is to develop fully and confront frankly the socioethical issues involved in abortion (and other similar problems, such as birth control or the death penalty). By espousing and embracing legislation based on traditional legal and social attitudes, psychiatrists actually make it more difficult for people, themselves included, to come to grips with the really significant issues. I submit that efforts to "liberalize" abortion laws by providing a broader spectrum of medical and psychiatric justifications for the procedure are, in effect, restrictive of human freedom. This is because medical and psychiatric "liberalization" of abortion laws would only increase the number of occasions on which other people could provide abortions for women; it would not increase the number of occasions on which pregnant women themselves could make this decision. Such measures, therefore, give assent to the proposition that it is good to deny people the right to determine for themselves how they should use their bodies.

III

Most problems posed by legislation pertaining to the sexual activities of adults may be condensed into a single question and the possible answers to it. The question is: Who owns one's body? In other words, does a person's body belong to his parents, as it did, to some extent, when he was a child? Or does it belong to the state? Or to the sovereign? Or, perchance, to God? Or, finally, does it belong to himself?[5]

Each of these choices is logically justifiable and empirically possible. Each reflects the rules of a particular socioethical system, or game of life. We must be clear, however, about which value system we favor. According to traditional Christian theology, for example, the body belongs to God. On the other hand, modern secular humanism implies—and, I believe, should explicitly affirm—that a person's body, if he is an adult, belongs to himself. This means that he may kill himself without thereby committing a crime. He may also exercise whatever controls he wishes over his procreative functions. From this point of view, then, having an abortion performed on oneself would fall in the same category as, say, having one's varicose veins ligated.

The foregoing attitude toward the human body, and particularly toward its procreative functions, is in sharp conflict with religious attitudes toward it. Whatever the differences among them, all Western religions agree that man is God's creation. This not only endows man with special importance and value, but also obligates him to adhere to God-given laws. For our present purposes it will suffice to consider briefly the Roman Catholic position on the issue of body-ownership, and, more specifically, on birth control.

The Catholic position, while it is the most extreme, is also the most consistent and logical among the various religious views on this subject. Briefly, Catholic teaching regards all "artificial" interferences with human procreation as sinful because of two fundamental ethical propositions: First, man's relation to virtually everything of importance, and especially the use of his sexual organs, is considered to be governed by "natural law"— that is, by law implicitly God-given. "Artificial" birth control is regarded as contrary to "natural law." Second, the beginning of human life is reckoned from the moment of fertilization. Thus, the embryo is regarded as "living" and as possessing a theologicolegal existence separate from that of the mother's. Be-

[5] See Szasz, T. S.: "The ethics of birth control; or, who owns your body?" *The Humanist,* 20:332–36 (Nov.–Dec.), 1960.

cause of this, Catholic doctrine places abortion, infanticide, suicide, and homicide in a single category, namely, "murder." It follows that lawbreaking and murder, however perpetrated, are bad. Hence, to ask a Roman Catholic to support artificial birth control or abortion is to ask him to approve of means leading to undesired ends.

Many non-Catholics, although subscribing to the thesis that considerations of health justify the use of artificial birth control measures, may nevertheless believe that the proper uses of the human body are, or should be, regulated by divine laws. Hence they, too, may be opposed to masturbation and the use of contraceptive devices when these serve only the pursuit of carnal pleasure, or to self-willed abortion when it serves merely the career aspirations of a woman.

The humanistic, secular view of man, no less than the Roman Catholic, rests on certain ethical premises. Fundamental among these is the proposition that the human embryo is considered to have no existence separate from the mother's. The decision of when "human existence" begins—that is, when the baby shall be considered an entity legally separate from the mother—must be an arbitrary one. The beginning of the baby's existence may thus be placed at the sixth month of life, when the fetus becomes viable, or perhaps at the time of delivery. The point is that, in the view here proposed, for some period of time after impregnation the uterine contents are regarded as part of the mother's body. According to this definition, there can be no such thing as the murder of a non-viable fetus.

Being human, then, is here regarded as primarily an ethical or psychological concept. This must be contrasted with theological or biological definitions of humanness. According to the theological (Roman Catholic) definition, for example, a fertilized egg is human, as is also an anencephalic (brainless) fetus. According to the biological definition, a viable fetus is human, but not a fertilized ovum. All definitions are to some extent arbitrary, and theological, biological, and psychosocial definitions of humanness are no exceptions. This brief discussion was intended only as a reminder of the criteria—which, although themselves arbitrary, can be described, inspected, and argued about—on the basis of which the quality of humanness is some-times ascribed to organisms, yet often withheld from people.

In the framework of an ethic that favors personal autonomy, responsibility, and self-reliance, the decision of whether a woman should or should not have an abortion would depend primarily on whether she wanted one. The matter would con-cern only her and her physician (and perhaps her husband, if she has one)—much as is the case today with elective surgical operations. Accordingly, providing an ever increasing range of psychiatric illnesses as justifications for performing therapeutic abortions is a liberalizing step only if we are fundamentally opposed to the principle of self-willed abortion and all that it implies. If, on the other hand, we regard self-determination over one's bodily functions and parts as an integral aspect of our ethic, then preserving legislation fundamentally opposed to abortion, and increasing the number of allowing conditions, is anything but desirable.

I believe it is a serious mistake to provide psychiatric inter-ventions, such as justifications for therapeutic abortion, without first seeking to clarify what one considers the desirable moral underpinnings of society. There are many serious scientific tasks for which psychiatric skills are sorely needed. Psychiatric justi-fications for abortions, however, belong in that class of phenom-ena that might appear to be scientific or technical, but are, in fact, strategic or tactical.[6]

IV

I have argued that therapeutic abortion on psychiatric grounds is a subterfuge, and that the psychiatrist who makes such abortions possible is a bootlegger of certain inexplicit moral values. I should like to amplify and perhaps further clarify this thesis.

When a psychiatrist recommends a therapeutic abortion, he does not, strictly speaking, bootleg abortion. A vast and flourish-

[6] In this connection, see Szasz, T. S.: "The rhetoric of rejection." This volume, pp. 49–68; "Psychiatric classification as a strategy of personal constraint." This volume, pp. 190–217.

ing bootleg market in this commodity is maintained by physicians and others who perform illegal operations. Although the psychiatrist who provides the grounds for an abortion is not an ordinary bootlegger like the abortionist, he may nevertheless be considered a bootlegger of a special kind: he is a legally authorized bootlegger. In his role as psychiatrist, he is empowered by law to grant permission for otherwise prohibited acts. The physician's role during Prohibition was similar. He could bootleg liquor by ordering it on a prescription blank. Hence, he did not have to smuggle it in from Canada. In much the same way, the psychiatrist need not violate the law to furnish an abortion. He is authorized to prescribe abortion as though it were treatment, provided he can find the pregnant woman to be mentally ill. Let us, at this point, suppose that there were no such thing as mental illness. Where would this leave us? What would we think if the basis for prescribing the banned product—whether liquor or abortion—were fictitious or contrived? Would this not be legalized bootlegging?

Some may object to this argument by rejecting the assertion that psychiatric diagnoses are fictitious or contrived. Psychiatric illnesses—they may reply—are every bit as real as medical illnesses. This is a crucial point. I can only say here that I consider the notion of mental illness a myth.[7] Asserting this, I do not mean to deny the obvious fact that people may suffer from, and may be disabled by, the difficulties that the task of coping with life presents to them. We must keep in mind, however, that mental illnesses are merely the names we give to certain strategies of living and their consequences. If this is true, the forms of behavior in the totality of social existence we define as mental illness—that is, the strategies we choose to so label—result from a profoundly moral and strategic decision. Let me briefly illustrate this aspect of psychiatry by citing an actual incident. I relate the episode from memory, but I believe the account is substantially accurate.

Some years ago, in a city on the eastern seaboard, there occurred a much publicized tragedy that was the result of an

[7] Szasz, T. S.: "The myth of mental illness," *supra*.

illegal abortion. The facts were briefly as follows: Against parental wishes, a woman from a wealthy family married a poor young man. She became first pregnant, then disillusioned with her husband. Thereupon she returned to the parental home and with her mother's aid obtained an illegal abortion. As a result of it, she died. The roles of the mother and of the abortionist in this tragedy were publicly exposed. The abortionist was tried and sentenced to a term in prison, but not the mother. She was said to have been severely depressed, and entered a psychiatric sanitarium. In spite of her complicity in the act, she was, to my knowledge, never brought to trial. Perhaps it was felt that she had suffered "enough" by the death of her daughter and that meting out additional penalty would be too harsh. Mercy and exemption from punishment were thus smuggled in under the guise of psychiatric diagnosis and treatment.

I am not advocating revengeful law-enforcement. This example is intended only as a reminder that what the law considers crime or mental illness is a matter of moral convention. In the example cited, the abortionist was like a bank robber who happened to kill a guard during a holdup, and the mother was like his accomplice who drove the getaway car. Both were engaged in the same prohibited, "criminal" act—the illegal removal of a fetus from a uterus in the one case, the illegal removal of money from a bank in the other. It is absurd to consider only one of the members of such a team a criminal, and not the other. Yet this is what was done with the abortionist and the grieving mother, and what is done generally in connection with prosecutions for illegal abortion.

From a psychological point of view, one could argue that having to bear a child she does not want is always deleterious for a woman. Hence, any woman's wish to have an abortion could be construed as psychiatric ground for permitting it. If this is true, therapeutic abortion for psychiatric reasons is clearly a smuggling operation. Merciful exemption from an otherwise harsh law—a law that prevents interference with certain physiological processes—is smuggled in under the guise of medical diagnosis, treatment, and prevention. The true character of this operation remains obscure so long as the quantity of the smuggled merchandise is relatively small. If the scale of the operation were stepped up, it would provoke the same resistance that motivates the law to oppose the principle of self-determined abortion.

I have by no means exhausted the uses to which the model of bootlegging may be put in connection with psychiatric interventions. For example, one could show that some psychiatrists who promote therapeutic abortions, believing that they function in a purely medical capacity, act as the unwitting stooges of the legislators. It is as though they drove the trucks that carried bootleg liquor (mercy), believing all the while that they transported some other, legitimate, product (psychiatric diagnosis and prevention). Such a psychiatrist alleviates the legislator's pangs of conscience for making laws that, without him, would be too hard on human beings. An example is the situation in which the victim of rape may be entitled to abortion only on psychiatric grounds.

v

I have tried to call attention to the hidden socioethical aspects of psychiatric-therapeutic abortion and similar methods of "bootlegging humanism." As I have shown, it is not so much abortion itself that is bootlegged by this strategy, but rather the right to determine for one's self whether to bring a child into the world. This is bad—though, of course, not wholly bad—if for no other reason than that the more efficiently bootlegging supplies a needed product, the less intense is the consciously experienced desire to change the law. This is a consequence of understandable human laziness. Knowing this, we should be especially cautious before we endorse or adopt psychiatric subterfuges to soften what may seem to us stupid or undesirable laws. For, by so doing, we may unwittingly delay and obstruct the reforms we really desire and need.

I dislike and disapprove of our abortion laws, but I also dislike evading laws by convenient subterfuges. To put it bluntly, I do not believe in "helping" patients by "pleading insanity" for them. It is out of this dilemma that I have evolved the ideas presented here.

Still, someone might object and say: "Well and good, but life cannot be lived in a social vacuum. Until existing laws are changed, we must live, if not within them, at least with them. We must play the game according to prevailing rules." This is a powerful argument on the level of everyday, practical living. It is difficult to adhere consistently to ideal principles. Compromises are sometimes necessary. Having said this, let us remember, however, that the more we compromise with our ideals, the more we play games by prevailing rules, and the more we perfect our skills in playing such games—the less eager, interested, and capable we shall be in developing and playing new games more fitting to the stature of civilized man.

8 · THE INSANITY PLEA AND
THE INSANITY VERDICT

In 1843, Daniel M'Naghten shot and killed Edward Drum-mond, private secretary to Sir Robert Peel, whom M'Naghten had intended to kill. The defense was insanity. Evidence was introduced showing that M'Naghten "was labouring under the insane delusion" of being hounded by enemies, among them Peel. Lord Chief Justice Tindal was so impressed by this evidence that he practically directed a verdict for acquittal. The jury found M'Naghten not guilty, on the ground of insanity.[1] As usually told, this is where the story ends. But what happened to Daniel M'Naghten?

Since M'Naghten was acquitted, the reader might think that he was discharged by the court. Until 1843, this is what the word "acquittal" meant in the English language. But M'Nagh-ten's "acquittal" was a precursor to that debauchment of lan-guage which, as Orwell taught us, is characteristic of modern bureaucratic societies. *De jure,* M'Naghten was acquitted; *de facto,* he was sentenced to life imprisonment in an insane asylum. He was confined at the Bethlehem Hospital until 1864, when he was transferred to the newly opened Broadmoor In-stitution for the Criminally Insane. M'Naghten died in Broad-moor in 1865, having been incarcerated for the last twenty-two years of his life.

According to traditional English and American Law, an illegal act is criminal only if it is committed with criminal intent. The law also holds that certain insane persons who com-mit forbidden acts are not capable of forming the necessary criminal intent and should therefore be judged "not guilty by reason of insanity." This judicial concept requires that some

[1] *Daniel M'Naghten's Case,* 10 Cl. & Fin. 200, 8 Eng. Rep. 718, 1843.

means be found to distinguish persons who commit forbidden acts with criminal intent from persons who commit them without such intent because of insanity. The purpose of psychiatric "tests" of criminal responsibility—one of the oldest of which is named after Daniel M'Naghten—is to do just this.

Actually, what does the M'Naghten rule say? It asserts that to establish a defense on the ground of insanity it must be clearly proved that at the time of committing the act the party accused was laboring under such a defect of reason, from disease of the mind, as not to know the nature and quality of the act he was doing, or, if he did know it, that he did not know he was doing what was wrong.

In 1954, the United States Court of Appeals for the District of Columbia, in an opinion by Judge David Bazelon, handed down a decision that displaced the M'Naghten rule and substituted for it what has become known as the Durham rule.[2] According to this decision, "An accused is not criminally responsible if his unlawful act was the product of mental disease or mental defect."[3]

In 1966, the United States Court of Appeals for the Second Circuit, in an opinion by Judge Irving R. Kaufman, handed down a decision replacing the prior rule for the circuit with a new test of criminal responsibility recommended by the American Law Institute.[4] Objecting especially to the M'Naghten rule's emphasis on "defect of reason," Judge Kaufman's ruling provided that "A person is not responsible for criminal conduct if at the time of such conduct as a result of mental disease or defect he lacks substantial capacity either to appreciate the wrongfulness of his conduct or to conform his conduct to the requirements of law."[5]

These new tests of criminal responsibility reflect a long-standing dissatisfaction, in both the legal and psychiatric community, with the M'Naghten rule, which is deemed unsatisfac-

[2] *Durham* v. *United States*, 214 F. 2d 862 (D. C. Cir.), 1954.
[3] Ibid., pp. 874–75.
[4] *United States* v. *Freeman*, 357 F. 2d 606 (2d Cir.), 1966.
[5] Ibid., p. 622; see also *Model Penal Code*, par. 4.01, final draft, 1962.

tory because, in Judge Kaufman's words, it is ". . . not in harmony with modern medical science which . . . is opposed to any concept which divides the mind into separate compartments—the intellect, the emotions, and the will."[6] This has been the gist of the argument against the M'Naghten rule: it is old-fashioned and unscientific.

All tests of criminal responsibility rest on the premise that people "have" conditions called "mental diseases," which "cause" them to commit criminal acts.[7] The value of these tests thus hinges on the soundness of this underlying concept.

II

What kind of illness is "mental illness"? Leaders in medicine, psychiatry, government, education, industry, and labor never tire of proclaiming that "mental illness is like any other illness," frequently adding that "mental illness is the nation's number one health problem." This concern about mental illness does not seem to be shared by those who suffer, or might suffer, from it. A 1966 Gallup poll on the question, "What disease or illness do you fear the most?" yielded the following results: On the top of the list: cancer (62%) and blindness (18%); on the bottom of the list: polio (3%) and deafness (1%); not on the list at all: mental illness.[8]

The explanation of this paradox lies in the nature of modern psychiatry and its concept of mental illness. Harold Visotsky, Director of the Department of Mental Health for Illinois, lists "[j]uvenile delinquency, school problems, problems of urban areas, community conflicts, marriage and family counseling, and well-being programs" as among the major concerns of the contemporary psychiatrist.[9] J. Sanbourne Bockoven, Superintendent of the Cushing Hospital in Framingham, Massachusetts, frankly

[6] *United States* v. *Freeman, supra,* p. 622.

[7] See also *United States* v. *Currens,* 290 F. 2d 751 (3rd Cir.), 1961.

[8] "Disease fear." *Parade,* Feb. 13, 1966, p. 14.

[9] Visotsky, H.: "Community psychiatry: We are willing to learn." *Amer. J. Psychiatry,* 122:692–93 (Dec.), 1965, p. 692.

acknowledges, "The condition designated as 'mental illness' is not primarily, basically, or essentially so much a medical concern or responsibility as it is a vital concern of the . . . state."[10] These statements by prominent psychiatrists—and many other similar opinions could be cited—illustrate the scope of modern psychiatry and the kinds of "illnesses" its practitioners treat.

In what sense, then, is a "mentally ill" person sick? To answer this question we must note the several ways in which social roles may be acquired. Some, like hereditary monarch, are inherited; others, like graduate student, are voluntarily assumed; and still others, like convicted criminal, are ascribed to the person against his will.

Typically, the role of medical patient is assumed voluntarily. In the usual course of events, an individual who suffers from pain, discomfort, or disability seeks out a physician and submits to examination by him; the diagnosis—say, diabetes mellitus—is the name the physician gives to the patient's illness.

My purpose in describing what might seem a rather self-evident chain of events, leading from personal discomfort to medical diagnosis, is to show that when we speak of illness we often mean two quite different things: first, that the person displays a certain ("abnormal") *biological condition;* second, that he occupies a certain ("deviant") *social role.* The hypothetical patient mentioned above displays signs and symptoms of his biological condition (for example, sugar in the urine and loss of weight); he also occupies the sick role (for example, he consults a physician and follows his therapeutic recommendations). It is worth emphasizing that biological conditions exist regardless of whether or not they are observed and recognized by human beings, whereas social roles exist only insofar as they are observed and recognized by human beings.

Whereas the role of the *medical* patient is typically assumed voluntarily (though it may sometimes be ascribed to an unconscious person)—the role of *mental* patient may either be assumed voluntarily or imposed on a person against his will. If

[10] Bockoven, S.: "The moral mandate of community psychiatry in America." *Psychiatric Opinion,* 3:32–39 (Winter), 1966, p. 34.

an individual assumes the role of mental patient voluntarily—
for example, by visiting a psychotherapist in his office—his social
role is essentially the same as that of a medical patient, or, for
that matter, of any client who purchases the services of an expert. If, however, an individual is pressed into the role of mental patient against his will—for example, by being committed to
a mental hospital—then his social role most closely resembles
that of the criminal sentenced to imprisonment.

III

Both psychiatry and law are concerned with defining which
roles are socially legitimate and which are not, and with enforcing conformity to prescribed roles. Institutional psychiatry
enforces role conformity by defining role deviance as mental
illness punishable by commitment. When, for example, a poor,
uneducated, overburdened housewife escapes from her life of
drudgery into the pretense that she is the Virgin Mary, the psychiatrist calls the woman "sick" and thus interferes with her
playing the role she has selected for herself.[11] This type of
prohibition, buttressed by the sanction of confinement in a mental hospital, is similar to the prohibition of the role of bank
robber, buttressed by the sanction of confinement in prison.

Why isn't all socially undesirable conduct proscribed by law
and punished by penal sanctions? And why isn't all other conduct allowed? Questions such as these are essential to a deeper
inquiry into our subject. It must suffice to remark here that our
age seems passionately devoted to *not* confronting problems of
good and evil, and prefers, therefore, the rhetoric of medicine
to the rhetoric of morals. It is as if modern judges had acquired
the disability their predecessors had attributed to M'Naghten.
M'Naghten, we are told, could not distinguish between right
and wrong. Many judges, we may infer from their words and

[11] For further discussion and documentation, see Szasz, T. S.:
"Psychiatric classification as a strategy of personal constraint." This
volume, pp. 190–217; "Involuntary mental hospitalization: A crime
against humanity." This volume, pp. 113–139.

acts, prefer not to distinguish between right and wrong. They speak of mental health and sickness rather than of good and evil, and mete out the penalty of commitment rather than of imprisonment.

In the above-mentioned case before the United States Court of Appeals for the Second Circuit, the moral problem was more difficult to evade than usual, but evaded it was. The defendant, Charles Freeman, had been convicted of selling heroin. He maintained that he was not guilty, by reason of insanity. In reversing the conviction, the court left open the possibility that under the new standards Freeman might be found insane. Yet, if ever there was a moral problem, this was it. The fundamental questions this case poses are whether it is good or bad to sell heroin, and whether or not such conduct should be prohibited by law. (By substituting cigarettes, alcohol, guns, birth control devices, or worthless drugs for heroin, we gain a broader perspective on the type of problem we must face here.) Judge Kaufman's decision is significant precisely because it shifts the emphasis from the moral to the medical. In doing so, it exemplifies the "hysterical optimism" that, according to Richard Weaver, "will prevail until the world again admits the existence of tragedy, and it cannot admit the existence of tragedy until it again distinguishes between good and evil."[12]

As mental illness is unlike medical illness, so the mental hospital is unlike the medical hospital. In contemporary American society, the situation of the medical patient vis-à-vis the medical hospital is essentially that of a buyer vis-à-vis a vendor. A customer need not buy any merchandise he does not want. In the same way, a sick person need not enter a hospital, or submit to an operation, or undergo X-ray treatment, or take drugs, unless he is willing to do so.[13] The patient must give "informed consent" to his physician for any diagnostic or therapeutic procedure; without such consent, the physician is committing an un-

12 Weaver, R. M.: *Ideas Have Consequences* [1948] (Chicago: Phoenix Books, 1962), p. 11.
13 See, for example, Shindell, S.: *The Law in Medical Practice* (Pittsburgh: The University of Pittsburgh Press, 1966), especially pp. 16–32.

authorized invasion of the patient's body and is subject to both civil and criminal sanctions.

It may be thought that the care of patients with communicable diseases constitutes a significant exception to this rule, but this is not so. For example, the *New York Public Health Law* (Paragraph 2223) provides: "1. Any person having tuberculosis, who shall dispose of his sputum, saliva, or other body secretion or excretion so as to cause offense or danger to any person or persons occupying the same room or apartment, house, or part of a house, shall on complaint of any person or persons subjected to such offense or danger, be deemed guilty of a nuisance, and any persons subjected to such a nuisance may make complaint in person or writing to the health officer of the local health district where the nuisance complained of is committed. 2. It shall be the duty of the local health officer receiving such complaint to investigate and if it appears that the nuisance complained of is such as to cause offense or danger to any person occupying the same room, apartment, house, or part of a house, he shall serve notice upon the person so complained of, reciting the alleged cause of offense or danger and requiring him to dispose of his sputum, saliva, or other bodily secretion or excretion in such a manner as to remove all reasonable cause of offense or danger. 3. Any person failing or refusing to comply with orders or regulations of the local health officer requiring him to cease to commit such nuisance, shall be deemed guilty of misdemeanor and on conviction thereof shall be fined not more than ten dollars." There are no provisions in the law authorizing tuberculosis hospitals to hold and treat patients against their will.

The opposite of this is the situation of the involuntary mental patient. (Approximately ninety per cent of hospitalized mental patients in the United States are confined involuntarily.)[14] The mental patient may be compelled, through the power vested in the physician by the state, to submit to psychiatric

[14] See *Hearings on Constitutional Rights of the Mentally Ill*, 87th Cong., 1st Sess., Part 1 (Washington, D.C.: U. S. Government Printing Office, 1961), p. 43.

incarceration and to interventions defined as therapeutic for him.[15]

There is evidence that, from the subject's point of view, confinement in a mental hospital is more unpleasant than imprisonment in jail. "One of my clients," said Hugh J. McGee, "who has served in the prison systems of Florida, Georgia, Virginia, and Maryland, and on road gangs, too, of those states, told me dead seriously that he would rather serve a year in any of them than 6 months in old Howard Hall [at St. Elizabeths Hospital in Washington, D.C.]."[16] The speaker, Chairman of the Committee on Mental Health of the District of Columbia Bar Association, was testifying, in 1961, before a Senate committee conducting hearings on "The Constitutional Rights of the Mentally Ill."

Testifying before the same committee in 1963, Mr. McGee's views were even stronger: "They [the psychiatrists] are punishing him [the defendant] by keeping him in a maximum security ward . . . , which . . . not only amounts to an unconstitutional deprivation of liberty but also amounts to cruel and inhuman punishment. The Court of Appeals has specifically designated persons pleading 'not guilty by reason of insanity' as second-class citizens. When a person acknowledges . . . that he might have had mental disease which caused his criminal conduct . . . he loses his rights—all rights. He loses more rights than a criminal in the penitentiary."[17]

Under New York State's civil commitment laws, an addict arrested for a misdemeanor and for certain felonies may "volunteer" before his trial for a maximum three-year commitment to a mental hospital for a "cure".[18] In doing so, he can avoid prison and a criminal record, because the charge will be dismissed. In

[15] See, for example, *New York Mental Hygiene Law*, par. 72 (1).

[16] McGee, H.: Statement, in *Hearings on Constitutional Rights of the Mentally Ill*, Part 2, *supra*, p. 659.

[17] *Hearings on S. 935 to Protect the Constitutional Rights of the Mentally Ill*, 88th Cong., 1st Sess. (Washington, D.C.: U. S. Government Printing Office, 1963), p. 215.

[18] *New York Mental Hygiene Law*, par. 206 (5), pp. 210–11.

practice, less than one in four arrested addicts have chosen commitment, and a large percentage of these have escaped from the hospital before their time was up.[19]

Hospitals for the criminally insane are especially unpleasant institutions. In March 1966 the New York Court of Claims awarded $115,000 to a fifty-seven-year-old man who had stolen $5 worth of candy when he was sixteen and, as a result, spent the next thirty-four years in mental institutions.[20] In his decision, Judge Richard S. Heller characterized the Dannemora State Hospital, where the claimant, Stephen Dennison, had been held for twenty-four years, as an institution that, "although called a 'hospital,' [is] essentially a prison. . . ."[21] In this hospital, continued Judge Heller, where the "illegality" of Dennison's confinement is unquestionable, ". . . the hospital records repeatedly described claimant's behavior as paranoid, or in lay terms, that he had delusions of persecution. If a person is, in fact, being treated unjustly or unfairly, the fact that he perceives, resents, and reacts to the inequity could hardly be regarded as competent and conclusive evidence of paranoia or paranoid tendencies. . . . In a sense, society labeled him as subhuman, . . . drove him insane, and then used the insanity as an excuse for holding him indefinitely."[22]

Excepting death, involuntary psychiatric hospitalization imposes the most severe penalty that our legal system can inflict on a human being: namely, loss of liberty. The existence of psychiatric institutions that function as prisons, and of judicial sentences that are, in effect, indeterminate sentences to such prisons, is the backdrop against which all discussion of criminal responsibility must take place. This is especially true in jurisdictions where there is no death penalty. For what does it matter whether or not the accused was, at the time of the

[19] See "Should addicts be locked up?" *New York Post Magazine,* March 6, 1966, p. 3.

[20] *Dennison* v. *State,* 49 Misc. 2d 533, 267 N.Y.S. 2d 920 (Ct. Cl.), 1966.

[21] Ibid., p. 924.

[22] Ibid.

offense, "sane" and criminally responsible, or "insane" and criminally not responsible?

IV

Most words, and certainly *all* words used during criminal trials in courts of law, have strategic import. Their meaning must be inferred mainly from their consequences. The consequences of pleading "guilty" and "not guilty" are clear and generally well appreciated. The consequences of pleading "not guilty by reason of insanity," however, are neither clear nor generally understood. Briefly, they are as follows: If the defense of insanity is not sustained and the defendant is found guilty, he is sentenced to punishment as prescribed by the law and meted out by the judge, much as if he had entered any other plea. If the defense of insanity is sustained, the defendant's fate varies from jurisdiction to jurisdiction. There are two basic possibilities. One is that acquittal by reason of insanity is regarded as being the same as any other acquittal; the defendant walks out of the courtroom a free man. This is what happened to the fictional hero of Robert Traver's *Anatomy of a Murder*.[23] It is what would have happened to Jack Ruby had Melvin Belli's defense strategy succeeded.[24] This outcome is unusual and is becoming rarer every day.

The other course of action, which has been gaining ground rapidly in recent years, is to treat the individual acquitted by reason of insanity as a dangerously insane person from whom society needs the utmost protection. Instead of walking out of the courtroom a free man, such a defendant is forthwith transported to an insane asylum, where he remains until "cured" or until "no longer dangerous to himself and others."[25] This concept and procedure are exemplified in the District of Columbia, where "If any person tried . . . for an offense is acquitted

[23] Traver, R.: *Anatomy of a Murder* (New York: St. Martin's Press, 1958).
[24] See Kaplan, J. and Waltz, J. R.: *The Trial of Jack Ruby* (New York: Macmillan, 1965).
[25] See, for example, *D. C. Code Ann.*, par. 24-301, 1961; *Ohio Rev. Code Ann.*, par. 2945.39, 1954.

solely on the ground that he was insane at the time of its commission, the court shall order such person to be confined in a hospital for the mentally ill."[26] The American Law Institute rule embodies the same principle of automatic commitment. "Throughout our opinion," wrote Judge Kaufman, "we have not viewed the choice as one between imprisonment and immediate release. Rather, we believe the true choice to be between different forms of institutionalization—between the prison and the mental hospital. Underlying today's decision is our belief that treatment of the truly incompetent in mental institutions would better serve the interests of society as well as the defendant's."[27]

Consider what this means. The judge recognizes the defendant as mentally competent to stand trial; he allows him to enter a plea and defend himself as best he can, and he considers the defendant sane enough to be sentenced to the penitentiary if found guilty. But should the defendant be found "not guilty by reason of insanity," that verdict immediately transforms him into a "truly incompetent" person, whom the judge feels justified in committing to a mental hospital. "In former days," observed John Stuart Mill in his famous essay On Liberty, "when it was proposed to burn atheists, charitable people used to suggest putting them in the madhouse instead; it would be nothing surprising nowadays were we to see this done, and the doers applauding themselves, because, instead of persecuting for religion, they had adopted so humane and Christian a mode of treating these unfortunates, not without a silent satisfaction at their having thereby obtained their deserts."[28] This was written when Freud was only three years old and when there was no "scientific psychiatry" to "illuminate" the problem of criminal responsibility.

In short, tests of criminal responsibility cannot be evaluated without knowing whether "acquittal" means freedom or commitment. More important than the semantic differences between

[26] D. C. Code Ann., par. 24-301 (d), 1961.
[27] United States v. Freeman, op. cit., p. 626.
[28] Mill, J. S.: On Liberty [1859] (Chicago: Regnery, 1955), p. 100.

the M'Naghten rule and its rivals are the personal consequences for the defendant of successfully pleading insanity. Indeed, preoccupation with the wording of the various rules, in both popular and professional discussions of the subject, only serves to distract attention from the basic issue of social control through legal psychiatry. Actually, where a successful insanity defense means commitment, the well-informed defendant rarely feels that the insanity plea serves his best interests. He tends to avoid this plea, preferring punishment in jail to "treatment" in the mental hospital.

V

What would happen, in jurisdictions where commitment follows automatically upon acquittal by reason of insanity, if the defendant clearly understood this choice? I venture to predict that such pleas would become very infrequent, and perhaps would disappear altogether. Although this is hardly the intention of the "liberalized" rules of criminal insanity, I would consider it a happy outcome. I do not believe that insanity should be an "excusing condition" for crime. The sooner the insanity plea is abolished, or the sooner it disappears because of its dire consequences for the defendant, the better off we shall all be.

But even if the defendant does not elect to plead insanity, so long as the law empowers physicians to incarcerate people in mental hospitals, the law enforcement agencies of the state will be tempted to make use of them. How this might happen was seen in the District of Columbia following the adoption of the Durham rule. Since the plea of "not guilty by reason of insanity" insured an indefinite stay at St. Elizabeths Hospital, judges chose in some cases not to allow the defendant to plead guilty and receive a minor prison sentence, but insisted instead that he plead not guilty by reason of insanity, and, following "acquittal," be committed to the mental hospital.[29] In a decision that side-stepped the constitutional issues involved, the Supreme Court ruled, in 1962, that this tactic was improper,

[29] See *Cameron* v. *Fisher*, 320 F. 2d 731 (D. C. Cir.), 1963; *Overholser* v. *Lynch*, 288 F. 2d 388 (D. C. Cir.), 1961.

and that, instead of foisting an involuntary plea of insanity on such a defendant, the court ought to initiate proceedings for his civil commitment.[30] This not only leaves commitment intact as a quasi-penal sanction, but recognizes it as the constitutionally proper alternative to a prison sentence.

Whether or not it is constitutional for the state to use mental hospitals to deprive citizens of their liberty is for the authorized interpreters of the Constitution to judge. Until now, the courts have found such detention constitutional. We might recall that earlier courts had found slavery constitutional.

Whatever the courts decide, responsible citizens must judge the matter for themselves. For, regardless of motives, the act of depriving a person of his liberty is a moral and political act. This is denied by the supporters of commitment, who maintain that the involuntary confinement of a person in a mental hospital is itself therapeutic, or that it is a condition necessary for the proper administration of some type of psychiatric treatment (for example, electroshock). In this view, held by many psychiatrists, commitment may be compared to the restraint of the patient on the operating table necessary for the proper performance of surgical treatment. The obvious difference, of course, is that the surgical patient consents to the restraint, whereas the mental patient does not. How, then, shall we decide? Is personal restraint, through commitment, therapy or punishment?

To ask the medical question "What is the proper drug for treating pneumococcal pneumonia?" presents a *technical problem* that the lay person *cannot* be expected to master. The best he can do is to select a competent expert and accept or reject his advice. In contrast, to ask the moral question "Is it justifiable to deprive a person of his liberty in order to treat him for mental illness?" presents an *ethical* problem that the lay person *can* master. If confronted with a choice between liberty and mental health (however defined), he must decide which one he values more highly.

It is an idle hope that a scientific psychiatry will save us from moral problems and moral decisions. If we only let ourselves

[30] *Lynch* v. *Overholser*, 369 U.S. 705, 1962.

see with the eyes God gave us and with the courage that only we can give ourselves, we shall see legal psychiatry and involuntary mental hospitalization for what they are: a pseudomedical system of social controls. This type of psychiatry (it should be kept in mind that it is not the only kind) is a servant of the bureaucratic state, whether it be a totalitarian or a democratic state. To Russian "scientific psychiatry," Valeriy Tarsis was mentally ill; to American "scientific psychiatry," Ezra Pound was mentally ill. A "scientific psychiatry" worthy of the name must begin by accounting for these facts. In doing so, it would lag by only sixty years behind Jack London, who wrote of a bishop who had "obeyed Christ's injunction and got locked up in a madhouse."[31] Why? Because "his views were perilous to society, and society could not conceive that such perilous views could be the product of a sane mind."[32]

VI

Neither the M'Naghten rule nor the Durham rule nor the American Law Institute rule is "humanitarian," for all diminish personal responsibility and thus impair human dignity; nor is any of them "liberal," for none promotes individual freedom under the rule of law. The centuries-old practice of using mental hospitalization as a means of punishing "offenders" has received fresh impetus in our day through the rhetoric of "scientific psychiatry." Contemporary concepts of "mental illness" obscure the contradictions between our pursuit of conflicting policies and objectives—individualism because it promises liberty, and collectivism because it promises security. Through the mental health ethic, psychiatry thus promotes the smooth functioning of the bureaucratic mass society and provides its characteristic ideology. According to this ideology, loss of liberty may be either punitive or therapeutic: If the individual offends because he is "bad," loss of liberty is punishment; but if he offends because he is "sick," it is therapy. From this point of view, deviance is

[31] London, J., *The Iron Heel* [1907] (New York: Sagamore Press, 1957), p. 174.
[32] Ibid., p. 163.

seen as sickness rather than badness, and the individual appears as a patient rather than as a citizen.

This psychiatric perspective on problems of living conceals the fundamental moral dilemma—the characteristic choice— facing us: Do we want to be free men or slaves? If we choose freedom, we cannot prevent our fellow man from also choosing to be free; whereas, if we choose slavery, we cannot permit him to be anything but a slave.

In the final analysis, the insanity plea and the insanity verdict, together with the prison sentences called "treatments" served in buildings called "hospitals," are all parts of the complex structure of institutional psychiatry, which, as I have tried to show, is slavery disguised as therapy. Those who value and wish to defend individual liberty can be satisfied with nothing less than the abolition of this crime against humanity.[33]

[33] See Szasz, "Involuntary mental hospitalization," *supra.*

9 · INVOLUNTARY MENTAL

HOSPITALIZATION:

A Crime Against Humanity

For some time now I have maintained that commitment—that is, the detention of persons in mental institutions against their will —is a form of imprisonment;[1] that such deprivation of liberty is contrary to the moral principles embodied in the Declaration of Independence and the Constitution of the United States;[2] and that it is a crass violation of contemporary concepts of fundamental human rights.[3] The practice of "sane" men incarcerating their "insane" fellow men in "mental hospitals" can be compared to that of white men enslaving black men. In short, I consider commitment a crime against humanity.

Existing social institutions and practices, especially if honored by prolonged usage, are generally experienced and accepted as good and valuable. For thousands of years slavery was considered a "natural" social arrangement for the securing of human labor; it was sanctioned by public opinion, religious dogma, church, and state;[4] it was abolished a mere one hundred years ago in the United States; and it is still a prevalent social practice in some parts of the world, notably in Africa.[5] Since its origin,

[1] Szasz, T. S.: "Commitment of the mentally ill: Treatment or social restraint?" *J. Nerv. & Ment. Dis.* 125:293–307 (Apr.–June) 1957.
[2] Szasz, T. S.: *Law, Liberty, and Psychiatry: An Inquiry into the Social Uses of Mental Health Practices* (New York: Macmillan, 1963), pp. 149–90.
[3] Ibid., pp. 223–55.
[4] Davis, D. B.: *The Problem of Slavery in Western Culture* (Ithaca, N.Y.: Cornell University Press, 1966).
[5] See Cohen, R.: "Slavery in Africa." *Trans-Action* 4:44–56 (Jan.–Feb.), 1967; Tobin, R. L.: "Slavery still plagues the earth." *Saturday Review*, May 6, 1967, pp. 24–25.

approximately three centuries ago, commitment of the insane has enjoyed equally widespread support; physicians, lawyers, and the laity have asserted, as if with a single voice, the therapeutic desirability and social necessity of institutional psychiatry. My claim that commitment is a crime against humanity may thus be countered—as indeed it has been—by maintaining, first, that the practice is beneficial for the mentally ill, and second, that it is necessary for the protection of the mentally healthy members of society.

Illustrative of the first argument is Slovenko's assertion that "Reliance solely on voluntary hospital admission procedures ignores the fact that some persons may desire care and custody but cannot communicate their desire directly."[6] Imprisonment in mental hospitals is here portrayed—by a professor of law!—as a service provided to persons by the state because they "desire" it but do not know how to ask for it. Felix defends involuntary mental hospitalization by asserting simply, "We *do* [his italics] deal with illnesses of the mind."[7]

Illustrative of the second argument is Guttmacher's characterization of my book *Law, Liberty, and Psychiatry* as ". . . a pernicious book . . . certain to produce intolerable and unwarranted anxiety in the families of psychiatric patients."[8] This is an admission of the fact that the families of "psychiatric patients" frequently resort to the use of force in order to control their "loved ones," and that when attention is directed to this practice it creates embarrassment and guilt. On the other hand, Felix simply defines the psychiatrist's duty as the protection of society: "Tomorrow's psychiatrist will be, as is his counterpart today, one of the gatekeepers of his community."[9]

These conventional explanations of the nature and uses of

[6] Slovenko, R.: "The psychiatric patient, liberty, and the law." *Amer. J. Psychiatry*, 121:534–39 (Dec.), 1964, p. 536.

[7] Felix, R. H.: "The image of the psychiatrist: Past, present, and future." *Amer. J. Psychiatry*, 121:318–22 (Oct.), 1964, p. 320.

[8] Guttmacher, M. S.: "Critique of views of Thomas Szasz on legal psychiatry." *AMA Arch. Gen. Psychiatry*, 10:238–45 (March), 1964, p. 244.

[9] Felix, op. cit., p. 231.

commitment are, however, but culturally accepted justifications for certain quasi-medical forms of social control, exercised especially against individuals and groups whose behavior does not violate criminal laws but threatens established social values.

II

What is the evidence that commitment does not serve the purpose of helping or treating people whose behavior deviates from or threatens prevailing social norms or moral standards; and who, because they inconvenience their families, neighbors, or superiors, may be incriminated as "mentally ill"?

1. *The medical evidence.* Mental illness is a metaphor. If by "disease" we mean a disorder of the physicochemical machinery of the human body, then we can assert that what we call functional mental diseases are not diseases at all.[10] Persons said to be suffering from such disorders are socially deviant or inept, or in conflict with individuals, groups, or institutions. Since they do not suffer from disease, it is impossible to "treat" them for any sickness.

Although the term "mentally ill" is usually applied to persons who do not suffer from bodily disease, it is sometimes applied also to persons who do (for example, to individuals intoxicated with alcohol or other drugs, or to elderly people suffering from degenerative disease of the brain). However, when patients with demonstrable diseases of the brain are involuntarily hospitalized, the primary purpose is to exercise social control over their behavior;[11] treatment of the disease is, at best, a secondary consideration. Frequently, therapy is nonexistent, and custodial care is dubbed "treatment."

In short, the commitment of persons suffering from "func-

[10] See Szasz, T. S.: "The myth of mental illness." This volume pp. 12-24; *The Myth of Mental Illness: Foundations of a Theory of Personal Conduct* (New York: Hoeber-Harper, 1961); "Mental illness is a myth." *The New York Times Magazine,* June 12, 1966, pp. 30 and 90-92.

[11] See, for example, Noyes, A. P.: *Modern Clinical Psychiatry,* 4th ed. (Philadelphia: Saunders, 1956), p. 278.

tional psychoses" serves moral and social, rather than medical and therapeutic, purposes. Hence, even if, as a result of future research, certain conditions now believed to be "functional" mental illnesses were to be shown to be "organic," my argument against involuntary mental hospitalization would remain unaffected.

2. *The moral evidence.* In free societies, the relationship between physician and patient is predicated on the legal presumption that the individual "owns" his body and his personality.[12] The physician can examine and treat a patient only with his consent; the latter is free to reject treatment (for example, an operation for cancer).[13] After death, "ownership" of the person's body is tranferred to his heirs; the physician must obtain permission from the patient's relatives for a postmortem examination. John Stuart Mill explicitly affirmed that ". . . each person is the proper guardian of his own health, whether bodily, or mental and spiritual."[14] Commitment is incompatible with this moral principle.

3. *The historical evidence.* Commitment practices flourished long before there were any mental or psychiatric "treatments" of "mental diseases." Indeed, madness or mental illness was not always a necessary condition for commitment. For example, in the seventeenth century, "children of artisans and other poor inhabitants of Paris up to the age of 25, . . . girls who were debauched or in evident danger of being debauched, . . ." and other "misérables" of the community, such as epileptics, people with venereal diseases, and poor people with chronic diseases of all sorts, were all considered fit subjects for confinement in the Hôpital Général.[15] And, in 1860, when Mrs.

[12] Szasz, T. S.: "The ethics of birth control; or, who owns your body?" *The Humanist,* 20:332–36 (Nov.–Dec.) 1960.

[13] Hirsch, B. D.: "Informed consent to treatment," in Averbach, A. and Belli, M. M., eds., *Tort and Medical Yearbook* (Indianapolis: Bobbs-Merrill, 1961), Vol. I, pp. 631–38.

[14] Mill, J. S.: *On Liberty* [1859] (Chicago: Regnery, 1955), p. 18.

[15] Rosen, G.: "Social attitudes to irrationality and madness in 17th and 18th century Europe." *J. Hist. Med. & Allied Sciences,* 18:220–40 (1963), p. 223.

Packard was incarcerated for disagreeing with her minister-husband,[16] the commitment laws of the State of Illinois explicitly proclaimed that ". . . married women . . . may be entered or detained in the hospital at the request of the husband of the woman or the guardian . . . , without the evidence of insanity required in other cases."[17] It is surely no coincidence that this piece of legislation was enacted and enforced at about the same time that Mill published his essay *The Subjection of Women*.[18]

4. *The literary evidence.* Involuntary mental hospitalization plays a significant part in numerous short stories and novels from many countries. In none that I have encountered is commitment portrayed as helpful to the hospitalized person; instead, it is always depicted as an arrangement serving interests antagonistic to those of the so-called patient.[19]

III

The claim that commitment of the "mentally ill" is necessary for the protection of the "mentally healthy" is more difficult to refute, not because it is valid, but because the danger that "mental patients" supposedly pose is of such an extremely vague nature.

[16] Packard, E. W. P.: *Modern Persecution, or Insane Asylums Unveiled*, 2 Vols. (Hartford: Case, Lockwood, and Brainard, 1873).

[17] Illinois Statute Book, Sessions Laws 15, Section 10, 1851. Quoted in Packard, E. P. W.: *The Prisoner's Hidden Life* (Chicago: published by the author, 1868), p. 37.

[18] Mill, J. S.: *The Subjection of Women* [1869] (London: Dent, 1965).

[19] See, for example, Chekhov, A. P.: *Ward No. 6,* [1892], in *Seven Short Novels by Chekhov* (New York: Bantam Books, 1963), pp. 106–57; De Assis, M.: *The Psychiatrist* [1881–82], in De Assis, M., *The Psychiatrist and Other Stories* (Berkeley and Los Angeles: University of California Press, 1963), pp. 1–45; London, J.: *The Iron Heel* [1907] (New York: Sagamore Press, 1957); Porter, K. A.: *Noon Wine* [1937], in Porter, K. A., *Pale Horse, Pale Rider: Three Short Novels* (New York: Signet, 1965), pp. 62–112; Kesey, K.: *One Flew Over the Cuckoo's Nest* (New York: Viking, 1962); Tarsis, V.: *Ward 7: An Autobiographical Novel* (London and Glasgow: Collins and Harvill, 1965).

1. *The medical evidence.* The same reasoning applies as earlier: If "mental illness" is not a disease, there is no medical justification for protection from disease. Hence, the analogy between mental illness and contagious disease falls to the ground: The justification for isolating or otherwise constraining patients with tuberculosis or typhoid fever cannot be extended to patients with "mental illness."

Moreover, because the accepted contemporary psychiatric view of mental illness fails to distinguish between illness as a biological condition and as a social role,[20] it is not only false, but also dangerously misleading, especially if used to justify social action. In this view, regardless of its "causes"—anatomical, genetic, chemical, psychological, or social—mental illness has "objective existence." A person either has or has not a mental illness; he is either mentally sick or mentally healthy. Even if a person is cast in the role of mental patient against his will, his "mental illness" exists "objectively"; and even if, as in the case of the Very Important Person, he is never treated as a mental patient, his "mental illness" still exists "objectively"— apart from the activities of the psychiatrist.[21]

The upshot is that the term "mental illness" is perfectly suited for mystification: It disregards the crucial question of whether the individual assumes the role of mental patient voluntarily, and hence wishes to engage in some sort of interaction with a psychiatrist; or whether he is cast in that role against his will, and hence is opposed to such a relationship. This obscurity is then usually employed strategically, either by the subject himself to advance *his* interests, or by the subject's adversaries to advance *their* interests.

In contrast to this view, I maintain, first, that the involuntarily hospitalized mental patient is, by definition, the occupant of an

[20] See Szasz, T. S.: "Alcoholism: A socio-ethical perspective." *Western Medicine,* 7:15–21 (Dec.) 1966.

[21] See, for example, Rogow, A. A.: *James Forrestal: A Study of Personality, Politics, and Policy* (New York: Macmillan, 1964); for a detailed criticism of this view, see Szasz, T. S.: "Psychiatric classification as a strategy of personal constraint." This volume pp. 190–217.

ascribed role; and, second, that the "mental disease" of such a person—unless the use of this term is restricted to demonstrable lesions or malfunctions of the brain—is always the product of interaction between psychiatrist and patient.

2. *The moral evidence.* The crucial ingredient in involuntary mental hospitalization is coercion. Since coercion is the exercise of power, it is always a moral and political act. Accordingly, regardless of its medical justification, commitment is primarily a moral and political phenomenon—just as, regardless of its anthropological and economic justifications, slavery was primarily a moral and political phenomenon.

Although psychiatric methods of coercion are indisputably useful for those who employ them, they are clearly not indispensable for dealing with the problems that so-called mental patients pose for those about them. If an individual threatens others by virtue of his beliefs or actions, he could be dealt with by methods other than "medical": if his conduct is ethically offensive, moral sanctions against him might be appropriate; if forbidden by law, legal sanctions might be appropriate. In my opinion, both informal, moral sanctions, such as social ostracism or divorce, and formal, judicial sanctions, such as fine and imprisonment, are more dignified and less injurious to the human spirit than the quasi-medical psychiatric sanction of involuntary mental hospitalization.[22]

3. *The historical evidence.* To be sure, confinement of so-called mentally ill persons does protect the community from certain problems. If it didn't, the arrangement would not have come into being and would not have persisted. However, the question we ought to ask is not *whether* commitment protects the community from "dangerous mental patients," but rather from precisely *what danger* it protects and by *what means?* In what way were prostitutes or vagrants dangerous in seventeenth century Paris? Or married women in nineteenth century Illinois?

It is significant, moreover, that there is hardly a prominent

[22] Szasz, T. S.: *Psychiatric Justice* (New York: Macmillan, 1965).

person who, during the past fifty years or so, has not been diagnosed by a psychiatrist as suffering from some type of "mental illness." Barry Goldwater was called a "paranoid schizophrenic";[23] Whittaker Chambers, a "psychopathic personality";[24] Woodrow Wilson, a "neurotic" frequently "very close to psychosis";[25] and Jesus, "a born degenerate" with a "fixed delusional system," and a "paranoid" with a "clinical picture [so typical] that it is hardly conceivable that people can even question the accuracy of the diagnosis."[26] The list is endless.

Sometimes, psychiatrists declare the same person sane *and* insane, depending on the political dictates of their superiors and the social demand of the moment. Before his trial and execution, Adolph Eichmann was examined by several psychiatrists, all of whom declared him to be normal; after he was put to death, "medical evidence" of his insanity was released and widely circulated.

According to Hannah Arendt, "Half a dozen psychiatrists had certified him [Eichmann] as 'normal.'" One psychiatrist asserted, ". . . his whole psychological outlook, his attitude toward his wife and children, mother and father, sisters and friends, was 'not only normal but most desirable.' . . . And the minister who regularly visited him in prison declared that Eichmann was "a man with very positive ideas."[27] After Eichmann was executed, Gideon Hausner, the Attorney General of Israel, who had prosecuted him, disclosed in an article in *The Saturday Evening Post* that psychiatrists diag-

[23] "The Unconscious of a Conservative: A Special Issue on the Mind of Barry Goldwater." *Fact*, Sept.–Oct. 1964.

[24] Zeligs, M. A.: *Friendship and Fratricide: An Analysis of Whittaker Chambers and Alger Hiss* (New York: Viking, 1967).

[25] Freud, S. and Bullitt, W. C.: *Thomas Woodrow Wilson: A Psychological Study* (Boston: Houghton Mifflin, 1967).

[26] Quoted in Schweitzer, A.: *The Psychiatric Study of Jesus* [1913] transl. by Charles R. Joy (Boston: Beacon Press, 1956), pp. 37, 40–41.

[27] Arendt, H.: *Eichmann in Jerusalem: A Report on the Banality of Evil* (New York: Viking, 1963), p. 22.

nosed Eichmann as "'a man obsessed with a dangerous and insatiable urge to kill,' 'a perverted, sadistic personality.'"[28]

Whether or not men like those mentioned above are considered "dangerous" depends on the observer's religious beliefs, political convictions, and social situation. Furthermore, the "dangerousness" of such persons—whatever we may think of them—is not analogous to that of a person with tuberculosis or typhoid fever; nor would rendering such a person "non-dangerous" be comparable to rendering a patient with a contagious disease non-infectious.

In short, I hold—and I submit that the historical evidence bears me out—that people are committed to mental hospitals neither because they are "dangerous," nor because they are "mentally ill," but rather because they are society's scapegoats, whose persecution is justified by psychiatric propaganda and rhetoric.[29]

4. *The literary evidence.* No one contests that involuntary mental hospitalization of the so-called dangerously insane "protects" the community. Disagreement centers on the nature of the threat facing society, and on the methods and legitimacy of the protection it employs. In this connection, we may recall that slavery, too, "protected" the community: it freed the slave-owners from manual labor. Commitment likewise shields the non-hospitalized members of society: first, from having to accommodate themselves to the annoying or idiosyncratic demands of certain members of the community who have not violated any criminal statutes; and, second, from having to prosecute, try, convict, and punish members of the community who have broken the law but who either might not be convicted in court, or, if they would be, might not be restrained as effectively or as long in prison as in a mental hospital. The literary evidence cited earlier fully supports this interpretation of the function of involuntary mental hospitalization.

[28] Ibid., pp. 22–23.
[29] For a full articulation and documentation of this thesis, see Szasz, T. S.: *The Manufacture of Madness: A Comparative Study of the Inquisition and the Mental Health Movement* (New York: Harper & Row, to be published in 1970).

IV

I have suggested that commitment constitutes a social arrangement whereby one part of society secures certain advantages for itself at the expense of another part. To do so, the oppressors must possess an ideology to justify their aims and actions; and they must be able to enlist the police power of the state to impose their will on the oppressed members. What makes such an arrangement a "crime against humanity"? It may be argued that the use of state power is legitimate when law-abiding citizens punish lawbreakers. What is the difference between this use of state power and its use in commitment?

In the first place, the difference between committing the "insane" and imprisoning the "criminal" is the same as that between the rule of man and the rule of law:[30] whereas the "insane" are subjected to the coercive controls of the state because persons more powerful than they have labeled them as "psychotic," "criminals" are subjected to such controls because they have violated legal rules applicable equally to all.

The second difference between these two proceedings lies in their professed aims. The principal purpose of imprisoning criminals is to protect the liberties of the law-abiding members of society.[31] Since the individual subject to commitment is not considered a threat to liberty in the same way as the accused criminal is (if he were, he would be prosecuted), his removal from society cannot be justified on the same grounds. Justification for commitment must thus rest on its therapeutic promise and potential: it will help restore the "patient" to "mental health." But if this can be accomplished only at the cost of robbing the individual of liberty, "involuntary mental hospitalization" becomes only a verbal camouflage for what is, in effect,

[30] Hayek, F. A.: *The Constitution of Liberty* (Chicago: University of Chicago Press, 1960), especially pp. 162–92.
[31] Mabbott, J. D.: "Punishment" [1939], in Olafson, F. A., ed., *Justice and Social Policy: A Collection of Essays* (Englewood Cliffs, N.J.: Prentice-Hall, 1961), pp. 39–54.

punishment. This "therapeutic" punishment differs, however, from traditional judicial punishment, in that the accused criminal enjoys a rich panoply of constitutional protections against false accusation and oppressive prosecution, whereas the accused mental patient is deprived of these protections.[32]

To support this view of involuntary mental hospitalization, and to cast it into historical perspective, I shall now briefly review the similarities between slavery and institutional psychiatry. (By the use of the term "institutional psychiatry" I refer generally to psychiatric interventions imposed on persons by others. Such interventions are characterized by the complete loss, on the part of the ostensible client or "patient," of control over his participation in his relationship with the expert. The paradigm "service" of institutional psychiatry is, of course, involuntary mental hospitalization.[33])

v

Suppose that a person wishes to study slavery. How would he go about doing so? First, he might study slaves. He would then find that such persons are generally brutish, poor, and uneducated, and he might accordingly conclude that slavery is their "natural" or appropriate social state. Such, indeed, have been the methods and conclusions of innumerable men throughout the ages.[34] Even the great Aristotle held that slaves were "naturally" inferior and were hence justly subdued. "From the hour of their birth," he asserted, "some are marked for subjection, others for rule."[35] This view is similar to the modern

[32] For documentation, see Szasz, T. S.: *Law, Liberty, and Psychiatry: An Inquiry into the Social Uses of Mental Health Practices* (New York: Macmillan, 1963); *Psychiatric Justice* (New York: Macmillan, 1965).

[33] For further discussion, and for a detailed exploration of the similarities between the Inquisition and institutional psychiatry, see Szasz, T. S., *The Manufacture of Madness, supra,* especially the Preface and Chap. 1–9.

[34] Davis, op. cit., passim.

[35] Ibid., p. 70.

concept of "psychopathic criminality" and "schizophrenia" as genetically caused diseases.[36]

Another student, "biased" by contempt for the institution of slavery, might proceed differently. He would maintain that there can be no slave without a master holding him in bondage; and he would accordingly consider slavery a type of human *relationship* and, more generally, a *social institution,* supported by custom, law, religion, and force. From this point of view, the study of masters is at least as relevant to the study of slavery as is the study of slaves.

The latter point of view is generally accepted today with regard to slavery, but not with regard to institutional psychiatry. "Mental illness" of the type found in psychiatric hospitals has been investigated for centuries, and continues to be investigated today, in much the same way as slaves had been studied in the ante-bellum South and before. Then, the "existence" of slaves was taken for granted; their biological and social characteristics were accordingly noted and classified. Today, the "existence" of "mental patients" is similarly taken for granted;[37] indeed, it is widely believed that their number is steadily increasing.[38] The psychiatrist's task is therefore to observe and classify the biological, psychological, and social characteristics of such patients.[39] This perspective is a manifestation, in part, of what I have called "the myth of mental illness,"[40] that is, of the notion that mental illnesses are similar to diseases of the body; and, in part, of the psychiatrist's intense need to deny the fun-

[36] Stock, R. W.: "The XYY and the criminal," *The New York Times Magazine,* October 20, 1968, pp. 30–31, 90–104; Kallman, F. J.: "The Genetics of Mental Illness," in Arieti, S., ed., *American Handbook of Psychiatry* (New York: Basic Books, 1959), Vol. I, pp. 175–96.

[37] Caplan, G.: *Principles of Preventive Psychiatry* (New York: Basic Books, 1964).

[38] See, for example, Srole, L., Langer, T. S., Mitchell, S. T., Opler, M. K., and Rennie, T. A. C.: *Mental Health in the Metropolis: The Midtown Manhattan Study* (New York: McGraw-Hill, 1962).

[39] Noyes, A. P. and Kolb, L. C.: *Modern Clinical Psychiatry,* 5th ed. (Philadelphia: Saunders, 1958).

[40] Szasz, T. S., *The Myth of Mental Illness, supra.*

damental complementarity of his relationship to the involuntary mental patient. The same sort of complementarity obtains in all situations where one person or party assumes a superior or dominant role and ascribes an inferior or submissive role to another; for example, master and slave, accuser and accused, inquisitor and witch.

The fundamental parallel between master and slave on the one hand, and institutional psychiatrist and involuntarily hospitalized patient on the other, lies in this: in each instance, the former member of the pair *defines* the social role of the latter, and *casts* him in that role by force.

VI

Wherever there is slavery, there must be criteria for who may and who may not be enslaved. In ancient times, any people could be enslaved. Bondage was the usual consequence of military defeat. After the advent of Christianity, although the people of Europe continued to make war upon each other, they ceased enslaving prisoners who were Christians. According to Dwight Dumond, ". . . the theory that a Christian could not be enslaved soon gained such wide endorsement as to be considered a point of international law."[41] By the time of the colonization of America, the peoples of the Western world considered only black men appropriate subjects for slave trade.

The criteria for distinguishing between those who may be incarcerated in mental hospitals and those who may not be are similar: poor and socially unimportant persons may be, and Very Important Persons may not be.[42] This rule is manifested in two ways: first, through our mental-hospital statistics, which show that the majority of institutionalized patients belong in the lowest socioeconomic classes;[43] second, through the rarity

[41] Dumond, D. L.: *Antislavery: The Crusade for Freedom* (Ann Arbor: Univ. of Michigan Press, 1961), p. 4.

[42] Henderson, D. and Gillespie, R. D.: *A Textbook of Psychiatry,* 7th ed. (London: Oxford University Press, 1950), p. 684.

[43] Hollingshead, A. B. and Redlich, F. C.: *Social Class and Mental Illness* (New York: Wiley, 1958).

with which VIPs are committed.[44] Yet even sophisticated social scientists often misunderstand or misinterpret these correlations by attributing the low incidence of committed upper-class persons to a denial on their part, and on the part of those close to them, of the "medical fact" that "mental illness" can "strike" anyone.[45] To be sure, powerful people may feel anxious or depressed, or behave in an excited or paranoid manner; but that, of course, is not the point at all. This medical perspective, which defines all distressed and distressing behavior as mental illness—and which is now so widely accepted—only succeeds in confusing the observer's judgment of the quality of another person's behavior with the observer's power to cast that person in the role of involuntary patient. My argument here is limited to asserting that prominent and powerful persons are rarely cast into the role of involuntarily confined mental patient—and for obvious reasons: The degraded status of committed patient ill befits a powerful person. In fact, the two statuses are as mutually exclusive as those of master and slave.

VII

A basic assumption of American slavery was that the Negro was racially inferior to the Caucasian. "There is no malice toward the Negro in Ulrich Phillips' work," wrote Stanley Elkins about the author's book *American Negro Slavery*, a work sympathetic with the Southern position. "Phillips was deeply fond of the Negroes as a people; it was just that he could not take them seriously as men and women; they were children."[46]

Similarly, the basic assumption of institutional psychiatry is that the mentally ill person is psychologically and socially inferior to the mentally healthy. He is like a child: he does not know what is in his best interests and therefore needs others

[44] See, for example, Rogow, op. cit.
[45] Ibid., pp. xxi, 44, 344–47.
[46] Elkins, S. M.: *Slavery: A Problem in American Institutional and Intellectual Life* [1959] (New York: Universal Library, 1963), p. 10.

to control and protect him.[47] Psychiatrists often care deeply for their involuntary patients, whom they consider—in contrast with the merely "neurotic" persons—"psychotic," which is to say, "very sick." Hence, such patients must be cared for as the "irresponsible children" they are considered to be.

The perspective of paternalism has played an exceedingly important part in justifying both slavery and involuntary mental hospitalization. Aristotle defined slavery as "an essentially domestic relationship"; in so doing, wrote Davis, he "endowed it with the sanction of paternal authority, and helped to establish a precedent that would govern discussions of political philosophers as late as the eighteenth century."[48] The relationship between psychiatrists and mental patients has been and continues to be viewed in the same way. "If a man brings his daughter to me from California," declares Braceland, "because she is in manifest danger of falling into vice or in some way disgracing herself, he doesn't expect me to let her loose in my hometown for that same thing to happen."[49] Indeed, almost any article or book dealing with the "care" of involuntary mental patients may be cited to illustrate the contention that physicians fall back on paternalism to justify their coercive control over the unco-operative patient. "Certain cases" [not individuals!]—writes Solomon in an article on suicide—". . . must be considered irresponsible, not only with respect to violent impulses, but also in all medical matters." In this class, which he labels "The Irresponsible," he places "Children," "The Mentally Retarded," "The Psychotic," and "The Severely or Terminally Ill." Solomon's conclusion is that "Repugnant though it may be, he [the physician] may have to act against the patient's

---

[47] See, for example, Linn, L.: *A Handbook of Hospital Psychiatry* (New York: International Universities Press, 1955), pp. 420–22; Braceland, F. J.: Statement, in *Constitutional Rights of the Mentally Ill* (Washington, D.C.: U. S. Government Printing Office, 1961), pp. 63–74; Rankin, R. S. and Dallmayr, W. B.: "Rights of Patients in Mental Hospitals," in *Constitutional Rights of the Mentally Ill*, *supra*, pp. 329–70.

[48] Davis, op. cit., p. 69.

[49] Braceland, op. cit., p. 71.

wishes in order to protect the patient's life and that of others."[50] The fact that, as in the case of slavery, the physician needs the police power of the state to maintain his relationship with his involuntary patient does not alter this self-serving image of institutional psychiatry.

Paternalism is the crucial explanation for the stubborn contradiction and conflict about whether the practices employed by slaveholders and institutional psychiatrists are "therapeutic" or "noxious." Masters and psychiatrists profess their benevolence; their slaves and involuntary patients protest against their malevolence. As Seymour Halleck puts it: ". . . the psychiatrist experiences himself as a helping person, but his patient may see him as a jailer. Both views are partially correct."[51] Not so. Both views are completely correct. Each is a proposition about a different subject: the former, about the psychiatrist's self-image; the latter, about the involuntary mental patient's image of his captor. In *Ward 7*, Valeriy Tarsis presents the following dialogue between his protagonist-patient and the mental-hospital physician: "This is the position. I don't regard you as a doctor. You call this a hospital. I call it a prison. . . . So now, let's get everything straight. I am your prisoner, you are my jailer, and there isn't going to be any nonsense about my health . . . or treatment."[52]

This is the characteristic dialogue of oppression and liberation. The ruler looks in the mirror and sees a liberator; the ruled looks at the ruler and sees a tyrant. If the physician has the power to incarcerate the patient and uses it, their relationship will inevitably fit into this mold. If one cannot ask the subject whether he likes being enslaved or committed, whipped or electroshocked—because he is not a fit judge of his own "best interests"—then one is left with the contending opinions of the practitioners and their critics. The practitioners insist that their

[50] Solomon, P.: "The burden of responsibility in suicide." *JAMA*, 199:321–24 (Jan. 30), 1967.

[51] Halleck, S. L.: *Psychiatry and the Dilemmas of Crime* (New York: Harper & Row, 1967), p. 230.

[52] Tarsis, V.: *Ward 7: An Autobiographical Novel* (London and Glasgow: Collins and Harvill, 1965), p. 62.

coercive measures are beneficial; the critics, that they are harmful.

The defenders of slavery thus claimed that the Negro "is happier . . . as a slave, than he could be as a free man; this is the result of the peculiarities of his character";[53] that ". . . it was actually an act of liberation to remove Negroes from their harsh world of sin and dark superstition";[54] and that ". . . Negroes were better off in a Christian land, even as slaves, than living like beasts in Africa."[55]

Similarly, the defenders of involuntary mental hospitalization claim that the mental patient is healthier—the twentieth-century synonym for the nineteenth-century term "happier"—as a psychiatric prisoner than he would be as a free citizen; that "[t]he basic purpose [of commitment] is to make sure that sick human beings get the care that is appropriate to their needs . . .";[56] and that "[i]t is a feature of some illnesses that people do not have insight into the fact that they are sick. In short, sometimes it is necessary to protect them [the mentally ill] for a while from themselves. . . ."[57] It requires no great feat of imagination to see how comforting—indeed, how absolutely necessary—these views are to the advocates of slavery and involuntary mental hospitalization, even when they are contradicted by facts.

For example, although it was held that "a merrier being does not exist on the face of the globe than the Negro slave of the United States,"[58] there was an ever-lurking fear of Negro violence and revolt. As Elkins put it, "the failure of any free workers to present themselves for enslavement can serve as one test of how much the analysis of the 'happy slave' may have added to Americans' understanding of themselves."[59]

The same views and the same inconsistencies apply to involuntary psychiatric hospitalization. Defenders of this system

[53] Elkins, op. cit., p. 190.
[54] Davis, op. cit., p. 186.
[55] Ibid., p. 190.
[56] Ewalt, J.: Statement, in *Constitutional Rights of the Mentally Ill, supra,* pp. 74–89, p. 75.
[57] Braceland, op. cit., p. 64.
[58] Elkins, op. cit., p. 216.
[59] Ibid.

maintain that committed patients are better off in hospitals, where they are contented and harmless; "most patients," declares Guttmacher, "when they get in a [mental] hospital are quite content to be there. . . ."[60] At the same time, such patients are feared for their potential violence, their escapes from captivity occasion intense manhunts, and their crimes are prominently featured in the newspapers. Moreover, as with slavery, the failure of citizens to present themselves for involuntary psychiatric hospitalization can serve as a test of how much the currently popular analysis of mental health problems has added to Americans' understanding of themselves.

The social necessity, and hence the basic value, of involuntary mental hospitalization, at least for some people, is not seriously questioned today. There is massive consensus in the United States that, properly used, such hospitalization is a good thing. It is thus possible to debate *who* should be hospitalized, or *how*, or for *how long*—but not whether *anyone should* be. I submit, however, that just as it is improper to enslave anyone —whether he is black or white, Moslem or Christian—so it is improper to hospitalize anyone without his consent—whether he is depressed or paranoid, hysterical or schizophrenic.

Our unwillingness to look at this problem searchingly may be compared to the unwillingness of the South to look at slavery. ". . . [A] democratic people," wrote Elkins, "no longer 'reasons' with itself when it is all of the same mind. Men will then only warn and exhort each other, that their solidarity may be yet more perfect. The South's intellectuals, after the 1830s, did really little more than this. And when the enemy's reality disappears, when his concreteness recedes, then intellect itself, with nothing more to resist it and give it resonance, merges with the mass and stultifies, and shadows become monsters."[61]

Our growing preoccupation with the menace of mental illness may be a manifestation of just such a process—in which "concreteness recedes . . . and shadows become monsters." A democratic nation, as we have been warned by Tocqueville, is

[60] Guttmacher, M.: Statement, in *Constitutional Rights of the Mentally Ill, supra,* pp. 143–60, p. 156.
[61] Elkins, op. cit., p. 222.

especially vulnerable to the hazards of a surfeit of agreement: "The authority of a king is physical, and controls the actions of men without subduing their will. But the majority possesses a power that is physical and moral at the same time, which acts upon the will as much as upon the actions, and represses not only all contests, but all controversy."[62]

VIII

There are essential similarities in relationships between masters and subjects—no matter whether plantation owners and Negro slaves or institutional psychiatrists and committed mental patients.

To maintain a relationship of personal or class superiority, it is necessary, as a rule, that the oppressor keep the oppressed uninformed, especially about matters pertinent to their relationship. In America the history of the systematic efforts by the whites to keep the Negro ignorant is well known. A dramatic example is the law passed in 1824 by the Virginia Assembly that provided a $50 fine and two months' imprisonment for teaching *free* Negroes to read and write.[63] Nor was the situation very different in the North. In January 1833 Prudence Crandall admitted to her private school in Canterbury, Connecticut, a young lady of seventeen, the daughter of a highly respected Negro family. Miss Crandall was thereupon ostracized and persecuted by her neighbors: "They dumped a load of manure in her well. They refused to sell her supplies and threatened her father and brother with mob violence, fines, and imprisonment if they continued to bring her food from their nearby farm. They piled refuse from a slaughter house on her front porch."[64] She was also accused of, and tried for, breaking a law that forbade the harboring, boarding, or instruction in any manner of any person of color, and was convicted. Finally, her school was set on fire.

[62] Tocqueville, A. de: *Democracy in America* [1835–40] (New York: Vintage Books, 1945), Vol. 1, p. 273.
[63] Dumond, op. cit., p. 11.
[64] Ibid., p. 211.

A similar effort to educationally degrade and psychologically impoverish their charges characterizes the acts of the managers of madhouses. In most prisons in the United States, it is possible for a convict to obtain a high-school diploma, to learn a trade, to become an amateur lawyer, or to write a book. None of these things is possible in a mental hospital. The principal requirement for an inmate of such an institution is to accept the psychiatric ideology of his "illness" and the things he must do to "recover" from it. The committed patient must thus accept the view that he is "sick" and that his captors are "well"; that his own view of himself is false and that of his captors true; and that to effect any change in his social situation he must relinquish his "sick" views and adopt the "healthy" views of those who have power over him.[65] By accepting himself as "sick," and his institutional environment and the various manipulations imposed on him by the staff as "treatment," the mental patient is compelled to authenticate the psychiatrist's role as that of a benevolent physician curing mental illness. The mental patient who maintains the forbidden image of reality that the institutional psychiatrist is a jailer is considered paranoid. Moreover, since most patients—as do oppressed people generally— sooner or later accept the ideas imposed on them by their superiors, hospital psychiatrists are constantly immersed in an environment where their identity as "doctors" is affirmed. The moral superiority of white men over black was similarly authenticated and affirmed through the association between slaveowners and slaves.

In both situations, the oppressor first subjugates his adversary and then cites his oppressed status as proof of his inferiority. Once this process is set in motion, it develops its own momentum and psychological logic.

Looking at the relationship, the oppressor will see his superiority and hence his well-deserved dominance, and the oppressed will see his inferiority and hence his well-deserved submission. In race relations in the United States, we continue to reap the

[65] Goffman, E.: Asylums: Essays on the Social Situation of Mental Patients and Other Inmates (Garden City, N.Y.: Doubleday Anchor, 1961).

bitter results of this philosophy, while in psychiatry we are even now sowing the seeds of this poisonous fruit whose eventual harvest may be equally bitter and long.

Convicts are entitled to fight for their "legal rights," but not involuntary mental patients. Like slaves, such patients have no rights except those granted them by their medical masters. According to Benjamin Apfelberg, Clinical Professor of Psychiatry and Medical Director of the Law-Psychiatry Project at New York University, "Our students come to realize that by fighting for a patient's *legal* rights they may actually be doing him a great disservice. They learn that there is such a thing as a person's *medical* rights, the right to get treatment, to become well."[66]

The "medical right" to which Apfelberg refers is a euphemism for the *obligation* to remain confined in a mental institution, not the opportunity to *choose* between hospitalization and no hospitalization. But calling involuntary mental hospitalization a "medical right" is like calling involuntary servitude in antebellum Georgia a "right to work."

Oppression and degradation are unpleasant to behold and are, therefore, frequently disguised or concealed. One method for doing so is to segregate—in special areas, as in camps or "hospitals"—the degraded human beings. Another is to conceal the social realities behind the fictional façade of what we call, after Wittgenstein,[67] "language games." While psychiatric language games may seem fanciful, the psychiatric idiom is actually only a dialect of the common language of oppressors.[68] Thus slaveholders called the slaves "livestock," mothers "breeders," their children "increase," and gave the term "drivers" to the men set over them at work.[69] The defenders of psychiatric imprisonment call their institutions "hospitals," the inmates

66 Quoted in "Attorneys-at-Psychiatry," *Smith, Kline & French Psychiatric Reporter,* July–August 1965, p. 23.

67 See Wittgenstein, L.: *Philosophical Investigations* (Oxford: Blackwell, 1953); and Hartnack, J.: *Wittgenstein and Modern Philosophy* (Garden City, N.Y.: Doubleday Anchor 1965).

68 On the language game of Nazi anti-Semitism, see Arendt, op. cit., especially pp. 80, 96, 141.

69 Dumond, op. cit., p. 251.

"patients," and the keepers "doctors"; they refer to the sentence as "treatment," and to the deprivation of liberty as "protection of the patient's best interests."

In both cases, the semantic deceptions are supplemented by appeals to tradition, to morality, and to social necessity. The proslavery forces in America argued that the abolitionists were wrong because "they were seeking to overthrow an ancient institution, one which was recognized by the Scriptures, recognized by the Constitution, and imbedded in the structure of southern society."[70] Thus, an editorial in the Washington Telegraph in 1837 asserted, "As a man, a Christian, and a citizen, we believe that slavery is right; that the condition of the slave, as it now exists in slaveholding states, is the best existing organization of civil society";[71] while another proslavery author, writing in 1862, defended the institution on mainly religious grounds: "Slavery, authorized by God, permitted by Jesus Christ, sanctioned by the apostles, maintained by good men of all ages, is still existing in a portion of our beloved country."[72] One has only to scan present-day psychiatric journals, popular magazines, or daily newspapers to find involuntary mental hospitalization similarly extolled and defended.

The contemporary reader may find it difficult to believe how unquestioningly slavery was accepted as a natural and beneficial social arrangement. Even as great a liberal thinker as John Locke did not advocate its abolition.[73] Moreover, protests against the slave trade would have provoked the hostility of powerful religious and economic interests. Opposition to it, as Davis observed, would therefore have required "considerable independence of mind, since the Portuguese slave posts were closely connected with missionary establishments and criticism of the African slave trade might challenge the very ideal of spreading the faith."[74]

[70] Ibid., p. 233.
[71] Elkins, op. cit., p. 36.
[72] Ibid.
[73] Davis, op. cit., p. 121.
[74] Ibid., p. 187.

Indeed, the would-be critic or opponent of slavery would have found himself at odds with all the tradition and wisdom of Western civilization. ". . . [O]ne could not lightly challenge," wrote Davis, "an institution approved not only by the Fathers and canons of the Church, but by the most illustrious writers of antiquity. . . . [T]he revival of classical learning, which may have helped to liberate the mind of Europe from bondage to ignorance and superstition, only reinforced the traditional justification for human slavery. . . . [H]ow could an institution supported by so many authorities and sanctioned by the general custom of nations be intrinsically unjust or repugnant to natural reason?"[75]

In Western nations and the Soviet Bloc alike, there are thus two contradictory views on commitment. According to the one, involuntary mental hospitalization is an indispensable method of medical healing and a humane type of social control; according to the other, it is a contemptible abuse of the medical relationship and a type of imprisonment without trial. We adopt the former view and consider commitment "proper" if we use it on victims of our choosing whom we despise; we adopt the latter view and consider commitment "improper" if our enemies use it on victims of their choosing whom we esteem.

IX

The change in perspective—from seeing slavery occasioned by the "inferiority" of the Negro and commitment by the "insanity" of the patient, to seeing each occasioned by the interplay of, and especially the power relation between, the participants—has far-reaching practical implications. In the case of slavery, it meant not only that the slaves had an obligation to revolt and emancipate themselves, but also that the masters had an even greater obligation to renounce their roles as slaveholders. Naturally, a slaveholder with such ideas felt compelled to set his slaves free, at whatever cost to himself. This is precisely what some slaveowners did. Their action had profound consequences in a social system based on slavery.

[75] Ibid., pp. 107, 115.

For the individual slaveholder who set his slaves free, the act led invariably to his expulsion from the community—through economic pressure or personal harassment or both. Such persons usually emigrated to the North. For the nation as a whole, these acts and the abolitionist sentiments behind them symbolized a fundamental moral rift between those who regarded Negroes as objects or slaves, and those who regarded them as persons or citizens. The former could persist in regarding the slave as existing in nature; whereas the latter could not deny his own moral responsibility for creating man in the image, not of God, but of the slave-animal.

The implications of this perspective for institutional psychiatry are equally clear. A psychiatrist who accepts as his "patient" a person who does not wish to be his patient, defines him as a "mentally ill" person, then incarcerates him in an institution, bars his escape from the institution and from the role of mental patient, and proceeds to "treat" him against his will—such a psychiatrist, I maintain, creates "mental illness" and "mental patients." He does so in exactly the same way as the white man who sailed for Africa, captured the Negro, brought him to America in shackles, and then sold him as if he were an animal, created slavery and slaves.

The parallel between slavery and institutional psychiatry may be carried one step further: Denunciation of slavery and the renouncing of slaveholding by some slaveowners led to certain social problems, such as Negro unemployment, the importation of cheap European labor, and a gradual splitting of the country into pro- and anti-slavery factions. Similarly, criticisms of involuntary mental hospitalization and the renouncing by some psychiatrists of relationships with involuntary mental patients have led to professional problems in the past, and are likely to do so again in the future. Psychiatrists restricting their work to psychoanalysis and psychotherapy have been accused of not being "real doctors"—as if depriving a person of his liberty required medical skills; of "shirking their responsibilities" to their colleagues and to society by accepting only the "easier cases" and refusing to treat the "seriously mentally ill" patient—as if avoiding treating persons who do not want to be treated were itself a kind of malpractice; and of undermining the profession of psychiatry—as if practicing self-control and eschewing violence were newly discovered forms of immorality.[76]

X

The psychiatric profession has, of course, a huge stake, both existential and economic, in being socially authorized to rule over mental patients, just as the slaveowning classes did in ruling over slaves. In contemporary psychiatry, indeed, the expert gains superiority not only over members of a specific class of victims, but over nearly the whole of the population, whom he may "psychiatrically evaluate."[77]

The economic similarities between chattel slavery and institutional psychiatry are equally evident: The economic strength of the slaveowner lay in the Negro slaves he owned. The economic strength of the institutional psychiatrist lies, similarly, in his involuntary mental patients, who are not free to move about, marry, divorce, or make contracts, but are, instead, under the control of the hospital director. As the plantation owner's income and power rose with the amount of land and number of slaves he owned, so the income and power of the psychiatric bureaucrat rise with the size of the institutional system he controls and the number of patients he commands. Moreover, just as the slaveholder could use the police power of the state to help him recruit and maintain his slave labor force, so can the institutional psychiatrist rely on the state to help him recruit and maintain a population of hospital inmates.

Finally, since the state and federal governments have a vast economic stake in the operation of psychiatric hospitals and

[76] See, for example, Davidson, H. A.: "The image of the psychiatrist." *Amer. J. Psychiatry*, 121:329–33 (Oct.), 1964; Glaser, F. G.: "The dichotomy game: A further consideration of the writings of Dr. Thomas Szasz." *Amer. J. Psychiatry*, 121:1069–74 (May), 1965.

[77] See Menninger, W.: *A Psychiatrist for a Troubled World* (New York: Viking, 1967).

clinics, the interests of the state and of institutional psychiatry tend to be the same. Formerly, the state and federal governments had a vast economic stake in the operation of plantations worked by slaves, and hence the interests of the state and of the slaveowning classes tended to be the same. The wholly predictable consequence of this kind of arrangement is that just as the coalition of chattel slavery and the state created a powerful vested interest, so does the coalition of institutional psychiatry and the state.[78] Moreover, as long as the oppressive institution has the unqualified support of the state, it is invincible. On the other hand, since there can be no oppression without power, once such an institution loses the support of the state, it rapidly disintegrates.

If this argument is valid, pressing the view that psychiatrists now create involuntary mental patients just as slaveholders used to create slaves is likely to lead to a cleavage in the psychiatric profession, and perhaps in society generally, between those who condone and support the relationship between psychiatrist and involuntary mental patient, and those who condemn and oppose it.

It is not clear whether, or on what terms, these two psychiatric factions could coexist. The practices of coercive psychiatry and of paternalistic psychiatrists do not, in themselves, threaten the practices of non-coercive psychiatry and of contracting psychiatrists. Economic relations based on slavery coexisted over long periods with relations based on contract. But the moral conflict poses a more difficult problem. For just as the abolitionists tended to undermine the social justifications of slavery and the psychological bonds of the slave, so the abolitionists of psychiatric slavery tend to undermine the justifications of commitment and the psychological bonds of the committed patient.

Ultimately, the forces of society will probably be enlisted on one side or the other. If so, we may, on the one hand, be ushering in the abolition of involuntary mental hospitalization and treatment; on the other, we may be witnessing the fruitless

[78] See Davis, op. cit., p. 193.

struggles of an individualism bereft of moral support against a collectivism proffered as medical treatment.[79]

XI

We know that man's domination over his fellow man is as old as history; and we may safely assume that it is traceable to prehistoric times and to prehuman ancestors. Perennially, men have oppressed women; white men, colored men; Christians, Jews. However, in recent decades, traditional reasons and justifications for discrimination among men—on the grounds of national, racial, or religious criteria—have lost much of their plausibility and appeal. What justification is there now for man's age-old desire to dominate and control his fellow man? Modern liberalism—in reality, a type of statism—allied with scientism, has met the need for a fresh defense of oppression and has supplied a new battle cry: Health!

In this therapeutic-meliorist view of society, the ill form a special class of "victims" who must, both for their own good and for the interests of the community, be "helped"—coercively and against their will, if necessary—by the healthy, and especially by physicians who are "scientifically" qualified to be their masters. This perspective developed first and has advanced farthest in psychiatry, where the oppression of "insane patients" by "sane physicians" is by now a social custom hallowed by medical and legal tradition. At present, the medical profession as a whole seems to be emulating this model. In the Therapeutic State toward which we appear to be moving, the principal requirement for the position of Big Brother may be an M.D. degree.

[79] Szasz, T. S.: "Whither psychiatry?" This volume, pp. 218–45.

10 · MENTAL HEALTH SERVICES

IN THE SCHOOL

The public school system is one of our major social institutions. Its aims and functions are of two kinds.

First, as in other large-scale bureaucracies, Parkinson's Law is at work: the institution seeks to enlarge its size and scope by increasing its personnel, its budget, the range of its services, and so forth. I shall not be concerned with this aspect of the problem, and mention it here only to explain why large institutions rarely reject opportunities to expand, even if doing so jeopardizes their primary functions. In the case of the public school system, this has meant that school boards, administrators, and teachers have generally embraced the "help" offered them by psychologists and psychiatrists.

Second, there are the socially acknowledged and codified aims and functions of the schools: to teach and to socialize. These are to some extent antagonistic to each other.

II

Is there evidence for the view that teaching and socialization are partly antagonistic processes? Or shall we rather assume—or assert, as many do—that these are not two separate educational functions but one, two faces of a single coin? Let me offer a brief defense of the former position.

Personality development is a complex biological, cultural, social, and personal affair. The kind of personality an individual develops depends partly on the kinds of values his family and his society cherish and despise—by word as well as by deed. The kind of personality modern Western man has grown to value in the last few centuries is embodied in the religions, laws, morals, and customs of this civilization: it is a person adequately socialized but possessing an authentic individuality. However, the precise proportion of the two ingredients necessary for a suitable balance is variously defined, and, regardless of the proportion, the achievement of such a balance is an exceedingly delicate task. This is why the concept of a "normal man"—or, more generally, of life as a well-executed dramatic production —is so elusive.

We must therefore try to be clear about the nature of the conflict between teaching and socialization. Of course, children are instructed in what society expects of individuals; in this sense, the process of socialization is part of teaching and learning. But this is trivial: what else could socialization be but an instructional enterprise? Moreover, teaching that does not go beyond socializing the pupil is better called indoctrination. In other words, only the simplest, psychologically most unsophisticated kind of teaching aims at socialization. In this type of teaching the student is required to imitate: the final aim is a performance that reproduces a standard model. A child may thus learn to control his bladder, use English words, or eat with a fork. Though such learning is essential, it is by no means representative of the scope of education. On the contrary, the broader aim of education is not so much socially correct performance as creative innovation, with its own, fresh standards of value. Particularly from the early teens onwards, the more serious and sophisticated the teaching, the more likely it is to create diversity rather than homogeneity among the students.

Nor is this the end of the process of education. The highest ideal of the teacher is nothing less than *subversion*. (I use the term advisedly, and with intentional precision.) This is not a new idea. Great teachers—from Socrates, through Jesus and Luther and Spinoza, to Marx and Freud and Gandhi—were all critical and, in this sense, subversive, of the existing socioethical order. To be sure, they were not nihilists: their subversion was but a proximal goal, or a means, to a distant end, the creation of a more rational, more just, more peaceful social order. Thus, teaching, especially critical teaching on a high level of competence and personal devotion, fosters many qualities and values antagonistic to those of simple socialization. Let me etch this dichotomy sharply.

In this critical sense, to teach means to encourage and reward competence, knowledge, skill, and the autonomous-authentic search for, and creation of, meaning (or "reality"). In the school, commitment to these values easily leads to an aristocratic style—in that the system encourages the development of elites of competence. Such an educational orientation creates tensions, in both teachers and students, for emphasis on competence leads to competitiveness—and frequently to envy, jealousy, and hostility among the competitors. The upshot is anything but a tranquil atmosphere conducive to an idyllic conception of "mental health."

If the goals of education are aristocratic, competitive, and instrumental, the goals of socialization are just the opposite: democratic, non-competitive, and institutional. To socialize the child, the teacher must emphasize the values of equality, consensus, popularity, and the acceptance of culturally shared myths. This aim is best achieved by discouraging idiosyncratic behavior and exploration, and by encouraging conduct favoring group solidarity. Thus, the reduction of choice and alternatives, though inimical to critical education, is essential to socialization, especially in a mass society.

Accordingly, the typical agent of socialization is not the critical teacher, but the modern advertiser—not he who clarifies, but he who mystifies. Whereas the former offers truth at the cost of spiritual turmoil and personal responsibility, the latter promises security and happiness for the sacrifice of an authentic search for meaning and truth.

In the end, the aim of critical teaching can only be to provide conditions favorable for the development of the autonomous personality, whereas the aim of socialization can only be the opposite—to provide the conditions favorable for the development of the heteronomous personality.

Though I have described education and socialization as if they were diametrically opposite endeavors, and autonomy and heteronomy as if they were mutually exclusive moral values and personality types, in actuality the situation is more complicated: The practical necessities of social life as we know it require a compromise between these goals and values. Reflecting such social realities, the school fosters and inhibits both autonomy and heteronomy; it exposes the child to a complex and constantly varying mixture of influences in which teaching and socializing are inextricably intertwined. As students of man, and more narrowly as students of education, our task is to be ever watchful of the fabric of education and to identify clearly those strands that belong to teaching and those that belong to socialization.

In this essay, I shall try to show that psychiatric services in the school promote the aims of socialization and retard the aims of critical education. If this is what those in control of our major educational enterprises desire, probably nothing can stop them from translating their wishes into action. The wisdom of this course of action, however, may be doubted.

It appears, moreover, that the progressive displacement of education by socialization in our schools is a part of a larger pattern—that is, of the steady drift of modern societies toward collectivism and statism. "The mass-man," wrote Ortega y Gasset more than thirty years ago, "sees in the State an anonymous power, and feeling himself, like it, anonymous, he believes that the State is something of his own. Suppose that in the public life of a country some difficulty, conflict, or problem presents itself, the mass-man will demand that the State intervene immediately and undertake a solution directly with its immense and unassailable resources."[1]

The lessons of recent European history should have taught us, however, that often such therapies are worse than the diseases they cure. Nevertheless, in the United States today it is considered bad taste—especially in intellectual and professional circles—to question the ever-increasing involvement of the state in every nook and cranny of social life, and the consequent ever-increasing cost, paid by tax monies, of maintaining the state apparatus. In short, the expansion of the schools, and

[1] Ortega y Gasset, J.: *The Revolt of the Masses* [1930] (New York: Norton, 1957), p. 120.

especially of the public schools, into the mental health field is thus but a symptom of the general expansion of the activities of the modern bureaucratic state.

III

Let us look at the actual operation of mental health services in educational institutions.[2] The psychiatrist in the school, like the psychiatrist in the public mental hospital or clinic, faces a conflict of interests. We know only too well that, in the latter situation, the individual patient and the psychiatric institution are often in conflict. When they are, the psychiatrist cannot serve the interests of both. The upshot is that he sides with the more powerful party to the dispute: he helps the system, and harms the patient.[3]

When psychiatric services are introduced into the school, the psychiatrist finds himself in a similar position. In general, the conflict is between the student and the teacher, or the student and the school administration. Since he is an employee of the school system, it is hardly surprising that the psychiatrist should take a position antagonistic to the student's (self-defined) interests. The literature on school psychiatry supports this contention. Though our interest here is mainly in psychiatric services in public grade schools and high schools, some of my data will be drawn from experiences reported by psychiatrists working in universities. This is justified by the fundamental similarities in what the school psychiatrist does, regardless of where he does it.

The alleged importance of the early treatment of "mentally disturbed" children received powerful impetus from the pub-

[2] See, for example, Bisgyer, J. L., Kahn, C. L., and Frazee, V. F.: "Special classes for emotionally disturbed children." *Amer. J. Orthopsychiatry*, 34:696–704 (July), 1964; Stogdill, C. G.: "Mental health in education." *Amer. J. Psychiatry*, 121:694–98 (Jan.), 1965; Stringham, J. A.: "Report on school psychiatry programs in five Central Schools." *New York State Journal of Medicine*, 61:3271–84 (Oct.), 1961.

[3] Szasz, T. S.: *Law, Liberty, and Psychiatry: An Inquiry into the Social Uses of Mental Health Practices* (New York: Macmillan, 1963).

licity given to Lee Harvey Oswald and his encounter with school psychiatry. When he was thirteen, Oswald allegedly suffered from a serious personality disorder for which he required expert help—which, however, was rejected by his mother. So far as I have been able to discover, no one—no columnist, commentator, or public figure—has questioned the propriety of releasing this presumably confidential "medical" information concerning Oswald. In view of what Oswald did—or, more precisely, of what he has been accused of doing—he presumably forfeited his right (if indeed anyone has this right) of having his childhood mental diagnosis kept out of the press. However, the implications of this episode for school psychiatry do not stop here. For Oswald's childhood "mental illness," and especially his mother's refusal to consent to its "treatment," have been interpreted—by men in the highest and most responsible echelons of our society—as grounds for suspecting all "mentally ill" children of being potential presidential assassins; and they have concluded, therefore, that such "illnesses" justify psychiatric measures of far-reaching significance.

In an article entitled "When Does A Child Need A Psychiatrist?" published in Parade magazine, 12 million families were informed: "The fact is that youth is the most important time to recognize and treat psychiatric problems. And if early warning signs are ignored, they can lead to great difficulties later—as the case of Lee Harvey Oswald demonstrated."[4]

The danger, because of the prevalence of this dread "disease" among children, is colossal: "Psychiatric problems among children are widespread. According to Dr. Stuart M. Finch, of the Children's Psychiatric Hospital, University of Michigan, about 7½ to 12 per cent of the grade school children in the United States—2½ to 4 million children—are sufficiently emotionally disturbed to require treatment. When you add in preschoolers, infants, and high school students who may need care, the number could be twice that."[5]

[4] Warshofsky, F.: "When does a child need a psychiatrist?" Parade, January 10, 1965, pp. 4–5; p. 4.
[5] Ibid., p. 5.

In another article, published in *Harper's Magazine*, Senator Abraham Ribicoff was even more alarmed and alarming. In tones bordering on psychiatric demagogy, he implied that every "mentally sick" child is a potential Oswald. Titling his essay "The Dangerous Ones," he began by citing Oswald's encounter with the school social worker at 13, and added: "Oswald never received that help [recommended by the social worker], the Warren Commission tersely reported in 1964. Oswald is dead and so is the beloved President he murdered. But there are—according to expert estimates—close to a half million American children as desperately sick as Oswald was, who, like him, are not getting the help they need today."[6]

Perhaps it is bad form to cavil about Senator Ribicoff's calling Oswald the President's murderer rather than his *alleged* murderer. But though Oswald's name is so blackened that any further maligning of him may have to be accepted uncritically—surely this is not true of a half million, or 4 million, or more, children whose only offense against the United States thus far may be nothing more serious than bed-wetting or nail-biting. The generalization suggested by Senator Ribicoff and others is demagogic and dangerous, for, if the enormity of Oswald's alleged crime justifies demarcating mentally ill children as members of a special class and treating them differently from the way we treat all other children, how can we object to the classic strategy of anti-Semitism, which justifies the special treatment of Jews as members of a special class, the descendants of the "murderers" of Christ?

We must be clear about the argument in favor of the wholesale treatment of "sick" children: the "disturbed" children are dangerous; our task is to render them harmless. This vulgarization of psychiatry must not go unrecognized and unchallenged. Not only does such a perspective malign and stigmatize the children—it also maligns and stigmatizes the psychiatrists. The more sharply we define mental illness in children as lack of so-

[6] Ribicoff, A.: "The dangerous ones: Help for children with twisted minds." *Harper's Magazine*, February 1965, pp. 88–90; p. 90.

cialization; and the risk they pose, as presidential assassination—
the more implicit is the "therapy" required: what such "patients" need is not a doctor or psychotherapist, but a policeman
or jailer.

The "treatment" of so-called emotionally disturbed children
is, according to Senator Ribicoff, "a problem of peculiar urgency
—as a matter both of humanity and of public safety. Week after
week, our newspapers report senseless killings, rapes, and acts
of sadism. For those who read beyond the headlines there
emerges a repetitive chronicle of neglect and inaction by a society that turned its back on deeply troubled children until it
was too late to save them or to protect the community."[7]

Here, then, is a distinguished and well-intentioned public
servant repeating the hoariest equation of crime and mental illness, and demanding that the control of delinquency and social
disorder be entrusted to physicians. While doing so, he also
blurs the differences between what "troubled" youngsters (and
their families) want, and what the pillars of society want. Frequently, the two do not want the same thing, no matter how
much Senator Ribicoff persists in maintaining that they do:
"[T]he statistics accumulate and the tragedies mount. What is
needed, it seems to me, is an all-out effort to make sure that
*potentially dangerous youngsters are identified early, effectively
brought into treatment, and continuously treated as long as
necessary to assure decent lives for themselves and safety for
society*" (italics added).[8]

This is a bold proposal. The best one can say about it is that
it is naive. Nowhere does Ribicoff mention that children or
their parents might have the right to refuse psychiatric examination, diagnosis, and treatment. One is forced to conclude that
Senator Ribicoff believes that the children have no such rights,
and that the parents, who now do possess these rights, should be
deprived of them. This surmise is supported by what Senator
Ribicoff says, and does not say, about a bill he had introduced
into the Senate of the United States in 1965.

[7] Ibid., p. 89.
[8] Ibid.

The purpose of that bill was "to develop community therapeutic centers for emotionally disturbed children, or children in danger of becoming disturbed. Up to 75 per cent of the cost would be borne by the federal government. These centers, cooperating with the schools and the courts, would offer a variety of services to children, all aimed at giving them accessible, comprehensive, and continuing care. A child might come to the center via a school, or a court, or a social agency, or a parent, or even a concerned neighbor. It would then be up to the center to use all the means at its disposal to make *sure* [italics in the original] that the child does not slip haphazardly through its fingers into the never-never land of neglect and remorse."[9]

Senator Ribicoff here speaks in the language typical of the mental health demagogue: he promises "therapeutic centers . . . [that] would offer a variety of services," but remains silent about whether the recipients of these "services" would have a right to reject the "benefits" so generously "offered" them by their government. It is a brazenly fraudulent rhetoric, like describing the Volstead Act (the Prohibition amendment) as a "therapeutic service offered" to American citizens for the cure of alcoholism.

Moreover, the kinds of psychiatric practices Senator Ribicoff advocates are already all around us. Perhaps it is precisely because children, and adults too, are so often treated as defective objects, without personal rights, that they become the kinds of persons that Senator Ribicoff wishes to cure by compulsory "therapy." This "therapy" may thus be the cause of the very "disease" it is supposed to alleviate.

The opinions cited and my remarks set the stage: they show that the advocates of large-scale psychiatric services for school children regard the psychiatrist as a policeman. Such a psychiatrist is an agent of the government: his task is to socialize, subdue, and, if necessary, segregate and psychologically destroy the "dangerous" child-patient in order to insure the safety and harmony of society. All this, of course, is done in the name of helping the clients become "mentally healthy."

[9] Ibid., p. 90.

IV

The effectiveness of psychiatric programs in schools is difficult to assess. They may not even be particularly useful for subduing recalcitrant children. For example, a ". . . six-year study [reported in 1965] has found that individual counseling of potentially delinquent high school girls is ineffective in improving their school behavior or in reducing the number of dropouts."[10]

Although the effectiveness of psychiatric programs in schools may be unclear, some of their effects are clear enough. We know that being cast in the role of mental patient is a form of personal degradation: it is a kind of stigmatization, like being classified as Negro in Alabama or Jewish in Nazi Germany. The psychiatric cant is that the aim of school psychiatry is to help the child; but the very definition of a student as someone in need of psychiatric help harms him. Nor is this harm limited to the stigmatization inherent in being publicly defined as mentally ill, as the following news item illustrates:

On May 5, 1964, *The New York Times* reported on the trial of the principal and two assistants of a Brooklyn school for emotionally disturbed children. The three had been charged with "permitting pupils to perform janitorial services and personal tasks for teachers. . . ." One of the teachers assigned to this school testified that "students were used to wash and wipe teachers' cars," and was further quoted as remarking, "This is the type of nonsense that they give Negro and Puerto Rican children who are labeled as emotionally or socially maladjusted." Another teacher, who had formerly been assigned to this school, stated "that on at least one occasion he had seen a student polishing the principal's shoes in his office."[11]

While I have made no empirical study of whether or not students categorized as mentally ill by school psychiatrists are

10 Jaffee, N.: "Counseling fails in delinquency test." *The New York Times*, February 20, 1965, p. 1.
11 Terte, R. H.: "Teacher charges misuse of pupils." *The New York Times*, May 5, 1964, p. 37.

mistreated, and, if so, in what ways, the question is: Which person's assertion requires fresh proof—the one who claims that a public diagnosis of mental illness is a stigma, or the one who claims that it is not?

The advocates of mental health practices in the schools ignore the stigma inherent in the mental-patient role and the coercion that they, as therapists, propose to employ. Here are some excerpts from a typical paper on psychiatric services for public school children. "The classroom teachers," the author tells us, "along with principal, school physician, school nurse, and visiting teacher, frequently call to the parents' attention the existence of a problem requiring psychiatric evaluation. The nature of the behavior which is symptomatic of deeper underlying disturbance is manifold, but may be grouped into several broad categories which rarely occur separately. (1) Academic problems—under-achievement, over-achievement, erratic, uneven performance. (2) Social problems with siblings, peers—such as the aggressive child, the submissive child, the show-off. (3) Relations with parental and other authority figures, such as defiant behavior, submissive behavior, ingratiation. (4) Overt behavioral manifestations, such as tics, nail-biting, thumbsucking . . . [and] interests more befitting to the opposite sex (such as tomboy girl and effeminate boy)."[12]

There is no childhood behavior that a psychiatrist could not place in one of these categories, thus classifying the child as requiring psychiatric attention. To categorize academic performance that is "under-achievement," "over-achievement," or "erratic performance" as pathological would be humorous were it not tragic. When we are told that if a psychiatric patient is early for his appointment he is anxious, if late he is hostile, and if on time, compulsive—we laugh, because it is supposed to be a joke. But here we are told the same thing in all seriousness.

Here are additional excerpts from this essay, to indicate the kinds of social interventions psychiatrists feel justified in engaging in after detecting so-called psychiatric symptoms in a child.

[12] Radin, S. S.: "Mental health problems in school children." *The Journal of School Health*, 32:390–97 (Dec.), 1962, p. 392.

"In most instances a careful history and clinical examination of the child and parents will be sufficient."[13] It does not seem to occur to this psychiatrist that a physician retained by the school system has no business "examining" parents, nor that parents may reasonably object to such an "examination" since it affords no protection for their privacy and confidences. On the contrary, the author asserts that an "important reason for carefully considering the child-parent unit is to ascertain who the patient is. . . . In some instances only the parent may require therapy."[14] In an abstract, psychoanalytic sense, this may be so, but we have long known this. What is more important here, it seems to me, is whether it is any of the school's business to make psychiatric diagnoses of, much less treat, adult persons who also happen to be the parents of school-age children. Again, we ought to be clear about the issues. For if membership in the group of persons called "parents of school-age children" justifies involuntary mental diagnosis and treatment by an agency of the government, why not also membership in other groups, such as the unemployed, or teachers, or judges, or Jehovah's Witnesses?

I use the term "involuntary" here to describe not only psychiatric procedures ordered by courts, but also psychiatric manipulations of people enforced by informal coercions—for example, by corporations, governmental agencies, or schools. Most parents are economically dependent upon the services of the public school system. Because of this dependence, and because of the sociopsychological authority of the school, any service recommended by the system will be experienced by the parents (and the children) as an order to which they must submit, rather than as an offer that they are free to accept or reject. In other words, if the parents have no alternatives, if they cannot send the child to a parochial or private school, they can easily be coerced by the public school system. This situation is often exploited by school psychologists and psychiatrists; however sin-

13 Ibid., p. 393.
14 Ibid.

cerely and in the "best interests" of the child they may do so does not matter.

The power of the public school to coerce, especially in matters of morals, is of course well recognized. It is one of the reasons why religious training is barred from such schools. For the same reason, I believe that the public school is the last place, not the first, for a psychiatric service.

The issue here is simply the use of the social power of the school system: should it be deployed for the promotion of "mental health"? The arguments justifying the placing of psychiatric services in schools may be applied to any interest or value that society might wish to promote—for example, birth control. If we wish to attain a particular social goal, it is indeed easier and usually more effective to coerce people to behave in a certain way than to provide them with alternatives among which they may freely choose.

The psychiatric invasion of the family contemplated by school psychiatrists, and actually carried out by them, recognizes no bounds. We are thus told that members of the "clinical team . . . acquire detailed information about the child and his family through social casework, psychological interviews, home visits, and psychiatric observations—all in an endeavor to understand not only the individual personality of the varied constituents of the family but also the manner in which members interact with one another in both healthy and neurotic fashions. *After an investigation and subsequent understanding of the family has been completed, a total plan for the child and his family is formulated.* This usually includes individual and/or group therapy of the child; social casework, group therapy, or psychiatric contacts with at least one parent; periodic meetings with teachers . . ." (italics added).[15]

If all these marvelous "therapies" are provided by an enlightened community for the benefit of families, why connect the services with the public school? Why not offer the psychiatric services in a separate setting and let the families take advantage of them if they wish? Could it be that the services pro-

[15] Ibid., p. 395.

vided are not really desired by the families affected? Indeed, that they are a means for manipulating the "clients," and for this the coercive power of the school is necessary?

The views I have cited are typical of those held by the advocates of community mental health, social psychiatry, and school psychiatry. According to Gerald Caplan, for example, the main task of the community psychiatrist is to provide more and better "sociocultural supplies" to people. And the "most obvious example of social action for the provision of sociocultural supplies is that of influencing the educational system."[16]

Caplan justifies this procedure by the following reasoning: "If the preventive psychiatrist can convince the medical authorities . . . that his operations are a logical extension of traditional medical practice, his role will be sanctioned by all concerned, including himself. All that remains for him to do so is to work out the technical details."[17]

Is Caplan aware that he proposes nothing new, but, on the contrary, advances the most discredited plea of the collectivist technocrat? The problem that confronts the community psychiatrist is the traditional problem of the politician and the moralist: it is a problem of ends, not of means. It has always been, and it still is, useful to deny this. For, as Isaiah Berlin so eloquently observed, "Where ends are agreed, the only questions left are those of means, and these are not political but technical, that is to say, capable of being settled by experts or machines, like arguments between engineers or doctors. That is why those who put their faith in some immense world-transforming phenomenon, like the final triumph of reason or the proletarian revolution, must believe that all political and moral problems can thereby be turned into technological ones. That is the meaning of Saint-Simon's famous phrase about 'replacing the governments of persons by the administration of things.' "[18]

[16] Caplan, G.: *Principles of Preventive Psychiatry* (New York: Basic Books, 1964), p. 63.

[17] Ibid., p. 79.

[18] Berlin, I.: *Two Concepts of Liberty* (Oxford: Oxford University Press, 1958), p. 3.

The collectivization of man, whether by political or psychiatric means, always comes to this: persons, having been transformed into things, can be controlled and manipulated by a technocratic elite.

v

I wish now to describe the operation of the psychiatric service at Harvard University. Because of the eminence of this institution, its mental health practices are likely to command wide respect and to serve as models for other schools and colleges.

The principles of "educational psychiatry" have been set forth by Dana L. Farnsworth, the director of the Harvard University Health Services. The following excerpts convey the essence of his views: "It is vitally important that nothing a student says to a college psychiatrist in confidence be divulged to anyone without the patient's permission. Of course, if a student is overtly psychotic, suicidal, or homicidal, the safety of the individual and people in the community must take precedence over maintaining confidence. . . ."[19]

In other words, whether or not the psychiatrist chooses to protect the patient's confidence depends on his judgment of what is "best," not only for the patient but for the community as well. As we shall see later, the college psychiatrist does not in fact protect the student's confidences.

Indeed, Farnsworth refers to a truly confidential psychiatrist-patient relationship in tones of condescension: "A psychiatrist who is comfortable only in the one-to-one relation with patients would not enjoy college psychiatry."[20] What, then, is the purpose of college psychiatry? Answers Farnsworth: "If the only purpose for having psychiatrists on the staff of a college health service were to treat those persons who became mentally ill, then they might as well not be there. Colleges could carry on their responsibilities by referring sick students to private psychiatrists.

[19] Farnsworth, D. L.: "Concepts of educational psychiatry." *JAMA*, 181:815–21 (September 8), 1962, p. 818.
[20] Ibid., p. 816.

. . . The presence of psychiatrists in a college health service is justified more because they learn about the institution, become familiar with the pressures encouraging or inhibiting maturity and independence, and thus *become able to consult with faculty members and administrators* in a constructive manner about any matters in which *abnormal behavior* is an issue than because they treat disturbed students" (italics added).[21]

It is, of course, not "abnormal behavior" in the abstract about which college psychiatrists consult administrators, nor—and let us be candid about this—is it the "abnormal behavior" of faculty or administration that concerns them; their business is only the "abnormal behavior" of the students. Farnsworth admits this much when he observes, "If they [i.e., the college psychiatrists] confine themselves to treating disturbed students only and *do not share their findings with faculty, with administrators . . . ,* then they might as well remain in their private offices and have those students who need help come to them there" (italics added).[22]

Is such a physician then a kind of psychiatric policeman and spy? According to Farnsworth he is just the opposite: a liberator! "A basic goal of psychotherapy"—he writes—"should be to free the individual from crippling inner conflict by *inculcating* the kind of honesty, sincerity, and integrity in him that will enable him to act with confidence and a sense of competence. In situations involving *inappropriate response to authority,* such *consultations between college officials and psychiatrists* have great value" (italics added).[23]

So much for the principles of "educational psychiatry." Its practices at Harvard University are described by Graham Blaine, Jr., one of the leading psychiatrists at the college, from whose article I shall now quote.

"[T]he college therapists," states Blaine, "have a responsibility to the institution they represent, the parents of their patients, and their government, and they must also be protective of their

21 Ibid.
22 Ibid.
23 Ibid., p. 818.

patients."[24] The order of responsibility is revealing—the patient comes last!

After noting the importance of confidentiality in psychotherapy, Blaine states that the college psychiatrist may ". . . give blanket promises about confidentiality that he may later regret. . . . [W]e know that in the life of a college phychiatrist instances arise almost daily in which some kind of information about a student is asked for by others, and in many of these instances the requests are legitimate and necessary. In the vast majority of cases it is in the best interests of the student to comply with these requests. Often professors want to know whether they can honestly excuse a student because of his emotional illness, or a dean may want to refrain from taking action if he knows that a student is earnestly working in therapy."[25]

The psychological implications and social effects of limiting communications in psychotherapy to therapist and client, as against diffusing them over third, fourth, and nth parties in accordance with the wishes of either or both participants, is a familiar problem, and I shall not dwell on it. Suffice it to note that even at this outstanding university it is considered the legitimate function of the school psychiatrist to obscure rather than to clarify, to compound rather than to separate, his loyalties to the student, the family, the school, and the government. "Over the years at Harvard," continues Blaine, "we have been able to establish certain customs that have contributed greatly to our effectiveness as therapists to individual students *and* the community at large. Important among these is a *medical administrative lunch* held weekly and attended by the therapy staff of the psychiatric services, members of the medical and surgical services, deans who are concerned with the students or the problems on the agenda, members of the local ministry who counsel students, our psychiatric social worker, the psychology staff, representatives from the student counseling office, and the *chief of University Police*. Originally, this meeting was kept more or

[24] Blaine, G. B., Jr.: "Divided loyalties: The college therapist's responsibility to the student, the university, and the parents." *Amer. J. Orthopsychiatry*, 34:481–85 (Apr.), 1964; p. 481.
[25] Ibid.

less *secret from the students,* but now it has become so well recognized as a forum where the students' interests are well served that it is openly discussed among them and an individual will ask his therapist to discuss his problems at the 'doctors' lunch'" (italics added).[26]

If the meeting served the best interests of the students, why was it kept a secret from them? And why does Blaine interpret the students' acceptance of the "doctors' lunch" as proof of its moral legitimacy and psychotherapeutic value, rather than as a symptom of the students' acquiescence in their debased role and of their attempt to turn it, however pitifully, to their own advantage? Did the presence of the Jewish Kapo in the concentration camp mean that the camp served the best interests of the inmates? Or the presence of the American POW who collaborated with his North Korean captors mean that the prison guards were really protecting the "best interests" of the prisoners? The total denial, by even as prominent an authority in the college mental health field as Blaine, of the school's *power* over the student, and the implications of this fact for therapy carried out under the auspices of the school, is astonishing. Most likely it is a sign of the moral capitulation of the expert: the college psychiatrist has come to feel at home in his role as an arm of the university police. He is a psychiatric spy. To be sure, he may try to "help" the student, if it is possible to do so without coming into conflict with the university; but, if it is not, the physician's loyalty is clearly to the school first, and to the student last.

How do we account for the existence of such a service, especially in an area like Boston, where there is no shortage of private psychiatrists? One would think that many, perhaps most, of the students at Harvard could afford private psychiatric therapy. Why, then, does the university provide them with psychiatric help? Blaine suggests that it is because the university psychiatric service is a means of keeping tabs on the students: "In the medical school and the divinity school all first-year students are interviewed for evaluation and also introduced personally to

26 Ibid., p. 482.

the therapist to whom they can turn later should they need help."[27]

Let us remember that we no longer deal here with children (not that I consider such procedures justified with them), but with young adults, many of whom are only a few years younger than junior faculty members. Why are there not similar "services" provided for Harvard faculty members (and their families), including compulsory psychiatric interviewing of all new teachers? I believe the answer is, again, that the students are a captive patient-group in a way that faculty members are not, or at least not yet.

The best way to illustrate the role of power in this type of psychiatric work is to cite some case material presented by Blaine.

A graduate student was taken into treatment following a suicide attempt. During therapy he became depressed again, and the therapist wanted to hospitalize him. The patient refused to go to the hospital; instead, he "wished to be allowed to return to his room and to make his own decision as time goes on about whether to live or die. Several different therapists interviewed the patient but were unable to persuade him to go to the hospital. Finally, his department head asked to speak to the student, and *by showing him that his future career at school depended upon his co-operation with the mental health service,* convinced him that he should follow our advice" (italics added).[28]

Are we really expected to believe that in such a case the Harvard University Student Health Service is concerned only about the student's "best interests" and is not also deeply concerned about the effect of student suicides on the public image of the school? The fact is that if such a student is committed to a mental hospital and there kills himself, his death may not even be mentioned in the local newspapers; but should he jump out of the window of his dormitory room, the news of his suicide is likely to be front-page news in Boston and be carried over the national news wires.

[27] Ibid.
[28] Ibid., pp. 483–84.

In this example, the college psychiatrist feels justified in using the school authorities to force a student to accept a type of "psychiatric treatment" he does not want. Surely, this does not solve the basic moral and psychiatric dilemma: Has the psychiatrist acted as the agent of the student or of the school? Has he helped or harmed the "patient"?

Another case is that of "a model student and good athlete [who] was caught stealing a small item in a local store. The college rule is that students caught stealing are required to withdraw for one year and then may be allowed to return. The dean requests our opinion about levying such a punishment on this boy. He asks, 'Is not such sudden uncharacteristic behavior evidence of illness rather than evil intent?' "[29]

Did Blaine suggest that, if the dean did not like the rule, he might propose to the administration that it be changed? Or that, if he did not like punishing students for infractions of rules, he might resign as dean? No. Instead, he acceded to the technocratic collusion proposed: "After interviews and psychological *tests* we were able to tell the dean that this student was suffering under a combination of stresses at the time of the stealing episode and that the *deed was a symptom* rather than an innate character trait. . . . We made no recommendation about the disciplinary action but we did suggest that *psychiatric treatment was indicated*" (italics added).[30]

Blaine seemed to be greatly pleased with his restraint in making no *direct* recommendation about disciplinary action. But is indirect action not also action? Indirect communication, not also communication?

The role-diffusion of the college psychiatrist and the corresponding diffusion of psychiatric information that Blaine considers justifiable have few limits. Not only does such a psychiatrist owe loyalties to the students, the parents, and the school —he must also co-operate with the FBI: "An FBI agent calls to discuss a former patient and has a signed release from the student who is now applying for a responsible government position.

29 Ibid., p. 484.
30 Ibid.

While in college this boy had sought help for homosexual pre-occupation. He had engaged in homosexual activity in high school and once in college."[31] The FBI agent wants to know if the student had engaged in homosexual practices.

"This is a difficult problem—one involving loyalty to patient and to country," says Blaine. His solution is to hedge, to double-talk—in sum, to inform on the patient, while, at the same time, telling himself that he hasn't really done so, but has instead protected the "best interests" of both student and country: "We have found that questions about homosexual practices usually can be answered in context without jeopardizing security clearance. Pointing out that an individual was going through a phase of development which involved him in temporary homosexual preoccupation and even activity does not seem to alarm these investigators."[32]

I find this a dismal picture indeed, and a terrifying example for other schools to follow. The Harvard University Health Services claim to be genuinely interested in providing psychiatric care for their students. But would the Services agree to distribute reprints of the paper from which I have quoted to all who apply for psychotherapy or are coerced into it? Or are the students at Harvard University not sufficiently intelligent or "mature" to receive complete and accurate information about the "medical" service supplied to them by the college?

Finally, insofar as student health services do not adequately protect the confidences of their clients, their practices pose not only moral but legal problems as well. The lack of confidentiality in this kind of psychiatrist-patient relationship represents, as we have seen, a special risk for the client. The courts have held that the physician is negligent if he undertakes the treatment of a patient without his "informed consent": "A physician violates his duty to his patient and subjects himself to liability if he withholds any facts which are necessary to form the basis of an intelligent consent by the patient to the proposed treatment. Likewise the physician may not minimize the known dangers of

[31] Ibid., p. 485.
[32] Ibid.

a procedure . . . in order to induce his patient's consent."[33] Clearly, the conduct of the psychiatrists at the Harvard University Health Services, as described by Blaine and Farnsworth, does not measure up to this standard.

VI

Many of these problems, although they may appear in novel forms in the school setting, are not new.

The methods of psychotherapy, especially psychoanalysis, are the products of a long history of moral, medical, and psychological ideas. What has taken centuries to develop has often been wrecked in years, even days. Cautionary examples seem superfluous. The social dynamics of the process has been described by Ortega y Gasset thus: "In the disturbances caused by scarcity of food, the mob goes in search of bread, and the means it employs is generally to wreck the bakeries. This may serve as a symbol of the attitude adopted, on a greater and more complicated scale, by the masses of today towards the civilization by which they are supported."[34]

What Ortega y Gasset says about bakeries has been happening to our public schools and to our individualistic-humanistic psychiatry: both are being wrecked—despite the claims of the wreckers that their aim is to improve education and psychiatric treatment.

Jacques Barzun, one of the most perceptive and incisive critics of our educational system, has perhaps said all there is to say about the twin aims of the school—education and adjustment. The moral imperative of equality on the one hand, and the practical necessity of assimilating a steady influx of immigrants on the other, have, he says, made it ". . . inevitable that our schools should aim at social adjustment first. . . ."[35] This being so, the schools were easy prey for the purveyors of psychological

[33] *Salgo* v. *Leland Stanford Board of Trustees*, 154 Cal. App. 2d 560, 578, 317 P. 2d 170 (Dist. Ct. App., 1st Dist.), 1957.

[34] Ortega y Gasset, op. cit., p. 60.

[35] Barzun, J.: *The House of Intellect* (New York: Harper & Row, 1959), p. 95.

and psychiatric scientism. Thus, "The notion of helping the child has in the United States displaced that of teaching him. Anyone who tries to preserve the distinction is obviously unhelpful, and is at once known for a declared enemy of youth. The truth is that even apart from its hostility to Intellect, systematic coddling is as dangerous as it is impertinent."[36]

The aim of the public school curriculum, continued Barzun, "is to round off edges, to work moral specifications—in short, to manipulate the young into a semblance of the harmonious committee, in accordance with the statistics of child development."[37] Given this character of the American elementary and secondary schools, is it not sheer madness to make them the purveyors of psychiatric services as well? What, after all, do we want our schools to be: houses of knowledge where the child acquires the discipline of learning—or day hospitals where he is lulled into believing that the best identity is no identity?

The pressures that force and the enticements that lure the growing child into relinquishing the risks of striving for a sharply defined personality, and, instead, taking refuge in the opacity of non-identity, have been discussed by many sociologists and writers—most eloquently, perhaps, by Edgar Z. Friedenberg in *The Vanishing Adolescent*. We have long encouraged the growth of what Ortega y Gasset called the "mass-man," or the other-directed or heteronomous personality. The introduction of formal psychiatric services into the schools is therefore not so much the cause of this process as it is a symptom of its final efflorescence.

The phrase "My house is my castle" may have accurately expressed the beliefs and values of our forebears; today it is virtually meaningless. In days past, it signified not only the sanctity of the home for the individual as person, but also the security of the mind as the abode of the soul. Solitude, however, is a source of comfort and strength only for the autonomous personality; for the mass-man it is just the opposite, a calamity and a threat. Those used to being watched by Big Brother expect to be on

[36] Ibid., p. 102.
[37] Ibid., p. 103.

stage; they know how to hide there behind a mask of imper-
sonation. Alone, without an audience, with no one watching,
they meet themselves—and, having met a ghost, are properly
frightened.

Institutional psychiatry, whether in the mental hospital or the
school, is perhaps the finest technique developed so far for driving the soul out of man. Mentally ill man is often said to have
lost his mind. The cure institutional psychiatry offers is to give
him back his mind—empty. The hospitalized mental patient
hounded by the specter of electroshock treatments, and the
child harassed by psychological testing and the threat of invidious psychiatric labeling, are exposed to the same dehumaniz-
ing influence. Usually they accept the solution the system offers
them: to adopt a rounded, rather than an edgy, identity, so that,
like greased pigs at a rodeo, they can be caught and subdued by
no one. But, having become shadows, they cast no shadows.
Social survival is their spiritual death.

It is pertinent, in this connection, to quote some of the
things Friedenberg says about this problem. "It is easier [he
writes], and less damaging, for a youngster to face bad grades,
disappointment at being passed over for a team or a club, or
formal punishment than it is for him to deal with gossip about
his character or his manners, with teachers who pass the word
along that he is a troublemaker or that he needs special patience
and guidance because his father drinks."[38]

The central developmental task of adolescence, according to
Friedenberg, is self-definition. As Freud saw it, and practiced
it, psychoanalysis—voluntarily sought by adult clients—served
the purpose of helping the individual sharpen his self-definition.
In another context, a seemingly similar method may serve the
opposite purpose: to confuse and undermine self-definition. In
my view, regardless of its aim, this is the effect of school psychiatry.

Nor should this surprise us. The surgeon's scalpel can heal
or wound—depending on who uses it and how. Similarly, if

[38] Friedenberg, E. Z.: *The Vanishing Adolescent* [1959] (New
York: Dell, 1963), p. 28.

psychiatric and psychotherapeutic methods are effective, as indeed they are, we cannot naively suppose that they may not be
put to various uses, depending on the aims and values of those
who employ them. "A society which has *no purposes* of its own
other than to insure domestic tranquility by suitable medica-
tion," Friedenberg warns, "will have no use for adolescents, and
will fear them; for they will be among the first to complain, as
they crunch away at their benzedrine, that tranquilizers make
you a square. It will set up sedative programs of guidance, which
are likely to be described as therapeutic, but whose apparent
function will be to keep young minds and hearts in custody till
they are without passion."[39]

This is a rather dark image. Is it correct? Perhaps feeling dis-
heartened by his own vision—which, however, may well be
20/20—Friedenberg adds: "We have by no means gone so far
as yet; but the sort of process of which I speak is already dis-
cernible."[40]

I think we have gone very nearly as far as Friedenberg has
indicated. If there is hope, as I believe there almost always is,
it does not lie in the moderation of the collectivistic aggressors;
rather, it lies in the resistance of some of the victims, in whom
each new assault on individuality seems to generate fresh determination to defend the individual. Though no doubt more complicated in its genesis, I surmise that the recent vast increase in
the use of illegal drugs among college students—often sensa-
tionally labelled "addiction"—is related to the increasing psychiatric surveillance of the youngsters. If political oppression
provokes political resistance, why should we be surprised if psychiatric oppression provokes psychiatric resistance?

Of course, psychiatric therapy need be neither oppressive nor
anti-individualistic. But, as Friedenberg himself so clearly saw,
the school is not the proper setting for a client-valuing therapy.
Noting that it is normal for a youngster to face crises in for-
mulating his identity, and that such a child might well benefit
from psychotherapy, he correctly states that what the child needs

[39] Ibid., p. 37.
[40] Ibid.

is the services of a ". . . skilled psychotherapist, not of a petty official. A civil service, in dealing with him, is most likely to constitute itself a Ministry of Adjustment; however sophisticated its staff may be about psychodynamics, its basic interest will be in the kind of problem the student creates for the school and for other people. This will serve as the real basis for classifying him and disposing of his case. It is almost impossible for a school guidance counselor or dean [or school psychiatrist—T.S.] to believe that his function in dealing with a particular student may *not* be to promote adjustment, but rather to help the youngster to find rational rather than destructive *alternatives* to adjustment, in circumstances where adjustment would cruelly violate his emerging conception of himself and the basis for his self-esteem."[41]

Thus has Freud's subversive psychotherapy been domesticated in America: an instrument for liberating man has been transformed into yet another technique for pacifying him. "That psychotherapy should be devoted to the ends of adjustment, rather than growth," comments Friedenberg, "is a tragedy that the indomitable Freud would have found ironical; but it is perhaps inevitable in a culture in which one must have an acceptable personality to succeed, and one must succeed to have self-esteem."[42]

In this I cannot fully agree with Friedenberg. To be sure, the culture must share in the blame. But the psychiatrists and psychoanalysts who use psychotherapy in this way—are they not also responsible?

VII

I have said it before and would like to say it again: I am not opposed to sound psychiatric practices. Just as the person critical of torture as a means of extracting confessions from alleged criminals is not opposed to law and order—so I, opposed to the practices of psychiatric fascism, am not opposed to the practices

[41] Ibid., p. 133.
[42] Ibid., p. 134.

of psychiatric humanism. Psychoanalysis, individual therapy, group therapy, family therapy, remedial counseling—all these and many other methods that students of psychotherapy have developed and may yet develop have a legitimate place in a free and pluralistic society. But, in my opinion, they have no place in social situations where they may be used as instruments of psychological deception and coercion against captive, unconsenting, or unwilling individuals. Hence, such procedures have no place *in the schools*.

Our society is still more capitalistic than socialistic. Those who wish to avail themselves of psychotherapeutic services, and can afford to pay for them, are free to purchase such help privately. They should be left undisturbed in their freedom to do so.

If society desires to make psychotherapeutic services available to those who cannot afford them, the way to do so is obvious: whether through philanthropy or through funds supplied by the government, society must supply a service for the client. But he must be left free to use it or reject it: such a society must be ready and willing to underwrite the services of a "private" therapist for the individual, or the family, and must not try to use the therapist as its spy or policeman. To be sure, society needs policemen, and perhaps spies as well. But it had better not use its psychiatrists and psychologists for such work unless it wishes to liquidate the individualistic uses of these professions.

11 · PSYCHIATRY, THE STATE,

AND THE UNIVERSITY

The Problem of the Professional Identity

of Academic Psychiatry

Among the subjects taught in universities, psychiatry occupies a singular position. It is the only modern scientific discipline whose leading theoreticians and practitioners were not, and often still are not, members of the university community. "Technical improvements in actual [mental] patient care," noted Robert Morison in his Alan Gregg Memorial Lecture for 1964, "have come almost entirely from outside the country and in a manner which bypassed much of academic psychiatry. . . ."[1]

I submit that this situation is more than the result of historical accident. It suggests, rather, that the university, which has been the traditional haven for scholars, has failed to provide a favorable soil for the development of the psychiatric academician. The main reason for this, in my opinion, is that, having remained under the direct or indirect control of social interests and institutions outside the academic fold, psychiatric education and research could not become integral parts of academic life.

II

Psychiatry has always been the unwanted problem child of medicine. It was accordingly ignored, demeaned, and, whenever possible, kept out of sight. This was the history of psychiatry from the dawn of scientific medicine in the second half of the

[1] Morison, R. S.: "Some illnesses of mental health. The Alan Gregg Lecture, 1964." *Journal of Medical Education*, 39:985–99 (Nov.), 1964.

nineteenth century until the First World War—the era of the alienist. The term is suggestive: the psychiatrist was expected to deal with persons who had become alienated from their society; at the same time, the psychiatrist himself was alienated from society in general, and from the medical profession (and other learned professions) in particular.

Freud attempted to hurdle this problem by creating a new discipline, psychoanalysis, which he sought to keep separate from medicine and psychiatry. Strengthened by the scholarly accomplishments and social prestige of psychoanalysis, psychiatry, the erstwhile stepchild of medicine, managed for a while to endear itself to its mother: during the Second World War, and for a decade or so afterward, psychoanalytic psychiatry, rechristened "dynamic psychiatry," was often treated as the favorite child, rather than the stepchild, of medicine. But this false relationship between medicine and psychiatry could not last. Psychiatry's position in the family of medicine became dubious once more. It then tried to regain its rapidly declining prestige by flirting with drugs and claiming that "mental illness", like any other illness, could be cured by chemistry. After only a few years, this claim, too, wore thin. Psychiatry next hitched its fortune to the growing national interest in problems of poverty and segregation, and staked its all on so-called community health practices. This is where we find our subject today.

I offer this thumbnail sketch of the history of modern psychiatry[2] to underscore, from the outset, psychiatry's lifelong problem of identity:[3] the nature and scope of psychiatry as a professional discipline, as well as its social role, have always been uncertain and shifting. It is against this background that I wish to examine the position of psychiatry as a scholarly discipline taught in universities.

[2] For further discussion, see "Whither psychiatry?" This volume, pp. 218–45.

[3] In this connection, see Erikson, E. H.: "The problem of ego identity." *Journal of the American Psychoanalytic Association*, 4:56–121, 1956.

III

Contemporary psychiatry is a mixture of two very different sorts of things: on the one hand, it is a science, both pure and applied (i.e., the study of man and the practice of psychological healing); on the other, it is a vested interest that controls vast sums of money (allocated to it by the federal and state governments) and wields vast powers (by means of its quasi-legal authority to hospitalize persons without their consent). These two aspects of what we call "psychiatry" have never been adequately separated; moreover, so long as they are not, it will be difficult, if not impossible, for psychiatry to be a "free" science —that is, to search for "truth" and to teach it without reference to the effect of such inquiry and instruction on the vested interests of psychiatric institutions. The obvious danger of nonseparation is that of fostering a pseudoscience—a system of assertions authoritatively defined as truth and promoted as mental health education to advance the power and prestige of the psychiatric establishment.

The reason for this state of affairs must be sought, at least in part, in the development of psychiatry. Organized psychiatry is little more than a hundred years old. It began, in the United States, with the development of the state hospital system: in 1844, thirteen superintendents of mental hospitals joined to form the Association of Medical Superintendents of American Institutions for the Insane—an organization that later became the American Psychiatric Association.

The history of psychiatry as a science thus differs radically from the history of other sciences, especially physics and chemistry. In psychiatry, there first developed a social institution— that is, the state hospital system—that society found useful for dealing with certain problems of deviant behavior; accordingly, society bestowed upon it a measure of prestige and power. Members of this vested interest group then formed an organization devoted in part to advancing the knowledge requisite for the intelligent discharge of their duties.

The legacy of this history is evident if one compares, for example, medical therapeutics with psychiatric therapeutics. The study of drug action, firmly based on the sciences of chemistry and physiology, is taught in medical schools. The interests of pharmacology as a science and academic discipline, and the interests of the pharmaceutical industry as a business enterprise, are accordingly clearly distinguished. Teachers and investigators in pharmacology in universities are equally free to discover favorable and unfavorable drug effects in men and animals. The study of toxic substances is as much in the domain of pharmacology as is the study of therapeutic agents.

In psychiatry, the situation is different. In the first place, the proper subject matter of psychiatry is not as clearly defined as that of pharmacology; nor are its methods or aims. Secondly, the distinction between psychiatry as a science and as an institution is frequently obscure. Some university departments of psychiatry are affiliated with the state hospital system; others, with psychoanalytic institutes. Ideologically, and often financially, such departments are then dependent on the affiliating system. This situation is comparable to the employment of a nominally scientific body by a vested interest group—for example, medical researchers by the tobacco industry. It is obvious that members of such a group do not have the freedom of research workers in an independent university department. In short, such affiliations render certain areas of psychiatry "off limits" for psychiatric investigation and inquiry. In most academic departments today this is true for certain practices in public mental hospitals and in psychoanalytic institutes.

IV

The questions I now wish to pose are these: What *was*, and what *is*, the role of psychiatry in the medical school of a university? And what *ought to be* its role?

George Packer Berry, former dean of the Harvard Medical School and one of the most distinguished medical educators of our day, has stated: "The psychiatrist is concerned primarily with behavior and interpersonal relationships. . . . Just as the physician needs the chemist, the physicist, and the other natural scientists to help him understand man's physical reactions, so he needs the social and behavioral scientists to help him understand man's way of life."[4]

To what extent is the psychiatrist in the medical school committed to the task of advancing our *understanding* of behavior, and to what extent to the task of perfecting means of *controlling* behavior?

We can no longer deny that, from its beginnings, psychiatry has always been engaged in the business of controlling human behavior—first through involuntary mental hospitalization alone, then through a series of additional measures such as physical restraints, chemical sedatives, electroshock, psychosurgery, tranquilizers, and, lately, milieu and group therapy. Nor can we deny that in the universities academic psychiatry never achieved a clear emancipation from the institutions entrusted by society with the practical task of controlling so-called mentally ill behavior. I shall briefly document these assertions.

Before the turn of the century and for several decades afterwards, here as well as abroad, the center of psychiatric activity was the state mental hospital. Departments of psychiatry in medical schools were at first mere appendages to state hospitals or to the mental hygiene system. These governmental health facilities controlled most of the funds and positions in psychiatry and, thereby, also the scope and content of psychiatric teaching in medical schools.

With the mounting influence of psychoanalysis in the United States that began in the 1930s and reached its peak shortly after the Second World War, the state hospital system lost its grip on the medical schools. But this does not mean that departments of psychiatry gained their independence. Instead of being handmaidens of the state hospital system, many of the best departments became handmaidens of organized psychoanalysis. Some still are. The nature and scope of psychiatry in the medical school—at both undergraduate and graduate levels—was hence-

[4] Berry, G. P.: "Valedictory comments about medical education." *Medical Tribune*, September 11-12, 1965, p. 6.

forth dictated by the theories and practices of psychoanalysis.

At present, we are witnessing the beginning of a new marriage and a new bondage: departments of psychiatry are becoming handmaidens of community mental health programs sponsored by the federal and state governments.

I contend that regardless of the merits of any or all of these psychiatric interests, the academicians in universities, medical schools, and departments of psychiatry who have accepted the role of merely interpreting and fostering such activities have defaulted on their obligations as scholars and teachers in academic institutions. For it is no more the proper function of a professor of psychiatry to help the state mental hospital system to care for large numbers of "mentally ill" people than it is for a professor of journalism to put out a newspaper. The community need is not in dispute here: the community may indeed need facilities for certain disabled persons, just as it may need a good newspaper. But is it the academician's task to meet this need?[5]

Because of the vast funds at its disposal, the community psychiatry movement promises to have a significant impact on departments of psychiatry. It is evident already that, in line with past practices, many departments will become interpreters and proponents of that psychiatric activity which possesses the most economic power and social prestige. That this kind of activity may be inappropriate to a university department, or that it may be harmful to its alleged beneficiaries, is socially suppressed and personally repressed. Compassion for the suffering of countless millions of poor, unemployed, physically handicapped, and socially disadvantaged people is used to silence inquiry: it must be nothing less than heartlessness, if not mindlessness, that would make a psychiatrist resist participation.

But the matter is not so simple. The poor and the disadvantaged have always been with us. The need, though unquestioned, is surely not an *acute* emergency, but on the contrary, a *chronic* difficulty that no crash program can possibly remedy. Moreover, regardless of the merits of the need, something else

[5] In this connection, see Barzun, J.: *The American University: How it Runs, Where it is Going* (New York: Harper & Row, 1968).

must be said about the direct participation of university departments of psychiatry in community mental health activities.

Because community mental health centers, like other large-scale public psychiatric facilities, offer "help" to both voluntary and involuntary mental patients—indeed, they make it a point of professional honor to refuse to make a distinction between these two groups—many of the persons thus "served" will regard the psychiatrist not as their doctor but as their adversary, and will prefer to be let alone. For example, a pregnant woman may want an abortion; society may choose to provide her with free psychiatric care. On which side of this conflict should academic psychiatry enlist itself? Clearly, to the extent that academic psychiatry becomes an extension of the political arm of the government, the support of the patient's self-defined interests will be rendered impossible; indeed, the mere acknowledgment of the patient's interests, as opposed to those of the society or the state, may be considered subversive and may tend to be suppressed.

If it is not the job of the academic psychiatrist to offer the kind of services that the state hospital psychiatrist, the psychoanalyst, and the community mental health worker provide, what is his job?

Berry put it well when he said that it is to promote our *understanding* of "man's way of life." Accordingly, the task of the university psychiatrist is to acquaint the medical student with past and present modes of approach to the so-called mentally ill patient, but not to teach him proficiency in the use of any of these methods. In short, the academic psychiatrist should never merely teach a specific technical activity, but instead should always maintain a critical attitude toward that activity.

Undergraduate psychiatric education should thus aim at imparting to the student conceptual understanding rather than practical mastery of specific skills. It should concentrate on the study and critical analysis of those aspects of human development and human relations that are relevant to medical practice and investigation. Medical students need to be acquainted with actual psychiatric practices only to the extent that this is necessary for their proper appreciation of the theoretical instruction. In this respect, psychiatric teaching must differ somewhat from medical or surgical teaching, and should more closely resemble instruction in jurisprudence: students of law do not "practice" the activities of legislator, judge, prosecution, or defense attorney, but are acquainted with these legal roles only to the extent that they are necessary for making theoretical instruction about the law meaningful to them.

v

At this point it may be useful to describe more fully the scope and implications of the Community Mental Health Centers Act of 1963, and also the psychiatric orientation that brought it into being and is, in turn, now bolstered by it.

On February 5, 1963, President Kennedy delivered his much-applauded message on mental illness and mental retardation. In it he stated: "I propose a national mental health program to assist in the inauguration of a wholly new emphasis and approach to care for the mentally ill. . . . Government at every level— Federal, state, and local—private foundations and individual citizens must all face up to their responsibilities in this area."[6] The President then sharply criticized the old-fashioned, custodial state hospitals, "from which death too often provided the only firm hope of release." He concluded by emphasizing that "We need . . . to return mental health care to the mainstream of American medicine."[7]

This was a lofty, and, I am confident, a sincere and well-intentioned proposal. But this does not prevent it from being naive, misleading, and even destructive in its consequences.

Almost to the day, 158 years earlier—on February 16, 1805— Prince Karl August von Hardenberg launched the Prussian mental hospital system with the following words: "The state must concern itself with all institutions for those with damaged minds, both for the betterment of the unfortunate and for the

---

[6] Kennedy, J. F.: *Message from the President of the United States Relative to Mental Illness and Mental Retardation*, February 5, 1963; 88th Cong., First Sess., House of Representatives, Document No. 58; reprinted in *Amer. J. Psychiatry*, 120:729–37 (Feb.), 1964, p. 730.
[7] Ibid.

advancement of science. In this important and difficult field of medicine only unrelenting efforts will enable us to carve out advances for the good of suffering mankind. Perfection can be achieved only in such institutions [that is, state mental hospitals]; here are found all the conditions necessary for conducting experiments to test basic theories and for using the results of such experimentation for the advancement of science."[8]

It is chilling to contemplate the similarities between these two statements.

Current proposals for community mental health services are thus misleading, because they are vague or silent about the rights of the prospective patient, not only to receive treatment he *allegedly needs,* but also to reject treatment he *explicitly repudiates.* There are no safeguards in any of the new legislation against involuntary mental hospitalization and treatment. It is reasonable to assume, therefore, that present laws and customs governing such procedures will prevail, and, if anything, will affect an ever-growing portion of the population (especially of the lower classes). Indeed, one of the prominent spokesmen for community psychiatry frankly acknowledges that "in many instances, those members of the community who need psychiatric care most, refuse such treatment, and there are so far no ways of enforcing psychiatric care where it is most needed"; and he then expresses the hope that "If public health workers have been successful in implementing legislation to make the treatment of contagious disease obligatory, the difficulties we encounter in the course of our parallel efforts on behalf of enforced psychotherapy should not prove insurmountable."[9]

Fifty years ago this idea, also, was considered scientifically daring and intellectually popular in Germany. "An autocrat in possession of our present knowledge," wrote Kraepelin in 1917, "would be able, if he showed no consideration for the lifelong

[8] Quoted in Kraepelin, E.: *One Hundred Years of Psychiatry* [1917] (New York: Philosophical Library, 1962), p. 152.
[9] Bellak, L.: "Epilogue," in Bellak, L., ed., *Handbook of Community Psychiatry and Community Mental Health* (New York: Grune & Stratton, 1964), pp. 458–60.

habits of men, to effect a significant reduction in the incidence of insanity within a few decades."[10] Here, then, is another melancholy illustration of the bitter saying, "We learn from history that we do not learn from history."

So much for the history and spirit of the community mental health movement. Let us now take a glance at its actual operation.

VI

The Community Mental Health Centers Act sponsored by President Kennedy was enacted into law in 1963. It authorizes the expenditure of $150 million to build mental health centers across the country. In 1965, Congress allocated an additional $224 million for the salaries of the people who staff these centers.

In an article in *Harper's Magazine,* the aims and operations of the mental health centers were described as follows: "There in the centers, it is hoped, treatment will become available to everybody who needs it—the poor as well as the rich. . . . In the process mental health services will have to be reorganized along lines that are both democratic and more efficient."[11]

The actual operations carried out in the centers are medical in name only. At the Lincoln Hospital, in Harlem, in a mental health center operated under the auspices of the Albert Einstein College of Medicine, "people usually come in to discuss a pressing practical emergency rather than serious emotional troubles." One client, for example, came in complaining that she was unable "to get new mattresses from Welfare." The worker who investigated her home situation found that "[O]f her nine children, only three were living at home—a seven-year-old girl, who weighed thirty-nine pounds (the normal weight of a three-year-old), an eleven-year-old daughter with an arrested case of TB, and a fourteen-year-old daughter who was three months

[10] Kraepelin, op. cit., p. 153.
[11] Pines, M.: "The coming upheaval in psychiatry." *Harper's Magazine,* October 1965, pp. 54–60; p. 54.

pregnant. Six sons, all drug addicts, had left home. . . . The mother was an alcoholic."[12]

The help given this family consisted, among other things, of getting the mother to attend Alcoholics Anonymous and placing the pregnant daughter in a home for unwed mothers. I do not mean to denigrate the quality of this help. Nevertheless, I believe it illustrates the fraudulence of the claim that community mental health centers will make the availability of psychiatric assistance more "democratic." If this family had been living in Scarsdale instead of Harlem, the daughter's baby would have been aborted, not adopted.

This practical, social-work approach to psychiatry raises many questions: Should such activity be considered "psychiatric"? Does it pertain to "mental health and illness"? Here is the reply of a worker at the Lincoln Hospital Mental Health Center: "Is it mental health? Oh sure! People come to you with problems they can't solve, and if you help to solve them while they are still *little* problems, actually what you are doing is securing their mental health."[13] The practical—social and legal—implications of this elastic definition of mental health, and therefore also of mental illness, seem not to worry most people, in and out of psychiatry. I shall not belabor the dangers of this practice here, for I have described them elsewhere.[14]

Moreover, there is no agreement—either in psychiatry in general, or in the community mental health field in particular—on the scope of community psychiatry or on the psychiatrist's role in it.[15] Though agreeing with the popular consensus of the day that "the primary challenge is for [state] hospital psychiatrists to join psychiatrists in the community in striving to create a single, uniform level of psychiatric treatment," Dr. James A.

[12] Ibid., p. 56.
[13] Ibid.
[14] See Szasz, T. S.: *Law, Liberty, and Psychiatry: An Inquiry into the Social Uses of Mental Health Practices* (New York: Macmillan, 1963).
[15] See, for example, Dunham, H. W.: "Community psychiatry: The newest therapeutic bandwagon." *Arch. Gen. Psychiatry*, 12:-303–13 (March), 1965.

Piel, assistant director of the Michigan Department of Mental Health went on to say, "Psychiatry is *not* sociology, social welfare, criminology, and other endeavors designed to help people in trouble. It *is* the application of specific skills to specific manifestations and symptoms of illness, including psychoses, neuroses, etc. . . . This removes from psychiatric practice hotel-keeping, finding homes for the homeless, raising children and immature adults, giving advice to the lovelorn, and protection of society from the socially marginal."[16]

In Leonard Duhl's view, however, the community psychiatrist "must learn how to be a consultant to a community, an institution, or a group without being patient-oriented. Rather, he must have the community's needs in central focus. . . . He must find himself at home in a world of economics, political science, politics, planning, and all forms of social action."[17]

In view of the beliefs and practices of the community psychiatrist, and of modern psychological and sociological insights into problems of so-called abnormal behavior, the claim that community psychiatry is, and ought to be, a branch of medicine, seems either foolish or hypocritical. In pleading for the return of "mental health care to the mainstream of American medicine," President Kennedy was thus merely echoing the sentiments—or perhaps better, the propaganda—of the mental health movement.

The division of opinion on the nature and scope of community psychiatry and the psychiatrist's proper role in it, as illustrated by the foregoing remarks, could be multiplied manyfold. Despite widely diverging views on this subject, agreement is unanimous on two propositions regarding community psychiatry: first, that mental illness is a vast social problem against which the solitary individual cannot adequately defend himself

[16] Quoted in "Challenge facing state mental hospitals in community programs." *Roche Report*, vol. 2, Sept. 1, 1965, p. 1.

[17] Duhl, L.: "Problems in training psychiatric residents in community psychiatry." Paper read before the Institute of Training in Community Psychiatry at the University of California (mimeographed, 1963).

—he requires the support of the community, that is, of the federal, state, and local governments; second, that the role of mental patient, like that of criminal, ought to be an assigned role rather than an assumed role only. In other words, society ought to have the right to force individuals into accepting the role of mental patient and into submitting to involuntary psychiatric hospitalization and treatment.

Where does all this leave academic psychiatry? In the face of such vexing theoretical uncertainties and compelling social pressures, what should be the proper function of a department of psychiatry in a university? Since the needs of medical students and psychiatric residents differ fundamentally, I shall discuss the roles of the medical school in undergraduate and postgraduate psychiatric education separately.

VII

The mandate entrusted to universities by the societies in which they operate and by which they are supported has changed from time to time and from place to place. Still, in the free West at least, it is widely accepted that the university should have a measure of independence from the major political and economic institutions of the nation: that is, it should not be a handmaiden either of big business or of big government. The traditional reference to the university as an "ivory tower," and to the scholar as one who dwells there, expresses precisely this aspect of the university as a place set apart from, and yet within, the arena in which the power struggles of public life take place.

Like all ideals, that of an independent university can never be reached; but it can be approximated—or abandoned.[18]

In the United States, medical schools, and especially departments of psychiatry, are entrusted by society to carry out not just one mandate, but two: to advance medical knowledge and

[18] In this connection, see Barzun, J.: *The American University: How it Runs, Where it is Going* (New York: Harper & Row, 1968); and Ridgeway, J.: *The Closed Corporation: American Universities in Crisis* (New York: Random House, 1968).

to train competent medical practitioners.[19] These two tasks are partly complementary, partly conflicting. To understand some of the difficulties that face academic psychiatry, it is necessary to grasp this conflict clearly.

Insofar as the medical school is concerned with the teaching and advancement of medical science, its function is similar to that of any other scholarly discipline: to impart a body of information and to foster the advancement of certain kinds of knowledge. Although practical aims never are, nor need be, relegated to oblivion, the principal concerns of such instruction need not be the immediate social usefulness of the student to society: for example, certain branches of mathematics may be taught regardless of whether students so trained will be useful to IBM or General Electric.

Insofar as the medical school is concerned with the training of competent medical practitioners, it has a quite different responsibility to society: to teach students a body of knowledge and skills that will be useful for alleviating and preventing human illness. There is nothing new about this. It is the familiar distinction between pure and applied science as it pertains to medical education. But these considerations are relevant to the problem of academic psychiatry.

To the extent that academic psychiatry is an extension of the state hospital or community mental health center system, its function is that of an applied science concerned with the *control* of human behavior. As such, it may succeed in discharging one of its duties to society, namely to train physicians to be adept in the social control of so-called mentally ill persons.

To the extent that academic psychiatry is an extension of the psychoanalytic movement, its function is that of a pure science concerned with the *understanding* of human behavior. As such, it may succeed in discharging another of its duties to society, namely to train physicians to understand so-called mentally ill persons.

[19] See Freyhan, A.: "On the psychopathology of psychiatric education." *Comprehensive Psychiatry*, 6:221–26 (Aug.), 1965; Romano, J.: "Psychiatry, the university, and the community." *Arch. Gen. Psychiatry*, 13:395–401 (Nov.), 1965.

The social utility of psychoanalysis to vast multitudes of "mentally sick" people is slight, whereas the social utility of a hospital system capable of accommodating four times the number of persons in our entire penal system is great; to this may now be added the social utility of a vast new hospital and clinic system, called community mental health centers.

In the past, academic psychiatry has been buffeted between the Scylla of trying to control people and the Charybdis of trying to understand them. The result has been a diffusion of identity from which academic psychiatry has long suffered, and from which it shows no signs of recovery.

There are additional difficulties in the psychiatric education of the physician. In practice, psychiatric undergraduate education has had to be a compromise, not only between the needs of social control and humane understanding, but also between the needs of those students who plan to pursue a career in organic medicine and those who plan to enter psychiatry. Whether or not we, as psychiatrists, like it, psychiatry is not as important a discipline to the medical student as physiology, internal medicine, or surgery. It is impossible to imagine a competent physician untrained in these fields, but it is quite easy to imagine one untrained in psychiatry. I believe that good obstetricians, surgeons, and even internists and pediatricians could be trained without exposing them to any *formal* psychiatric education in medical school.

The current belief that medical students need a great deal of formal psychiatric education rests on a basic misconception. It is assumed that, since physicians deal with patients, they ought to learn about the doctor-patient relationship; or that, since they do a certain amount of common-sense counseling, they ought to learn about psychotherapy. But the fact is that there are many professional activities in which the medical student might ultimately engage that are not a part of the medical school's required curriculum. The most striking example is medical education itself: many of the best students in the best schools become medical teachers; despite this, instruction in medical education is never included in the medical curriculum, nor do I believe that it should be.

This is not to say that psychiatry is unimportant. What I am trying to say is that psychiatry is both *less* and *more* important than is now generally recognized: for the student who is not interested in it, and plans a strictly medical career, it is less important; and for the student who is interested in it, and plans a psychiatric (or public health or administrative) career, it is far more important. In actual practice, medical schools strike a compromise between the needs of both groups. The result is that for some students too much psychiatry is taught; for others, too little.

Finally, academic psychiatry suffers from trying to reach still another compromise—about the nature of its subject matter. Psychiatry has not decided whether it ought to study and treat pathological conditions, social performances, or both.[20] If the former, it would be a discipline essentially like pathology and internal medicine; if the latter, it would be a discipline more like sociology and politics; if both, it would be—as, indeed, it often is—like a bigamist, who claims love for two women, but neither understands nor is truly committed to either.

In short, then, undergraduate psychiatric education is now a triple compromise: (1) between the needs of those students who neither desire nor require psychiatric instruction and the needs of those who do; (2) between psychiatry as social control and as social science; and (3) between psychiatry as the study and treatment of medical conditions (diseases) and as the study and influencing of social roles (games).

VIII

Societies, like individuals, often have several conflicting needs. This fact affects the education of psychiatric residents as it does perhaps few others in contemporary American society. The two needs of society that must be reconciled here are the education of psychiatric scientists, capable of critical thinking

[20] In this connection, see Szasz, T. S.: *The Myth of Mental Illness: Foundations of a Theory of Personal Conduct* (New York: Hoeber-Harper, 1961); "The myth of mental illness." This volume, pp. 12–24.

and independent investigation; and the training of psychiatric practitioners, capable of performing those skills deemed appropriate for the profession. Actually, residency programs in psychiatry, in and out of the universities, have tended to rank these two goals in an inverse order: training practitioners first, educating scientists second.

This conflict, moreover, is not one between the aspirations of individuals and the requirements of society. Instead, it is a conflict between two different needs on the part of society itself—the need for practitioners as well as for scientists.

The tension between these two goals and needs—not only in psychiatry, but in medical education generally—has only recently become a matter of concern to medical educators. In 1965, a committee of the Association of American Medical Colleges reported that "Much formal education, beyond the granting of the M.D. degree, is a matter of relatively limited concern to the medical school and university. . . . Hence, the conclusion is inescapable that total medical education in the United States, even today, really is not fully a unversity function, even though most medical schools and their teaching hospitals add the word 'university' to their names."[21]

Pressures in the other direction—pushing medical schools toward dispensing services rather than fostering critical and creative education and scholarship—now come mainly from the state and federal governments. For example, as a result of the Medicare amendment to the Social Security Act, the federal government will—so a medical writer tells us—make fresh efforts "to involve medical schools ever more deeply in provision of care. . . . The medical schools themselves are certain to undergo profound changes because of the new federal programs. Not only are they being drawn into accepting more responsibility for community health services, but they are likely to be strengthened by the new direct operating assistance."[22]

Perhaps in response to these renewed pressures for service,

[21] "The critical issues in MD education." *Medical Tribune*, Oct. 23–24, 1965, p. 14.
[22] O'Neil, M. J.: "Capital rounds." *Medical World News*, October 22, 1965, p. 93.

the needs of scholarship are also becoming more clearly articulated. Thus, Robert H. Ebert, dean of the Harvard Medical School, has complained that, even at this late date in the history of medical education, "Medical faculties curiously have not taken on the responsibility for the continuing education of the student after graduation from medical school. They have too long assumed that postgraduate training is not the business of the university."[23] And he expressed the hope that medical school faculties would become directly involved in the physician's postgraduate education, to meet "his particular needs and the special needs of the community, without regard to the source of financial support or the vested interests of a variety of paraeducational institutions."[24]

This statement shows fine understanding of the complexities of this problem. The community, unless it proposes to sacrifice its long-range needs for scholarship and the advancement of knowledge and skills to its short-range needs for public services, requires a medical school as a source both of medical scholarship and of medical practitioners. These two goals must coexist in a constructive compromise—or society will be the loser.

At present, training programs for psychiatric residents try to effect a compromise between two of the three conflicting social and professional needs that I listed earlier: that is, between psychiatry as social control and as social science, and between psychiatry as the study and treatment of diseases and as the study and influencing of social roles.

The freedom of departments of psychiatry to offer an eclectic program, including instruction in all the varied elements that now constitute the discipline of psychiatry, or a program selectively geared to one or another theoretical and practical task, depends also on external circumstances—such as certification requirements, legal regulation of medical and specialty practice, economic opportunities in various branches of psychiatry, and so forth.

In the final analysis, what distinguishes the psychiatrically in-

[23] Ebert, R. H.: "Faculties have not taken responsibility." *Medical World News*, October 22, 1965, p. 53.
[24] Ibid.

formed student of man from the political scientist, the psychologist, the sociologist, or the social worker is *the practical task* he tries to master and *the methods* he uses: as the task and the methods vary, so does the "psychiatry." Community psychiatry and individual psychotherapy will thus differ—and must be expected to differ—in much the same way as the control of syphilis through public health measures differs from the beautification of a nose by plastic surgery.

IX

Academic psychiatry is now on the threshold of another identity crisis. As in earlier crises, the question once again is: Who will shape the identity of academic psychiatry—the psychiatric academicians, or persons outside the academic fold representing other social interests?

"It is only through the resolution of moral perplexities," said Eliseo Vivas, "that a man can discover, *by creating*, what he is."[25] Similarly, it is only through the resolution of moral perplexities that a group, or an institution, can discover, *by creating*, what it is. Only an individual with a well-defined sense of identity can resist the blandishments and threats of outside interests. We have seen that, in the past, academic psychiatry has not been able to maintain and develop a self-defined identity: in the face of pressure, it has allowed one interest after another to define its social role and function—in short, its professional identity. Unless it is conscious of this threat, and prepared to defend itself from it, academic psychiatry seems ill-prepared to resist the pressures that are likely to flow from the community psychiatry movement.

The problem is not new, and we ought to try to learn from the lessons of history. In the past few decades, the power of the purse has been dramatically demonstrated in two areas: social welfare legislation and practices, and the relationship between government and the physical sciences.

25 Vivas, E.: *The Moral Life and the Ethical Life.* (Chicago: Regnery-Gateway, 1963), p. 40.

"Paradoxical though it may seem," observed Wilcox, "the most serious threat to freedom in our programs of public services and public benefits is to the freedom of the recipient. . . . It is sometimes possible, by paying people to do things or not to do them, to control their actions as effectively as by threatening to send them to jail."[26]

The Community Mental Health Centers Act of 1963, like the Social Security Act, is a program of public benefits. Thus, it is likely to spawn another mammoth bureaucracy, holding its employees in bondage economically and its psychiatric clients legally. The scope of what has been dubbed "government by bribery" may in this way be extended still further.

The problem here is not simply the risk of aid *from* government leading to regulation *by* it; in psychiatry, it is rather the danger of the shifting definition of what the aid is *for*. As we have seen, the community mental health movement, with federal support, is pushing toward the establishment of centers for providing "mental health care" for masses of people, especially poor people. This enterprise may be a social necessity. So is the training of policemen. But would an increasing crime rate justify turning the law schools of our universities into training schools for policemen? Nearly everyone would consider this unjustified, for the law school must serve other social functions—namely, to train persons to be defense attorneys, prosecuting attorneys, judges, corporation lawyers, legal scholars, and so forth. Yet, this kind of redefinition of the purposes of academic departments of psychiatry is now widely advocated and justified by the argument that we must combat the increasing "incidence" of "mental illness," especially among the poor and disadvantaged.

The dangers to psychiatry as a science of man may be even graver. Physics, a highly developed discipline with a clear sense of identity, was severely bent under the weight of large-scale federal support for research and development; psychiatry is likely to break under it. Why should this be so? The main reason

[26] Wilcox, A. W.: "Patterns of social legislation: Reflections on the welfare state." *J. Public Law,* 6:3-24 (Spring), 1957.

for a conflict between science and government is that scientists are basically interested in knowledge, and politicians in power. As James R. Newman observed: "Where scientists and politicians meet there should be conflict; and so there was for a time. This healthy condition no longer prevails. Scientists and politicians now dance together, advance dos-à-dos, bow, scrape, exchange compliments; a regrettable spectacle."[27]

The joining of forces of government and atomic physics, suggested Newman, has helped the national defense, but not physics. Science has been "slanted and corrupted by federal support; scientists have lost their independence; education has suffered." Concluded Newman: "The relationship between science and the Federal Government is unhealthy and the ills I have pointed to are getting worse. They are not in the long run self-curing, and they require much more honesty, candor, and disinterested thought than either the scientific community or the government has been willing to devote to them. That science needs some measure of federal support is certain. It is no less certain that to use federal funds to turn science into little more than an instrument for the continuation of politics by other means is to debase and degrade it."[28]

Because psychiatry is a moral science, its need for independence from those who wield economic and political power is even greater than that of a natural science. I shall not dwell further on what might become of psychiatry if massive federal support transformed it into an "instrument for the continuation of politics."[29]

x

Academic psychiatry now faces a two-pronged attack on its integrity: blandishments—consisting of vast sums of money,

[27] Newman, J. R.: "Big science, bad science." *The New York Review of Books,* August 5, 1965, pp. 10–12; p. 11.

[28] Ibid., p. 12.

[29] In this connection, see Szasz, T. S.: "The mental health ethic." This volume pp. 25–48; "Whither psychiatry?" This volume, pp. 218–45.

available to those willing to train cadres of mental health workers; and accusations—consisting of criticisms leveled at those unwilling to lend their own, and their institutions', talents and resources to the waging of the all-out "war against mental illness."

In the final analysis, the survival of academic psychiatry will depend on the support it receives from its own ranks, from the larger academic community, and from society. The public health physician has resisted social pressures to define his role as social work: he does not, for example, consider it his task to protect the poor against their landlords (though such protection may well enhance their health). Nor has the legal scholar succumbed to social pressures to define his role as social engineering: he does not, for example, consider it his task to interpret the Constitution in such a way as to make life easier for the greatest number of people (though such interpretation might well make many people more comfortable).

It devolves first, therefore, on the academic psychiatrist to resist social pressures to define his role as practicing social control: he must not, for example, consider it his task to retrain improperly socialized adults so that they will be productive workers (though such retraining might benefit many persons). In short, he must be faithful to the integrity of his social role. And what is that role? It is nothing new. It was eloquently restated by Christopher Lasch when he asserted that "Intellectuals are not policy makers, they are not Senators, they are not arbitrators of international disputes. They are critics, and whatever power they have derives from that fact. . . ."[30] Hence, if the psychiatric academician is not an intellectually independent critic, he has in fact *no role* that he could expect society to protect.

The survival of academic psychiatry (even in its presently embryonic form), and its further development, thus depend on the psychiatric academician's awareness of the special nature of his role as critical scholar and on his loyalty to that role. But this is not enough. The larger academic community, and society in general, must recognize the nature and value of academic en-

[30] Lasch, C.: "Democratic vistas." *The New York Review of Books,* September 30, 1965, pp. 4–6; p. 6.

deavors, and must protect them from encroachments by zealous social reformers. It is necessary, therefore, that people both within and outside of psychiatric, medical, and professional circles comprehend and appreciate the differences between *understanding persons* and helping them to live *as they see fit—* and *controlling persons* and making them behave *as society sees fit.* If they don't appreciate this difference, academic psychiatry has no *raison d'être,* and psychiatric academicians have no valid claims to the special privileges that Western society bestows on its scholars.

12 · PSYCHIATRIC CLASSIFICATION

AS A STRATEGY

OF PERSONAL CONSTRAINT

Man is the only animal that classifies. Everything we apprehend or do must be placed in its proper category. In former days, when theology was the supreme arbiter among men with conflicting opinions, things were simpler. Man did not classify. Only God could do that. In that era, the scientist's task was like the safecracker's: to unlock the mysterious combination built into nature by God.

Modern science unseated the Master Classifier. It did so by suggesting an opposite view of the world—one in which all is "buzzing and booming confusion," until man brings order and harmony into it. Thus, the distinction between animals and men, rocks and trees, is not the result of a divine production schedule, as set forth in Genesis—but the manifestation of man's power to create categories by means of symbols. However, if we *create* categories, rather than *discover* them, how can we be certain that we have got things in the right classes?

In psychiatry, all discussion of the problem of classification rests on the fundamental premise that there exist in nature abnormal mental conditions or forms of behavior, and that it is scientifically worth while and morally meritorious to place persons suffering from these conditions, or displaying such behavior, into appropriately named categories.

My experiences and reflections have led me to question these assumptions. Of course, it is not the existence of wide variations in personal conduct that I doubt, nor the feasibility of attaching various labels to them. What I question is the logical basis and moral status of the premise behind all existing systems of psychiatric classification: that human behavior is a natural event; and, like other such events, can and should be classified.

Yet, on the face of it, the position of the psychiatric nosologist may seem impregnable. We live in a scientific age and have unbounded faith in the methods of the physical sciences. If we can classify the behavior of stars and animals, why not the behavior of men?

The lure of positivism may be difficult to resist, but the student of man must resist it or fail as a humanist. For in behavioral science, the logic of physicalism is patently false: it neglects the differences between persons and things and the effects of language on each.

The special language of physics helps us understand and manipulate physical objects. If we conceive of psychiatry (or psychology) similarly, then its special language must serve a like purpose: to help us understand and control people. But, unless carefully circumscribed, is the control or manipulation of people a morally legitimate endeavor? In particular, is it a morally legitimate enterprise for scientists? If the purpose of the science of man is to manipulate people, how does it differ from law and religion, or from advertising and politics? Clearly, the nature, scope, and ethics of the science of man require further clarification.

We can be sure of this: only man creates symbols and is influenced by them. Accordingly, being placed in certain classes affects people, whereas it does not affect animals and things. You call a person "schizophrenic," and something happens to him; you call a rat "rat" and a rock "granite," and nothing happens to them. In other words, in psychiatry and in human affairs generally, *the act of classification* is an exceedingly significant event.

II

The problem of psychiatric classification is as old as psychiatry itself. It is appropriate, therefore, before setting forth on a new path and toward unknown destinations, to consider the existing paths and their familiar destinations.

There is no shortage of nosological schemes in psychiatry. In general, these are based on one or more of the following conceptual and methodological models: (1) medicine (or pathological anatomy and physiology), (2) constitution or heredity, (3) ethics and law, (4) statistics, (5) psychobiology, (6) psychology, and (7) psychoanalysis. In its current form, the official nomenclature of the American Psychiatric Association is a mixture of all these elements.

Much as these systems may differ in detail, they agree in one fundamental characteristic: the act of classification must *not* be scrutinized. The adherents to each of these nosological schemes accept the view that it is the psychiatrist's task to examine and classify *patients*. Why the psychiatrist occupies the role of classifier and the patient the role of classified is never asked. Nor does anyone question the effect of classification on the subsequent behavior of patients and psychiatrists. In brief, behavioral scientists classify people as if they were things. This is almost as true for the psychoanalytic approach as for the purely organic approach. Nor is this surprising. It is not due to any lack of humane feeling in psychiatrists, but rather to the fallacy of thinking in terms of natural science. I mean by this the attempt to study, explain, and control people as if they were animals or things. This was the aim of the "scientific" student of man a hundred years ago. It is still his aim. Writing in a recent issue of *Science,* a prominent medical investigator asserts, "[We] should not be debating whether a man is a machine but rather . . . should ask, 'What kind of machine is a man?' "[1]

From Charcot to the present, psychiatric nosologists have thought of man as a machine that can be taken apart and "explained" mechanistically. Thus, in a memorable essay on his great teacher, Freud observed: "But the pupil who spends many hours with him going round the wards of the Salpêtrière—that museum of clinical facts, the names and peculiar characteristics of which were for the most part derived from him—would be reminded of Cuvier, whose statue, standing in front of the Jardin

[1] Potter, V. R.: "Society and science." *Science,* 146:1018–22 (Nov. 20), 1964; p. 1022.

des Plantes, shows that great comprehender and describer of the animal world surrounded by a multitude of animal forms; or else he would recall the myth of Adam, who, when God brought the creatures of Paradise before him to be distinguished and named, may have experienced to the fullest degree that intellectual enjoyment which Charcot praised so highly."[2]

Freud here compares Charcot to Cuvier, who had classified various types of animal life, and to Adam, who, in the Biblical view of Creation, named and grouped the objects God had "manufactured." In each case, classifier and classified are on different existential planes: one up, the other down.

It may be thought that this approach represents the primitive beginnings of any science. But that would be a mistake. Today we have more refined methods of observation; we may use different words; but the fundamental approach is the same. Referring to German institutional psychiatrists of the mid-nineteenth century, Kurt Kolle, one of the foremost contemporary European psychiatrists, stated: "Doctors who worked in these institutions were dedicated men of science; through methodical and yet *benevolent* observations of their patients, they put together a composite portrait of insanity. The pioneering psychiatrist resembled *a child sorting stones or shells* according to size and color" (italics added).[3]

The dilemma of the natural scientist studying insanity is nicely revealed by the word *benevolent*. One would not describe Galileo's observations as benevolent, or Newton's, or Einstein's. Why, then, the observations of the early psychiatrists? The answer can only be: Because their objects of observation were people, not stars. But if the psychiatrist works with people, should his attitude toward his subjects be like that of a "child sorting stones"? According to Kolle, it should. He pays homage to Kraepelin for "his great contribution to medicine—a classification of mental disorders." The telling question, he con-

[2] Freud, S.: "Charcot" [1893], in *The Standard Edition of the Complete Psychological Works of Sigmund Freud*, Vol. III, pp. 7–23 (London: Hogarth Press, 1962), p. 13.

[3] Kolle, K.: *An Introduction to Psychiatry* (New York: Philosophical Library, 1963), p. 2.

tinues, "which Kraepelin explored painstakingly, was this: How does the disease progress? This method of inquiry enabled him to bring order into the confusing plethora of clinical symptoms by dividing them into separate categories; though thirty years have passed since his death, the system devised by this eminent researcher is still valid."[4]

What does the term "valid" mean here? Still in use? We must be exceedingly careful on this point. The psychiatric method is but one of many by which people classify other people. Some of these classifications have been employed for much longer than thirty years and, in this sense, have been proved "valid." For example, more than five thousand years have elapsed since the Jews classified themselves as the "Chosen People"—and others, by inference, as God's stepchildren; many Jews and gentiles still believe this. Similarly, the Negro in America was classified as an inferior being more than three hundred years ago; he is still considered so by many. Are these therefore "valid" classifications?

It is appropriate to mention here some of the phenomena Kraepelin regarded as mental diseases, to be classified by psychiatrists. His much-applauded nosology included such "diagnoses" as "sexual abnormalities: masturbation," "the born criminal," and "pathological liars and swindlers."[5]

Nor is this naturalistic view a matter of psychiatric history only—a position held some time ago, but now discarded. After devoting seven pages of small-type text to a review of Kraepelinian classification, Karl Menninger concludes with the judgment, "Kraepelin's lifelong work represents probably the greatest nosologic synthesis ever accomplished in psychiatry. . . . Kraepelin succeeded in bringing about some degree of fusion of psychiatry and medicine, which had been the goal and ideal of psychiatric workers since the time of Hippocrates."[6]

If Kraepelin's nosology is "the greatest ever accomplished in psychiatry," how irrational and destructive of human values can

[4] Ibid., p. 3.
[5] Quoted in Menninger, K.: *The Vital Balance: The Life Process in Mental Health and Illness* (New York: Viking, 1963), p. 462.
[6] Ibid., p. 463.

the others be? Moreover, if Kraepelin was able to achieve a "fusion of psychiatry and medicine"—a goal that Menninger and many other contemporary psychiatrists consider wholly desirable—perhaps we ought to question the unquestionable: the unification of psychiatry and medicine.[7]

Kolle's present view—which is representative of what I have called the standard approach to classification—is this: "Whoever earnestly wishes to gain understanding of the basic tenets of psychiatry must first become acquainted with the system through which the psychiatrist—and here we adhere closely to the teachings of Kraepelin—attempts to interpret mental illness and abnormalities as *states determined by nature.*"[8]

It is not clear what Kolle means here by the word *nature*. One usage of it is this: We distinguish between things that occur in nature, like the sea, the mountains, or coal and oil—and things that are man-made, like tables, chairs, or nylon and the jet engine. Does Kolle mean that mental illnesses are like the sea or the mountains, given in nature, and not the products of human action?

In another usage, the word *nature* means the physical world, as against the human (moral and social) world—for example, physical law as against moral law. If this is what Kolle means, he asserts that mental illness is a natural or impersonal event, like an earthquake, rather than a personal act, like a decision to pretend that one is Christ. Kolle expresses this view in the following passage: "In setting up a classification of diseases (nosology)—whether we are concerned with disorders of the internal organs, skin, nervous system, or mind—we must seek to identify the cause of each disease, for in the science of medicine we must always be guided by the axiom, 'no cure unless the cause is first diagnosed.'"[9]

This position is at least clear: Mind is like skin. Things happen to each. Some of these happenings we call "diseases." We investigate their *causes* and, if possible, remove them. But what

[7] See Szasz, T. S.: *The Myth of Mental Illness: Foundations of a Theory of Personal Conduct* (New York: Hoeber-Harper, 1961).

[8] Kolle, op. cit., p. 7.

[9] Ibid.

is the status of human action in this scheme? The answer is: None. There is no such thing as action to attain a goal—only behavior determined by causes. Herein lies the fundamental error of the medical and mechanomorphic[10] approach to human behavior and to psychiatric classification. Nothing short of a fundamental reorientation in our approach to psychiatric classification will extricate us from this dilemma.

III

To gain a new perspective on the problem of psychiatric nosology, let us begin at the beginning: by examining the act of classification.

Classification is not reserved for science or the scientists. It is a fundamental human act. To name something is to classify it. But why do men name things? The answer often is: To gain control over the thing named, and, more generally, over one's power to act in the world.

Consider some basic concepts, present even in the most primitive cultures: food, drink, wife, enemy. To separate things that are edible from those that are not aids survival; to separate the woman with whom one may have sexual congress from those with whom one may not aids social co-operation; and so forth.

The sophisticated ideas of modern science may be viewed in a similar way. Concepts like atom or bacterium aid us in mastering the world about us: for example, to synthesize new compounds and cure infectious diseases. The act of naming or classifying is intimately related to the human need for control or mastery. There is nothing novel about this. It is another way of saying that man's superiority over other animals lies in his ability to use language.

This leads to the source of some of our troubles in psychiatry. It is one thing to gain control over animals, for example to learn to domesticate cattle; it is another to gain control over human beings, for example to learn to enslave the Negro. How-

[10] See, in this connection, Matson, F. W.: *The Broken Image: Man, Science, and Society* (New York: Braziller, 1964).

ever, before turning to the problem of classification as constraint, let us examine the act of classification in the sorting of non-human objects.

As a rule, the motive for classifying is to gain control over a part of nature. Therefore, the classificatory act is unlike the child's play at the seashore—exploratory and indifferent. It is more like the tiger's lying in wait for an antelope—purposeful and strategic. As classifier, man also "attacks" the object of his classificatory interest—not to devour it, but to control it.

Sartre describes this perceptively. An only child and bookish, he did not chase butterflies and catch them in his net; instead, he chased and tried to catch all of "reality" in a net fashioned of words: "Caught in the trap of naming, a lion, a captain of the Second Empire, or a Bedouin would be brought into the dining room; they remained captive there forever, embodied in signs. I thought I had anchored my dreams in the world by the scratchings of a steel nib."[11]

Later, he makes the same point: "To exist was to have an official title somewhere on the infinite Tables of the Word; to write was to engrave new beings upon them or—and this was my most persistent illusion—to catch living things in the trap of phrases: if I combined words ingeniously, the object would get tangled up in the signs, I would have a hold on it."[12]

Often it is obvious that classification serves a strategic or tactical purpose. When primitive man attributes the death of his cattle to the curse laid on them by his neighbor, he has classified the cattle's illness in strategic terms: he cannot cure his cattle, but he can kill his neighbor. Classification is like a lever: it gives one a purchase on whatever it is one wants to move.

Of course, it is better to base classification on fact than on illusion—to attribute the death of one's cattle to hoof-and-mouth disease rather than to the evil eye of one's neighbor. I do not deny or minimize the empirical or scientific basis of various systems of classification. However, my concern here is different: it is to clarify the strategic intent and import of systems of clas-

11 Sartre, J. P.: *The Words,* transl. by Bernard Frechtman (New York: Braziller, 1964), p. 142.
12 Ibid., p. 182.

sification regardless of their content. Thus, when men do not know about hoof-and-mouth disease, they attribute the death of their cattle to the machinations of their neighbors or their gods, rather than acknowledge their ignorance about the nature of the calamity that has befallen them. Any classification, even a false one, promises hope of successful mastery; on the other hand, the lack of classification requires the admission of helplessness. This admission is a rare and highly sophisticated human achievement: it requires control of the incessant human striving for mastery, at least temporarily. This is a luxury that only those who feel secure enough to acknowledge their insecurity can afford. However difficult it may be to classify things, and especially to classify them accurately, it is even more difficult not to classify things: to suspend judgment and delay the act of classification.

IV

Science may be regarded as the sum total of human effort to understand nature and thus gain a measure of control over it. The process of naming, or symbolic identification, is perhaps the basic building block of science. Classification is a refinement over naming, as brick and concrete are over rock and timber. How does classification help us to master the world about us? By providing us with certain regularities: as a result, we are spared recurrent surprise over various happenings about us. In temperate climates, the sequence of the seasons is such an occurrence; at the seashore, the ebb and flow of the tides. The naming of animals and plants, the ordering of elements, and the classification of human diseases are other, more complex patterns of regularities; each helps us to master certain aspects of the world about us. In some cases, mastery is attained by having the power to predict future events, and, hence, to prepare for and adapt to them—for example, meteorology; in others, by having the power to bring about certain future events by judiciously planned action—for example, agriculture.

In broad outline, this has always been the attitude of rational man toward the world of rocks, of plants, and of animals. Wherever this attitude is most highly developed, man is most success-ful in "conquering" nature. This is the background against which we must view the problems of psychiatric classification.

The aims of natural science, and the main criteria of the validity of its assertions, are prediction and control. Naming and classification—and the construction of hypotheses, theories, or so-called natural laws—help to achieve these goals. But it is not enough for man to understand and thus be able to plan for, or alter, the movement of planets, the growth and decay of plants, and the behavior of animals. There is another source of mystery and danger for man: other men.

Man's efforts to understand and control his fellow man have a long and complicated history. Here I shall remark briefly on but one part of the story—the past three hundred years. This period encompasses the development of most of modern physi-cal science, and all of modern social science. Of special interest is the scientist's attitude toward the similarities and differences between describing, predicting, and controlling natural events and human behavior.

The idea of a "unified science" is not as new as we some-times think. In a sense, primitive man's view of the world is unified: his attitude is the same toward animate and inanimate nature, toward man, animals, and things. We call this *anthro-pomorphism*: the primitive tries to understand the physical world as if it were animated by human spirits. Physical events, whether desired or disastrous, are viewed as the consequences of willed action. Consequently, the control of such events cen-ters around efforts to propitiate the gods or spirits believed to have caused them.

Since the advent of modern science, beginning with men like Galileo and Newton, the image of nature as a harmoni-ously functioning mechanical machine inspired another view of man. Instead of "projecting" himself into nature, man now "introjects" nature into himself. Whereas primitive man per-sonifies things, modern man "thingifies" persons. We call this *mechanomorphism*: modern man tries to understand man as if "it" were a machine. Thus, the student of man must take apart this machine and understand its parts and functions, so that he may predict and control its behavior as he would that of any other machine.

Is this the proper way to study man? The history of the dialogue between the yea-sayers and the nay-sayers to this question constitutes the history of social science. Since I cannot review or even summarize this dialogue here, a few remarks on its general nature must suffice.

Those who have considered the prediction and control of human behavior logically possible and morally desirable have, in general, tended to advocate its coercive social control. Their rank begins with Saint-Simon and Comte and extends to contemporary men like Harold D. Lasswell in political science and B. F. Skinner in psychology. In contrast, those who have been skeptical about the range of the predictability of human behavior, and about the moral desirability of making such predictions, have tended to advocate freedom from arbitrary or personal social restraints. Their rank begins with Locke and Jefferson and extends to contemporary figures like Ludwig von Mises in economics and Karl Popper in philosophy.

Where do psychiatrists, especially nosologists, stand on this issue? On the whole, they are mechanomorphists of the first rank: they view man, especially mentally ill man, as a defective machine. This is especially clear in the view of Kraepelin and his followers. They regard mental diseases as they do physical diseases: as "entities" that "progress" from one phase to another—usually from bad to worse. Bleuler also regarded mental illnesses in a naturalistic light. Indeed, to think of such "diseases" in any other way would have been unscientific, a sure sign of quackery. This undoubtedly accounts for Freud's ambiguous position on so-called mental illness. Although he viewed psychoanalysis as a natural science, and mental abnormalities as causally determined, his chief interest was not to classify and constrain his patients, but to understand and liberate them. He was therefore compelled to devise a method of approach to the so-called mentally ill (though not a theory or a vocabulary) totally different from the existing methods of psychiatry, medicine, and the natural sciences.[13] To understand this essential difference between the Kraepelinian and Freudian positions, and their implications for psychiatric nosology, it is necessary to review the purposes of classifying human behavior, especially so-called mentally deranged behavior.

V

As modern science progressed in its conquest of nature, it became clear—by the end of the nineteenth century and increasingly thereafter—that, among all the unpredictable events in the universe, human behavior was one of the most baffling. Nor is this surprising. Among all the objects and creatures in the world, man is the only one endowed with free will: his behavior is not only *determined* by antecedent events but is also *chosen* by him, in accordance with his view of himself and of the goals he seeks to attain. Or is this an illusion? Is personal freedom an ethical concept, unworthy of inclusion in the vocabulary of science?

I shall not engage in the futile controversy about the nature of "real science." Our interest in this problem lies in the concept of freedom it introduces. What is its import for psychiatric classification? The answer, it seems to me, may be briefly stated: *To classify human behavior is to constrain it.* Let me explain what I mean.

One of man's basic strivings is for order and harmony in a potentially chaotic universe. The classification of physical objects and of living but non-human things serves this need. It must be noted now that the behavior of these non-human objects is essentially independent of symbolic acts, and is, therefore, unaffected by the act of classification itself. A cow is a mammal regardless of what we call it or how we classify it. To affect the cow's behavior, we must act directly upon the animal: for example, by milking it or slaughtering it. This kind of sepa-

[13] See Szasz, T. S.: *The Ethics of Psychoanalysis: The Theory and Method of Autonomous Psychotherapy* (New York: Basic Books, 1965).

ration between physical action and symbolic action exists in all realms where man acts upon non-human objects. However, in situations where man acts upon his fellow man, this separation is either absent or radically different in character: here language becomes a kind of action.

Viewed in this light, social role emerges as a classificatory prison, with personal identities as the cells in which men confine each other. This helps explain the persistent difficulties that psychiatric classifications pose for us. As a rule, medical diagnoses do not define an individual's personal identity, whereas psychiatric diagnoses do. What a difference there is between calling a person a "leukemic poet" and a "schizophrenic poet"! In other words, psychiatric diagnoses define personal identity in much the same way as descriptive adjectives like "existential," "Kantian," or "linguistic" define the noun "philosopher" and the person to whom it is applied.

It would be absurd for anyone, and especially for students of man, to disregard the ways in which men use language and respond to it. The expressions "hysterical mother" or "paranoid senator" differ fundamentally from "obese mother" or "diabetic senator." Again, Sartre has illuminated this issue. "The homosexual," he observed, "recognizes his faults, but he struggles with all his strength against the crushing view that his mistakes constitute for him a destiny. He does not wish to let himself be considered a thing. He has an obscure but strong feeling that a homosexual is not a homosexual as this table is a table or as this red-haired man is red-haired."[14]

It is precisely this defacing, this rendering of the person into a thing, that the psychiatric nosologist inflicts on his subject. Thus, according to the experts, the proper psychiatric method of treating a "patient" like Secretary of Defense Forrestal is to treat him like any other patient—that is, as a non-human object bearing a psychiatric label.[15] Of course, when the "patient" is a

[14] Sartre, J. P.: *Existential Psychoanalysis* [1953], transl. by Hazel E. Barnes (Chicago: Regnery-Gateway, 1964), p. 193.

[15] Rogow, A. A.: *James Forrestal: A Study of Personality, Politics, and Policy* (New York: Macmillan, 1964).

Very Important Person, this is impossible, but the command to do so is revealing. For when the "patient" lacks the social power of an important personage, as is usually the case, he can be and is treated in this fashion.[16] Thus, when a hospital psychiatrist classifies a newly admitted patient as a paranoid schizophrenic, he does exactly what Sartre described. The diagnostic label imparts a defective personal identity to the patient. It will henceforth identify him to others and will govern their conduct toward him, and his toward them. The psychiatric nosologist thus not only *describes* his patient's so-called illness, but also *prescribes* his future conduct.

In short, we must choose between two radically different attitudes toward personal conduct. First, human behavior may be regarded as an event, essentially similar to other, non-human events; for example, as an astronomer can predict an eclipse of the sun, so a criminologist can predict the incidence of "recidivism" among discharged prisoners. Although this approach commits the investigator to treating people as essentially no different from things, it is not without merit. It is especially useful for certain kinds of statistical analyses and predictions of behavior.

Second, human behavior may be regarded as a unique achievement of which only man is capable. Personal conduct is based on the free choices of a sign-using, rule-following, and game-playing person whose *action* is often largely governed by his future goals rather than by his past experiences. This view of man casts efforts to predict his behavior in a new perspective. For, to the extent that man is free to act—that is, free to choose among alternative courses of action—his conduct is, and must be, unpredictable: after all, this is what is meant by the word "free." Trying to predict human behavior is, therefore, likely to result in efforts to constrain it.

[16] See, for example, Goffman, E.: "The Moral Career of the Mental Patient," in Goffman, E., *Asylums: Essays on the Social Situation of Mental Patients and Other Inmates* (Garden City, N.Y.: Doubleday Anchor, 1961), pp. 125–70.

VI

Wherever we turn, there is evidence to substantiate the view that most psychiatric diagnoses may be used, and are used, as invectives: their aim is to degrade—and, hence, socially constrain —the person diagnosed. A dramatic example is the poll of psychiatrists conducted by *Fact* magazine during the 1964 presidential campaign.

On July 24, 1964, one week after Senator Goldwater received the Republican nomination for President, *Fact* sent a questionnaire to each of the 12,356 psychiatrists in the United States, asking: "Do you believe Barry Goldwater is psychologically fit to serve as President of the United States?" The explanation accompanying the question left no doubt that the editors of *Fact* did not think he was.[17]

In all, 2,417 psychiatrists, or approximately 20 per cent of those polled, responded. Two out of three were willing to have their names printed. By a vote of 1,189 to 657, the psychiatrists declared the Republican candidate unfit for the Presidency.

The majority diagnosed Goldwater as suffering from paranoid schizophrenia or some similar condition. Here are some typical comments: "Senator Goldwater impresses me as being a paranoid personality or a schizophrenic, paranoid type . . . he is a potentially dangerous man." (From an anonymous psychiatrist at the Cornell Medical Center in New York City.) ". . . Goldwater is basically a paranoid schizophrenic who decompensates from time to time." (From an anonymous psychiatrist in Boston.)

Another group of psychiatrists saw in Senator Goldwater a totalitarian leader, mainly of a fascist or Nazi type. Sample opinions: "Hitler had his Jews, and Goldwater has his Negroes." (From an anonymous psychiatrist in San Francisco.) ". . . I salute your effort to present some highly essential facts to the public. It is good to know that psychiatrists of this nation will

[17] "The Unconscious of a Conservative: A Special Issue on the Mind of Barry Goldwater." *Fact*, September-October 1964.

not be blamed for their silence later, should Goldwater emerge as another Hitler." (From an anonymous psychiatrist in Topeka, Kansas.)

In a third type of reply, the respondents offered "diagnostic" opinions about other prominent persons, both living and dead (for example, Abraham Lincoln and Theodore Roosevelt). One psychiatrist characterized Goldwater's running mate, Congressman William E. Miller, as "a man as hostile and semi-paranoid as [Goldwater] himself." Others hinted darkly at the psychiatric abnormalities of other living persons: "I know nothing firsthand regarding Barry Goldwater, but I do regarding one of our recent Presidents and his wife. He was under psychiatric care just before taking office and she still is a chronic alcoholic." (From an anonymous psychiatrist in California.)

Lastly, there was a group of psychiatrists who favored Senator Goldwater for the Presidency. Many, however, were not content to do this on political grounds, but denigrated Mr. Johnson either psychiatrically or personally. Sample comment: ". . . Does not his [Mr. Johnson's] behavior behind the wheel of his automobile betray his lack of judgment and an irresponsibility sufficient to warrant impeachment? I value my reputation as a psychiatrist but I am willing to stake it on the opinion that Barry Goldwater is qualified—psychologically and in every other way—to serve as President of the United States." (From a professor of psychiatry in Georgia.)

It would be a mistake to dismiss all this as the foolish mistakes of a few psychiatrists, for these opinions illustrate the very essence of psychiatric diagnosis as a social act. The psychiatrist is here revealed in his basic social role: he legitimizes and illegitimizes the social aspirations and roles of others. Thus, when a psychiatrist declares that Senator Goldwater is unfit to be President, he does not do something unusual; his act is not the miscarriage of some other, fundamentally different sort of psychiatric performance. On the contrary, it is indistinguishable from declaring one person unfit to stand trial, another to execute a will, a third to drive a car, a fourth to serve in the Peace Corps. In each of these instances, the psychiatrist plays his characteristic social role: he brands as illegitimate the roles or role-aspirations of certain people. Of course, sometimes psychiatrists legitimize certain roles or role-aspirations—for example, when they declare a defendant fit to stand trial, a recruit to serve in the armed forces, or an Eichmann to be executed. The power to declare a role illegitimate must include the power to declare it legitimate.

Because of the uses and abuses of psychiatric diagnoses, one might conclude that they are meaningless. This is not so. There *are* certain differences in the way human beings are "put together." When psychiatrists call people "paranoid" or "compulsive," they often refer to something just as real as the black skin of a Negro or the pink skin of a white man.

The point is not that psychiatric diagnoses are meaningless, but that they may be, and often are, swung as semantic blackjacks: cracking the subject's respectability and dignity destroys him just as effectively, and often more so, as cracking his skull. The difference is that the man who wields a blackjack is recognized by everyone as a public menace, but one who wields a psychiatric diagnosis is not.

It is curious that this method of defamation and character assassination—often leading to the destruction of the victim—has so long escaped detection. Undoubtedly, one reason for this is that it is practiced by doctors of medicine. Yet, the nature of an ostensibly medical enterprise is determined not by who performs it, but rather by its social context and practical consequences.

Consider the case of a psychologically well-informed individual who consults a psychiatrist in private practice in an effort to pursue his life goals more freely and effectively. There may come a day in the relationship between the therapist and his patient when they might find it useful to describe some of the patient's tendencies with the word "paranoid." At best, this use of the English language will increase the patient's self-understanding; at worst, it will injure his self-esteem.

Suppose, however, that a husband summons a psychiatrist to examine his wife, who, he claims, is excessively jealous; or that a district attorney summons a psychiatrist to examine a defendant who, he maintains, is mentally unfit to stand trial;

or that a newspaper editor asks a group of psychiatrists whether a candidate for public office is mentally fit for it. What will be the effect if the psychiatrist calls any of these persons "paranoid"? I need not belabor the answer.

If Senator Goldwater can be diagnosed as suffering from paranoid schizophrenia, which renders him suicidal and homicidal—and can be diagnosed so easily, with so much assurance, and by so many psychiatrists—what chance does an ordinary citizen have when a label like this has been pinned on him? How can he gain his freedom from a mental hospital, private or public, civil or criminal, where he may be incarcerated for no reason other than this "diagnosis"? How can he assert his right to trial, taken from him because of this diagnosis (made, possibly, by psychiatrists retained and paid by his adversaries)? Again, the answers are painfully obvious.[18]

VII

Human behavior is almost infinitely plastic. Potentially, man is capable of learning to speak hundreds of tongues and performing a great variety of roles. One of the functions of culture and tradition is to narrow this vast potential freedom. Soon after birth, the child is exposed to influences that channel his capacities; he is discouraged from indulging in some forms of behavior and encouraged to engage in others. Like soft clay, behavior becomes molded and assumes various shapes. This is most evident in primitive culture: a man becomes a hunter and warrior; a woman, a wife and mother. Such behavior is, of course, highly predictable. Somewhat less obviously, similar processes also operate in more highly developed cultures.

The need to classify behaviors and persons is an important manifestation of this process. Terms like "waiter," "shoe salesman," "stenographer," and "judge" not only classify occupations but also define role-expectations. To the extent that they do, they constrain conduct and render it predictable.

[18] Szasz, T. S.: *Law, Liberty, and Psychiatry: An Inquiry into the Social Uses of Mental Health Practices* (New York: Macmillan, 1963).

We find support for this thesis in several quarters. One is our everyday language. The term "to pigeonhole" is a synonym for "to classify," and expresses the imprisoning of something elusive in a tight little space, where it may be easily located. I submit that one of the essential functions of classifying people is just this: to "imprison" them.

People may be constrained in two basic ways: physically, by confining them in jails, mental hospitals, and so forth; and symbolically, by confining them in occupations, social roles, and so forth. Actually, confinement of the second type is more common and pervasive in the day-to-day conduct of society's business; as a rule, only when the symbolic, or socially informal, confinement of conduct fails or proves inadequate, is recourse taken to physical, or socially formal, confinement.

Let us see how this process of informal, or symbolic, confinement works. An excellent model is the armed forces. There are a group of people in the service—I shall call them "classification officers"—whose task is to assign each recruit to a specific duty, such as clerk, cook, machine gunner, or mechanic. In this way, each man is imprisoned in a role. If he remains in this pigeonhole and proves, by good performance, that he belongs in it, he is rewarded; if he tries to break out of it, either by poor performance or outright flight, he is punished. Thus do we all, the classification officers of everyday life, classify and control personal conduct.

Some may claim that this is not true in civilian society. True, the pigeonholing is not as crude. But it is carried out nevertheless. The role of the classification officer, entrusted to a few individuals in the army, is now diffused over all of society. The need to assume specific roles—to choose one occupation or another, to marry or remain single—is impressed upon the individual by the combined weight of "social opinion." Everyone must be "somebody." The one thing one cannot be is *unclassified*. The person who is too eclectic in his choices and conduct, and does not fit into one of society's pigeonholes, becomes the object of suspicion and hostility. By refusing to conform to a stereotype, he remains an individual. Much as we may like individualism as an abstract ethical idea, we tend to dislike individuals. This is because we are often baffled by them: we cannot understand their behavior and, what is even worse, cannot predict it. Frequently, such an individual is regarded as a threat to others.

VIII

The institutional psychiatrist's role in society is comparable to that of the classification officer in the army. In the public mental hospital, it is his task to classify the people brought there. Such a psychiatrist has a practical problem: he needs to know how different "patients" will behave in the hospital; also, how they should be "treated," to effect certain kinds of behavior change in them. What he cannot tolerate—and let us keep this clearly in mind—is uncertainty. The ostensible diagnosis of mental patients is covertly, and sometimes even explicitly, also their prognosis.

As we have seen, we usually identify and classify personal conduct to help us predict it. In the ordinary course of events this process of pigeonholing conduct is so firmly established, and functions so smoothly, that we are completely unaware of it. We become cognizant of it only when it breaks down. Even then, our awareness is fleeting: no sooner do we recognize the problem than we obscure it by creating a new class of behaviors —the class known as mental diseases. Let us see how we do this.

When people perform their social roles properly—in other words, when social expectations are adequately met—their behavior is considered normal. Though obvious, this deserves emphasis: a waiter must wait on tables; a secretary must type; a father must earn a living; a mother must cook and sew and take care of her children. Classic systems of psychiatric nosology had nothing to say about these people, so long as they remained neatly imprisoned in their respective social cells; or, as we say about the Negroes, so long as they "knew their place." But when such persons broke out of "jail" and asserted their liberty, they became of interest to the psychiatrist.

In human rather than psychiatric terms this is how the individual, now a suspected mental patient, and the psychiatrist, his diagnostician, confront each other.

The waiter refuses to wait on tables. He sits in the back of the café and scribbles endlessly on scraps of paper. When asked what he is doing, he either scowls condescendingly and refuses to answer, or confides to friends that he is writing a treatise on philosophy that will save the world. He is taken to a mental hospital by the police.

The mother presents a different picture. She sits dejectedly and cries. Occasionally she paces the floor and exclaims that she is unworthy to live. Her husband takes her to a doctor, who commits her to a mental hospital. A few days after admission, she whispers in the ear of one of the attendants that she is the Holy Virgin.

I have cited these vignettes of "psychiatric cases" to illustrate that people like this are called "mentally sick" mainly because they behave in ways in which they are not supposed to behave. We may look upon such persons as individuals who have discarded one social stereotype only to assume another, like the prisoner who digs a tunnel to escape from jail and ends up in another cell. In other words, the "psychiatric patient" is a person who fails, or refuses, to assume a legitimate social role. This is not permitted in our culture, nor, for that matter, in any other culture. A person unclassified is unpredictable and not understandable, and hence a threat to the other members of society. This is why people who choose this path to personal freedom pay dearly for it: although they succeed in breaking out of their particular cells, they do not remain long at liberty. They are immediately recaptured, first symbolically, by being classified as mentally ill; and then physically, by being brought to the psychiatrist for processing into formal psychiatric identities and for psychiatric detention.

Confronted by persons like these, what can the psychiatrist do? As behooves any good classification officer, he classifies them. Some he calls "schizophrenics," some "manic-depressives," some "hysterics," and so forth. The essential purpose of this type of psychiatric classification is strategic: first, to separate those who require or warrant admission to the mental hospital from those who do not; and second, to separate those who are willing and able to co-operate with the managers of the institution from those who are not. Clearly, this kind of classification serves solely the interests of the psychiatrists. It does not help the patients, nor is it intended to. The reason for this lies not in some moral defect in the psychiatrist, but rather in the situation: one cannot be a classification officer without classifying. The psychiatrist who assumes this role is like the judge: he must pass public judgment on other people or relinquish his role.

As classification officer, the psychiatrist fulfills important functions for both the mental hospital and the society he serves. Above all, he legitimizes and defines the institution as a "mental hospital," in which only mentally sick individuals are confined. Psychiatrists often assert that there are no "normal" people in mental hospitals. Moreover, the public likes to be re-assured that no one is ever "railroaded" into such a hospital. Remarked a judge in Chicago: "This is the only court where the defendant always wins. If he is released, it means he is well. If he is committed, it is for his own good."[19]

The difference in our attitude toward a finding of criminality and one of mental illness is instructive. In a criminal trial, the jury plays the role of classification officer: it decides who should be convicted and who acquitted. If the defendant is found guilty, he may be sent to prison. It is thus understood that prisoners are people who have been found guilty of a crime; and it is also understood that this "diagnosis" is a human judg-ment, not a natural event. A judgment is open to error. Rec-ognizing this, the law provides elaborate safeguards for detecting and correcting such errors.

In contrast, there is intense pressure today to regard mental illness as a fact, not a judgment. Thus, the assertion that there are no mentally normal people in mental hospitals is unlike the statement that there are no innocent people in jails. In-stead, it is more like the declaration that there are no French Impressionist paintings in zoos: by definition, the objects stored

[19] Quoted in *Time*, November 20, 1964, p. 76.

and classified in zoos are animals—not paintings. What I mean is that *in psychiatry the classificatory act functions as a definition of social reality.* As a result, no one committed to a mental hospital can be "normal," because his very commitment defines him as "mentally ill." This is like saying that if we should see a canvas by Renoir in a cage at the zoo, it *must* be an animal. Having defined all objects stored in such cages as animals, we can arrive at no other conclusion.

Surely, it cannot be an accident that all the great names in psychiatry, save Freud's and Adler's, belong to persons who had worked in state mental hospitals or similar institutions. Indeed, Kolle observes with pride that "Modern psychiatry traces its origins to institutional psychiatry. . . . Kraepelin, like all other nineteenth-century alienists, had served an apprenticeship in institutions for the insane."[20]

The chains removed from the insane by Pinel were re-attached by the great psychiatric nosologists. To be sure, the new chains conformed to modern hygienic and humanitarian standards: they were not made of iron, but of words; their ostensible aim was not to imprison, but to cure. But, as Emerson observed more than a century ago, "We die of words. We are hanged, drawn, and quartered by dictionaries. . . . It seems as if the present age of words should naturally be followed by an age of silence, when men shall speak only through facts, and so regain their health."[21]

Though Emerson's "diagnosis" was astute, his "prognosis" could hardly have been more mistaken. He believed that the semantic disease he diagnosed had reached a crisis, and that the patient was now on the road to recovery; but, in fact, what he saw was a mild malady that did not reach epidemic proportions until nearly one hundred years later. In Emerson's day, the real debauchment of language in the service of the enslavement of man lay neither in the past nor in the present, but in the future.

---

[20] Kolle, op. cit., pp. 2–3.
[21] Emerson, R. W.: "Apothegms" [1839], in Lindemann, E. C., ed., *Basic Selections from Emerson: Essays, Poems, Apothegms* (New York: Mentor Books, 1960), p. 173.

IX

I have argued that to classify another person's behavior is usually a means of constraining him. This is particularly true of psychiatric classification, whose traditional aim has been to legitimize the social controls placed on so-called mental patients. However, if one person wants to constrain another, it is necessary that he have the power to do so. If what I have said about psychiatric classification is true, we should find such classification imposed more often on the poor and helpless than on the rich and powerful. And this is precisely what we do find.

In our society, there are two types of membership that may be foisted on people against their will: criminality and mental illness. These classes differ from those in which membership must be sought or may be declined by the prospective member. It is also true that the incidence of criminality and mental illness is highest in the lower classes, and lowest in the higher classes. There is a cynical saying: a person who steals five dollars is a thief, but one who steals five million is a financier. The reason is obvious: it is easier to constrain the petty thief than the influential financier. The same is true for the human events we call mental illness. The problem that sends the rich woman to Reno is likely to send the poor woman to the state hospital. When the butcher, baker, or candlestick maker thinks that the Communists are after him he is easily dispatched to the mental hospital; when a Secretary of Defense thinks so, who will constrain him? These examples illustrate that to make a psychiatric diagnosis of a person is to constrain him. But how can the weak constrain the strong?

Many of these ideas are not new. For example, Sartre has expressed the view, in his writings as well as in his life, that to categorize a person is to constrain him. He observed that the essential difference between a thing and a person is that a thing does not react to the attitude we have toward it, whereas a person does. "It is not accurate to hold," he wrote, "that the 'id' is . . . a thing in relation to the hypotheses of the psychoanalyst, for a thing is indifferent to the conjectures which we make concerning it, while the 'id' on the contrary is sensitive to them when we approach the truth."[22]

Emphasizing the "ceremonial" nature of what we call social roles, Sartre also noted that the role is an essential limitation on personal freedom: "There are indeed many precautions to imprison a man in what he is, as if we lived in perpetual fear that he might escape from it, that he might break away and suddenly elude his condition."[23] Perhaps this fear is caused not so much by our anxiety lest the role-occupant escape his condition as by the dread that we will be unable to classify him. Loss of identity has been viewed as if it were a threat only to the person concerned. But it is also a threat to those who witness his performance: They are faced with an actor who plays a role they do not comprehend in a play they cannot identify. At this, the audience panics: It arrests the actor, declares his role illegitimate, and imprisons him in a mental hospital until he is willing to play roles that the audience can recognize.

In principle, any assigned role, not only that of the mental patient, may be experienced as a constraint. Even the role of a Nobel prize winner! This, as I understand it, was Sartre's reason for refusing the prize. "I don't align myself with anybody else's description of me," he told the correspondent of *Life* magazine. "People can think of me as a genius, a pornographer, a Communist, a bourgeois, however they like. Myself, I think of other things."[24] In Sartre's view, then, any classification of a person without his consent is a violation of that individual's personal integrity, just as a surgical operation without his consent is a violation of his bodily integrity.

To be captured in a category, to be diagnosed as this or that kind of person, is here seen as an essential deprivation of personal freedom. And, of course, that it is. But most people find freedom too much to bear. They escape from it into the security of a *fixed identity*.

Yet, Sartre has an identity: that of the fearless thinker, for whom nothing is unthinkable. He states this in terms indis-

[22] Sartre: *Existential Psychoanalysis, supra,* p. 164.
[23] Ibid., p. 183.
[24] Quoted in "Existentialism." *Life,* November 6, 1964, p. 88.

tinguishable from Freud's: "I am not, as has been said, a pessimist; I am a person who tried to make people more lucid vis-à-vis themselves, and it is for this that I am disliked. I frighten people. I would say that the majority of people have always been afraid to think. Stendhal, in his time, wrote, 'all good reasoning is offensive'—that is still very much true."[25]

What is meant here by "good reasoning" is the refusal to accept conventional categories. Appropriately, Sartre wishes, as did Freud before him, to place himself in a category that is a metacategory: he constructs, scrutinizes, and reshuffles categories, but does not himself belong in any. In other words, man is a person only as the subject who categorizes; as the object categorized, he becomes a thing.

Sartre's refusal of the Nobel prize evoked a curiously sour comment in *Science*.[26] Described as an "atheist existentialist," his views were compared with Bergson's: "While Bergson is overtly antiscience, Sartre appears rather to accept the effect of science but ignores it." After a series of such vaguely critical comments about Sartre as a person and as a thinker, the article concludes with the following significant sentence: "It may say something about the transcendental qualities of science that nobody has felt constrained to turn down a Nobel prize in physics, chemistry, or medicine."[27]

This is a striking commentary on the differences between natural science and moral science, between the study of things and the study of men. Though I would hesitate before calling science "transcendental," it is true that natural science seeks to master the universe by means of accurate description and appropriate scientific strategy. The science of man cannot have the same goal and remain a morally dignified enterprise. Instead of aiming to control the object of its investigations, it must seek to set it free. To achieve this requires methods unlike those of the physical sciences.

[25] Ibid.
[26] Walsh, J.: "Sartre, J. P.: French philosopher is model of literary intellectual by two cultures definition." *Science*, 146:900–2 (November 13), 1964, p. 901.
[27] Ibid.

Indeed, in one crucial respect, the central problem of natural science is the opposite of that of moral science: though both seek to understand the objects of their observation, in natural science the purpose of this is to be able to control them better, whereas in moral science it is to be better able to leave them alone.

We noted earlier that however difficult it may be to classify things, it is even more difficult not to classify them: to suspend judgment and delay the act of classification. We may now supplement this by asserting that however difficult it may be to control men, it is even more difficult not to control them: to acknowledge their autonomy and respect their liberty.

x

I have been developing the view that to classify a person psychiatrically is to demean him, to rob him of his humanity, and thus to transform him into a thing.

At first glance, this view may appear nihilistic. It may be objected that, after all, there are variations in human behavior. Is it not irrational and anti-scientific to refuse to classify them?

Let me repeat: I do not question the "existence" or "reality" of differences in human behavior. To assert that John is depressed and James paranoid may be just as "true" as to assert that John is fat and James slim. But this is not our problem.

The problem that has plagued psychiatry and society and to which I have addressed myself here is not the existence or reality of diverse modes of personal conduct, but *the context, nature, and purpose of the classificatory act*. In other words, it is one thing to agree that Negroes have black skin, and whites pink; it is another, to call a Negro a "nigger" and accord him the inferior status appropriate to this label. I hold that the reality of behavioral variations is similar to the reality of variations in the pigmentation of the skin; and that, in general, psychiatric diagnoses have the same linguistic and social function as the word "nigger." Refusal to call Negroes by that name does not imply a refusal to acknowledge racial differences between blacks and whites. Likewise, refusal to degrade people by means of psychiatric diagnoses does not imply a refusal to acknowledge moral, psychological, and social differences among people. It only makes it more difficult for men considered mentally healthy to degrade and mistreat men considered mentally sick.

13 · WHITHER PSYCHIATRY?

Before offering speculations about the future of psychiatry, it seems appropriate to review some aspects of its recent past and its present status. I shall limit myself to American psychiatry and to its history since 1908.

I have selected 1908 as my point of departure because it was in that year that the Connecticut Society for Mental Hygiene was organized. Out of this group was formed, a year later, the National Committee for Mental Hygiene. By one of those curious coincidences that one occasionally finds in history, this year, 1909, also saw Freud's visit to Clark University, in Worcester, Massachusetts.

These two events, occurring almost at the same time and within a few hundred miles of each other on the eastern seaboard of the United States, symbolize, in my mind at least, the two major forces that were henceforth to shape American psychiatry: the mental hygiene movement and psychoanalysis. Let us look at each separately.

II

Founded and initally sparked by Clifford Whittingham Beers, the mental hygiene movement was a typical social reform movement. As is true of many such movements, its psychological leitmotiv was contempt for man—in this case, for the so-called mentally ill person. The basic premise of this movement is that the madman deserves help, indeed must be helped—whether he likes it or not; but respect he deserves not. To some, this view might seem harsh or unjust; I do not believe it is either. A few illustrations in its support should suffice here.

"An insane man is an insane man," wrote Beers, "and while

insane, should be placed in an institution for treatment."[1] One of the first and main objectives of the mental hygiene movement was stated to be "to work for the conservation of mental health."[2] And how was this lofty aim to be achieved? The first official business of the Committee "was the adoption of a resolution urging Congress to provide for adequate mental examination of immigrants."[3] This, I should like to remind the reader, was in 1912, when the inscription on the Statue of Liberty was not yet rendered into a historical relic by the immigration laws enacted after the First World War. How the mental health of prospective immigrants was to be improved by their exclusion from this country on psychiatric grounds is not exactly obvious.

Historically, the mental hygiene movement is a direct descendant of a larger intellectual-social movement whose "father" is said to be Saint-Simon, and which Hayek has aptly dubbed "the counter-revolution of science."[4] Briefly, the characteristics of this movement, and especially of the type of social science based on it, are: first, that the individual is regarded as object, rather than subject; second, that the individual is considered unimportant, whereas the group—whether it be the community, society, nation, or mankind as a whole—is considered supremely important; and third, that, in imitation of the physical sciences, the aim of social science (and psychiatry) is the prediction and control of human behavior. Inherent in this approach is a contempt for man as an autonomous individual: we thus witness the aspiration by a "scientific" elite to control the masses of mankind, whom they consider their inferiors.

The mental hygiene movement is a link in this ideological chain. Its founder, Beers, was contemptuous of man—especially if mentally ill or poor—and was implacably opposed to the idea that mentally deranged behavior was meaningful and under-

[1] Beers, C. W.: *The Mind That Found Itself: An Autobiography* [1908] (Garden City, N.Y.: Doubleday, 1956), p. 218.

[2] Ridenour, N.: *Mental Health in the United States: A Fifty-Year History* (Cambridge: Harvard University Press, 1961), p. 1.

[3] Ibid., p. 18.

[4] Hayek, F. A.: *The Counter-Revolution of Science: Studies on the Abuse of Reason* [1955] (New York: The Free Press of Glencoe, Paperback Edition, 1964).

standable. To him, such behavior was just as senseless as cancer or pneumonia. It was as simple as that. It is not surprising that this view found favorable reception among the leading medical figures of the time. Indeed, Beers intended that it should: the mental hygiene movement was a movement *for* mental patients, *not by* them: Its organizers and leaders were psychiatrists and medical administrators. Their aim was to control mental patients —not to understand them.

This point of view has continued to attract many followers. Indeed, it may be more powerful today than at any time in American psychiatry. I shall cite only a few highlights in its later course.

In 1924 the American Orthopsychiatric Association was founded. Its formation was initiated by Karl Menninger, who sent a letter to twenty-six psychiatrists urging them to participate in establishing a new organization of "representatives of the neuropsychiatric or medical view of crime."[5] Thus, criminal behavior, too, was no longer to be treated as essentially human and understandable, but rather as "sick" and, as such, having causes rather than reasons. The name "orthopsychiatry" is itself suggestive, pointing to the arrogant belief that a group of physicians is entitled to undertake the "straightening out" of the "crooked" behavior of a group of their fellow men.

The medical view of "mental illness" as well as of all kinds of behavior thus became the hallmark of the mental hygiene movement. In true Saint-Simonian style, this posture was defined as essentially metaethical—beyond and superior to "morals." In his influential book *The Human Mind,* published in 1930, Karl Menninger expressed this view as follows: ". . . the declaration continues about travesties upon *justice* that result from the introduction of psychiatric methods into courts. But what science or scientist is interested in *justice?* Is pneumonia just? Or cancer? . . . The scientist is seeking amelioration of an unhappy situation. This can be secured only if the scientific laws controlling the situation can be discovered and complied with, and not by talking of 'justice,' not by debat-

[5] Ridenour, op. cit., p. 39.

ing philosophical concepts of equity based on primitive theology."[6]

In retrospect, it seems clear that few people took seriously
the moral implications of this position. Even today, the similarities between the "therapeutic" morality of mental hygiene
and of totalitarian politics are curiously neglected.

By the time the Second World War broke out, the image
of the psychiatrist as a utopian social engineer was well
established and strongly supported. (The voices of dissent were
few and barely audible.) An article by Harold D. Lasswell,
published in 1938, exemplifies how the psychiatrist and the
social scientist were exhorted to trade understanding for control,
truth for power:

". . . the most far-reaching way to reduce disease is for the
psychiatrist to cultivate closer contact with the rulers of society,
in the hope of finding the means of inducing them to overcome
the symbolic limitations which prevent them from utilizing their
influence for the prompt rearrangement of insecurity producing
routines.

"So the psychiatrist may decide to become the advisor of
the 'king.' Now the history of the 'king' and his philosophers
shows that the king is prone to stray from the path of wisdom
as wisdom is understood by the king's philosophers. Must the
psychiatrist, then, unseat the king and actualize in the realm of
fact the 'philosopher-king' of Plato's imagination? By grace of
his psychiatry, of course, the modern philosopher who would
be king knows that he may lose his philosophy on the path to
the throne, and arrive there empty of all that would distinguish
him from the king whom he has overthrown. But, if sufficiently
secure in his knowledge of himself and his field, he may dare
where others dared and lost before."[7]

The gospel that men like Menninger, Lasswell, and others
were preaching was arrogant and grasping: they claimed that
Lord Acton's famous phrase should be amended to read: "Power

[6] Menninger, K. A.: *The Human Mind* (New York: The Literary Guild of America, 1930), p. 428.

[7] Lasswell, H. D.: "What psychiatrists and political scientists can
learn from one another." *Psychiatry*, 1:33–39, 1938; p. 34.

corrupts, and absolute power corrupts absolutely—except psychiatrists."

During the Second World War psychiatry was enlisted to help the war effort. Understandably, perhaps, it placed the welfare of the group over that of the individual.

In recent American psychiatry, there are two important developments: psychopharmacology and community psychiatry. Each carries with it its own moral and philosophical judgments about the nature of man and human relations.

III

Inherent in the psychiatric interest in psychopharmacology is a desire to control human behavior—in this instance, by means of chemical agents that "energize" and "tranquilize." But let us ask: How are these drugs actually used? What are the implications, not of their pharmacologic effects, but of their social uses?

In the first place, like other substances considered medically dangerous, most of the new psychopharmacologicals are available to patients only when prescribed by physicians. The use of tranquilizers thus supports the medical credentials of psychiatrists; it does this, moreover, just when these credentials are, because of a previous strong identification of American psychiatry with individual psychotherapy, badly frayed. Whatever might be the effects of modern psychopharmacologicals on so-called mentally ill patients, their effects on the psychiatrists who use them are clear, and unquestionably "beneficial": they have restored to the psychiatrist what he had been in grave danger of losing—namely, his *medical identity*.

"How else could the use of these drugs be regulated?" someone might counter. Our traditional medical practices with respect to drugs constitute a strong precedent for the new psychopharmacological agents. I recognize this. But the argument in favor of strict medical control of drugs is not as simple as it may seem at first glance.

In a modern society individuals can regulate and control their behavior in at least two basic ways: first, by learning certain skills, like driving a car, or by purchasing certain substances, like alcohol; second, by placing themselves under the control of a person, like a physician, or an institution, like the Catholic church.

In the first instance, the individual makes use of impersonal aids, such as drugs; in the second, of personal assistance, such as a therapist. With minor exceptions, the modern state leaves the individual free to act as he chooses in the former area, but regulates his conduct in the latter (for example, by licensing members of the healing professions). It is by no means obvious why all drugs that affect the "mind" should be treated by the law as if they were "dangerous" narcotics.

The sole reason cannot be that such drugs are potentially injurious to the user: so are automobiles, cigarettes, guns, and a host of drugs and chemical agents available to the public. Nor can the reasons be that the effects of psychopharmacologicals are specifically "medical," and that for this reason they can be taken safely only under medical supervision. To be sure, this may be true for *some* of these drugs. But many other substances that are far from harmless are available without medical supervision (for example, vitamins A and D, household sprays of DDT, lozenges of penicillin, and so forth; these are as easy to obtain as alcohol—with, at most, a warning on the label that medical supervision is advisable for the habitual user). Is it then so far-fetched to contemplate placing the responsibility for the safe use of drugs, including those that influence behavior, in the hands of the user, rather than upon the government or the medical profession? The lessons of Prohibition may well apply here.

Moreover, because of the nature of psychiatric practice, drug control inevitably affects people in a twofold and paradoxical fashion. On the one hand, many persons who might benefit from self-medication—and thus avoid both the economic cost and social stigma of assuming the role of psychiatric patient—cannot do so, because they cannot obtain the drugs. On the other hand, many persons who do not wish to be drugged—for example, patients committed to mental hospitals and others treated involuntarily—cannot refuse being tranquilized into submission.

This paradox flows logically from the fact that once a procedure is socially accepted as "psychiatric treatment," it may be imposed on involuntary patients. Accordingly, regardless of the alleged medical-psychiatric merits of these drugs for the treatment of mental illness, whenever a person is given such a drug against his will, it is because those in charge of him wish to alter his behavior. Whether or not this alteration will subsequently be considered beneficial by the subject is another matter. Despite its medical appearance, we face here the same moral dilemma as that posed by the justifiability, or lack of it, of coerced religious conversion.

Let us leave the problem of government controls over the use of psychopharmacological agents by posing two questions: What kinds of rights and obligations, of freedoms and responsibilities, should adult citizens have for the use of drugs? And, if we deprive persons of the availability of certain drugs, and hence of the responsibility for their proper use, how do we affect individuals and society?

IV

Community psychiatry, the newest fad of the psychiatric ideologist, complements and reinforces the posture of a drug-oriented, quasi-medical approach to human problems.[8] Under the protective coloration of this label, the mental health professional becomes an unabashed moralist. As such, his values are clear: collectivism and social tranquility. As with the early Saint-Simonians and their later disciples, from Comte through Marx to Pavlov and Skinner, the individual should be allowed to exist only if he is socially well adapted and useful. If he is not, he should be "therapized" until he is "mentally healthy"— that is, uncomplainingly submissive to the will of the elites in charge of Human Engineering. The aim of community psychiatry is to transform our poorly functioning society—beset by such manifestations of "mental illness" as poverty, juvenile

[8] See Szasz, T. S.: "The mental health ethic." This volume, pp. 25–48.

delinquency, political strife, and the assassination of a President and then of his alleged assassin—into, to paraphrase Skinner, a Walden Three, the Psychiatrically Healthy Society.

But I want to do more than criticize this scientistic utopia. I want to call attention to the authoritarian and collectivistic ethic of community psychiatry, and to the coercive, controlling social roles of the psychiatrists who support it.

However much the advertisers of community psychiatry strain to make their program appear novel and radically different from traditional mental hygiene, the two are but variations on a single theme. It cannot be an accident that the same persons and organizations that supported the mental hygiene movement and its therapeutic triumphs in the past—that is, insulin coma and electroshock in the 1940s and the tranquilizers in the 1950s—now advocate community mental health centers as the latest "breakthrough in psychiatric research."

The essential aim of community psychiatry is social rehabilitation of the mentally ill—that is, conversion of a social misfit into a socially useful citizen. The basic methods are those of traditional psychiatry—social control through ostensibly medical measures.

All this, I submit, is neither new nor good. The community psychiatrist simply picks up where the mental hygienist leaves off. Writing in 1938, when the mental hygiene movement was preparing to "celebrate its twenty-ninth anniversary," Kingsley Davis sagely observed, "Mental hygiene possesses a characteristic that is essential to any social movement—namely, that its proponents regard it as a panacea. Since mental health is obviously connected with the social environment, to promote such health is to treat not only particular minds but also the customs and institutions in which the minds function. To cure so much is to cure all."[9]

Nearly thirty years have passed since Davis was moved to observe, "Mental hygiene turns out to be not so much a science for the prevention of mental disorder, as a science for the pre-

9 Davis, K.: "Mental hygiene and the class structure." *Psychiatry,* 1:55–65, 1938; p. 55.

vention of moral delinquency. . . . Mental health being defined in terms of conformity to a basic ethic, the pursuit of mental hygiene must be carried on along many fronts. Also, since the fiction of science is maintained, the ethical character of the movement can never be consciously and deliberately stated—hence the goals must be nebulous and obscurantist in character."[10]

The actual function and purpose of the mental hygienist, according to Davis, follow from what he does: he "enforces in a secular way and under the guise of science the standards of the entire society. . . . Thus the diffuseness of the mental hygiene goal is integrally related to the hygienist's actual function. Mental hygiene can plunge into evaluation, into fields the social sciences would not touch, because it possesses an implicit ethical system which, since it is that of our society, enables it to pass value judgments, to get public support, and to enjoy an unalloyed optimism. Disguising its valuational system (by means of the psychologistic position) as rational advice based on science, it can conveniently praise and condemn under the aegis of the medico-authoritarian mantle."[11]

Insofar as mental illness presents itself as a social problem, it is—among other things—an expression of human freedom: in this instance, the freedom to "misbehave," to break personal and social rules of conduct. The desire to correct such misbehavior and thus replace social disorder by social order is hardly new. Comte, as Hayek reminded us, asserted, ". . . the purpose of the establishment of social philosophy is to reestablish order in society."[12] In Comte's day the behaviorist despot wore the mask of the "social physicist"; today, he wears the mask of the public health physician—working for the "mental health" of the community, the nation, the whole world.

The essential point of the community mental health approach is the emphasis on the supreme value of the collective; to this value, the individual, if he is to become and remain "mentally healthy," must subordinate himself. This, of course, was the

10 Ibid., pp. 60–61.
11 Ibid., pp. 64–65.
12 Hayek, op. cit., p. 182.

essential thesis of the Fourierists and Saint-Simonians. To Fourier, the couple—man and woman together—constitute the true social individual. To Comte, the very concept of individual rights is "immoral"; his aim is to create a new social order in which such rights would disappear, and would be replaced by social duties.[13] The early French utopian socialist, the Soviet psychiatrist, and the American community psychiatrist thus strive after the same goal: to "cure" the disorderly free individual by "teaching" him to become a socially integrated and useful member of society.

But who shall say what is socially useful behavior? Growing tobacco? Advertising cigarettes? Providing federal subsidies for tobacco growers?

And who shall say what is socially integrated behavior? Marrying at eighteen? Having more children than one can properly care for? Or who contributes more to society: the whiskey-manufacturer or the prohibitionist? The demonstrator for disarmament or the nuclear scientist?

And what of the pressures that many societies exert on some of their members (in our case, on the Negro and on the elderly) to be not integrated into society, but just the opposite—to be segregated from it?

My point is simply that any kind of plan for a "sane society" confronts us with fundamental moral problems about the quality of human life. Attempts to solve such problems by taking recourse to the ideology of mental health are at once naive and dangerous.

v

I have viewed American psychiatry of the past half century as a tapestry woven with two types of thread: one is the neurologic-medical approach to mental illness, which, combined with the custodial, has become our contemporary community psychiatry; the other is psychoanalysis, which, together with the work of many modern psychotherapists and students of man,

[13] Ibid., p. 183.

has become our quest for a science of moral man, or for a moral science. Having reviewed the history of the former, we are ready now to examine the latter.

Freud's work received early recognition in the United States. In 1909, he gave his famous series of lectures at Worcester. In 1911, the New York Psychoanalytic Society was founded. It was the first one formed after the Viennese Society, preceding by many years the formation of analytic societies in Berlin, Budapest, Zurich, London, and elsewhere.[14]

The initial influence of psychoanalysis on American psychiatry was as clear as it was strong: it was individualistic and liberal (in the classic, libertarian—not the modern, interventionist—sense). It moved the psychiatrist away from viewing the mentally sick man as a patient, and toward viewing him as a fellow man; away from viewing him as medically ill, and toward viewing him as morally striving, and hence as psychosocially deviant or rebellious; and, perhaps more importantly, away from trying to control and suppress a person's conduct for the benefit of society, and toward trying to understand and liberate the individual so that he would be free to make responsible choices for his own benefit.[15]

This individualistic-humanistic orientation was, unfortunately, burdened by the deterministic-mechanistic superstructure of classic Freudian theory. It was burdened still further, in the United States especially, by an increasingly rigid medical affiliation of organized psychoanalysis; this has resulted not only in the repudiation of non-medical analysts as full-fledged practitioners of psychoanalysis, but also in a consistent slighting of the moral, philosophical, and psychosocial *meanings* of personal conduct, as against its instinctual and genetic *causes*.

By the end of the 1920s American psychoanalysis had succeeded in excluding non-physicians from the ranks of those who could be trained in psychoanalysis. In the 1930s it made strong

[14] Oberndorf, C. P.: *A History of Psychoanalysis in America* (New York: Grune & Stratton, 1953).

[15] See Szasz, T. S.: *The Ethics of Psychoanalysis: The Theory and Method of Autonomous Psychotherapy* (New York: Basic Books, 1965).

efforts to become reintegrated into medicine and psychiatry, a goal that was crowned with near-success during the Second World War. Since then, a slow but progressive mutual disillusionment has set in, bringing this marriage of convenience to the brink of divorce. Apparently, more and more analysts are beginning to recognize that it may have been a political mistake and a scientific disaster to sacrifice psychoanalytic integrity for medical prestige. Recently some members of the American Psychoanalytic Association took some halting steps to re-embrace a few carefully selected lay analysts.[16] For American psychoanalysis, however, this may well be a case of "too little, and too late."

In short, because of the scope and nature of contemporary American psychiatry, and because of the social forces that impinge upon it, its future course may take one of two general directions. One, though seemingly forward, toward Science, would actually carry it backward, toward the social scientism of the Saint-Simonians; the other, though seemingly backward, toward Moral Philosophy, would actually carry it forward, toward a science of man as moral being. Let us examine each of these possibilities.

VI

The attempt to explain and control human behavior "scientifically" is surprisingly recent. It originates with the French philosophers of the eighteenth century, especially with Condorcet, Saint-Simon, and Comte. As early as 1783 Condorcet stated, in astonishingly modern terms, the credo of the positivist social scientist: ". . . a stranger to our races, [he] would study human society as we study those of the beavers and the bees." His advice to the student of man was ". . . to introduce into the moral sciences the philosophy and the method of the natural sciences."[17]

16 "Report of the Ad Hoc Committee on a Proposal of Special Membership." *Journal of the American Psychoanalytic Association,* 12:856–57, 1964.

17 Hayek, op. cit., p. 108.

With the French Revolution safely out of sight, and with Napoleon as the model of the enlightened and "rational" ruler, Saint-Simon did not hesitate to announce, in the early years of the nineteenth century, the political aim of Social Science: the establishment of an intellectual-scientific elite as the ruler of France, and indeed of all of mankind. At first, in 1803, he proposed a "Newtonian Council" to be composed of twenty-one scholars and artists, to become, in their collective capacity, "the representatives of God on earth."[18] But this was not "scientific" enough. Saint-Simon went on to insist "that the physiologists chase from their company the philosophers, moralists, and metaphysicians just as the astronomers have chased out the astrologers, and the chemists have chased out the alchemists."[19]

Sobering words, these. They reveal the social origins and contexts of the scientific ideals and moral aspirations of the modern neurophysiologist who tries to understand anger by studying the temporal lobe, and of the research psychiatrist who tries to cure schizophrenia by studying neurohormones. However, today we can no longer indulge ourselves in the luxury of merely praising or condemning those who propose to study man as if he were an animal.

Man *is* an animal; of this there can be no doubt. Accordingly, his body, and especially his brain, determine a great deal of his behavior. Contributions to our understanding of the bodily *causes* of man's behavior will thus remain valuable additions to our scientific knowledge of nature—that is, of man as animal. This will be so until we have as complete an understanding of the machinery of the human body as we have, for example, of the chemical structure of sodium chloride, or of the physical functioning of the electron tube. This day is nowhere in sight. It seems likely that a good deal of work that we now consider psychiatric will develop along these lines, and will serve to augment our understanding and mastery of our bodies. Whether such work ought to be called psychiatric is a matter of semantic convention.

18 Ibid., p. 120.
19 Ibid.

We are concerned here, however, not only with scientific understanding, but also with its practical use. Though physics and chemistry are sciences, their uses pose moral problems where the practical application of physical and chemical knowledge affects human beings; the same is true, of course, of biology and the social sciences, except that in these disciplines, especially where the objects studied are men, the separation between abstract knowledge (theoretical science) and practical application (engineering) becomes indistinct. Thus, the question is: How will a psychiatry that is biologically more sophisticated affect human beings?

I do not know the answer. But I do know that we have no guarantee that those who possess such knowledge, or who feel deeply about its importance, will use it to enhance the moral quality of human life. There remains a fundamental logical dichotomy between man as person and as thing, and a corresponding moral dilemma of using science for or against the self-defined interests of the individual. We have seen the uses and abuses of Reason and Science before, and are likely to see them again. How will a psychiatry preoccupied with the physico-chemical basis of behavior, and with its social control, fare in terms of moral values? We have, I think, grounds for concern.

Here is an example of the kinds of dangers that may befall us, perhaps on an ever-increasing scale. In the initial decades of this century much was learned about epilepsy. As a result, physicians gained better control of the epileptic process (which sometimes results in seizures). The desire to control the disease, however, seems to go hand in hand with the desire to control the diseased person. Thus, epileptics were both helped and harmed: they were benefited insofar as their illness was more accurately diagnosed and better treated; they were injured insofar as they, as persons, were stigmatized and socially segregated.

Was the placement of epileptics in "colonies" in their best interests? Or their exclusion from jobs, from driving automobiles, and from entering the United States as immigrants (note here the similarity with one of the first aims of the National Committee for Mental Hygiene)? It has taken decades of work, much of it still unfinished, to undo some of the oppressive social effects of "medical progress" in epilepsy, and to restore the epileptic to the social status he enjoyed before his disease became so well understood. Paradoxically, then, what is good for epilepsy may not be good for the epileptic.

The fate of the epileptic is not isolated. It illustrates the moral bias of the medical view of man: persons are fully acceptable only if healthy; if sick, they must strive to recover, or be penalized.

For the future of psychiatry, as the medical discipline most intimately concerned with the regulation of human behavior, these considerations point to a particular danger: under the guise of a health ethic and the protection of the medical profession, psychiatry may easily become an all-powerful social force for regulating human behavior. The influence of the mental health ethic on children is already considerable, and is likely to grow with the increasing penetration of psychiatry into the public schools. Its influence on adults is no less and is also growing—as penal authorities, business executives, and university administrators increasingly delegate the task of social control inherent in their positions to psychiatrists in their employ.

Again, the early history of social science is instructive. In Revolutionary and post-Revolutionary France, the exponents of Reason and Science first celebrated individual liberty and human dignity—then their opposites, the "scientific" organization of communal life and social usefulness. The transition from the one to the other required less than a generation.

The danger I speak of is not new; it has long been recognized by economists, historians, and political scientists. Indeed, much of what I have said is merely an extension of their views into psychiatry and the mental health disciplines. In particular, men like Friedrich Hayek, Ludwig von Mises, and Karl Popper have warned of the dangers of historicism and scientism in human affairs.[20] Recently Floyd Matson adumbrated their thesis and

[20] Hayek, F. A.: *The Road to Serfdom* [1944] (Chicago: Phoenix Books, 1957); Mises, Ludwig von: *Human Action: A Treatise on Economics* (New Haven: Yale University Press, 1949); Popper, K. R.: *The Open Society and Its Enemies* [1945] (Princeton: Princeton University Press, 1950).

Szasz's ideology prevents and limits his apprehension of the social — still atomistic/economic man

noted its relevance to psychology and psychiatry. Speaking about Saint-Simon and Comte, he observed, "The comprehensive attempt to apply scientific method to the rationalization of human conduct—what might be termed the first systematic program of behavioral engineering—turned out to be, not a dispassionate and positive science of behavior, but a wholly passionate and negative campaign to make men behave."[21] And he concluded, ". . . In the hands of its most devoted missionaries, the natural scientists of behavior, this faith in social and political physics has produced with impressive regularity the vision of a techno-scientific future . . . and with it a corresponding image of man—manipulated and managed, conditioned and controlled—from whom the intolerable burden of freedom has been lifted."[22]

So much for the possible future of a collectivistic-scientistic psychiatry—committed to valuing the community above the individual, and to regulating human behavior by drugs and medical penalties rather than by personal conscience and legal sanctions. Whatever such a psychiatry might be called, it would be the handmaiden of a closed and ordered society, as was envisioned by Saint-Simon and Comte. We have seen the Social Physics of eighteenth-century France, with its view of the individual as a social atom, spawn the totalitarian regimes of the twentieth century, with their views of the citizen as the obedient servant of his political masters. What began modestly as medical psychiatry in eighteenth- and nineteenth-century Europe, with its view of man moved by physicochemical processes inside his brain, may yet become, perhaps in the United States, a tyranny based on neurological scientism and psychoanalytic historicism.

VII

It is also possible, however, that psychiatry will develop along individualistic and libertarian lines. Or it may split into two distinct disciplines—one collectivistic and devoted to enslaving

21 Matson, F.: *The Broken Image: Man, Science, and Society* (New York: George Braziller, 1964); p. 52.
22 Ibid., p. 115.

man, the other individualistic and devoted to liberating man.

The roots of an individualistic and libertarian psychiatry are shallow and tender. As against the tradition of alienists and psychiatric nosologists, like Kahlbaum and Kraepelin, the exemplars of this humanistic spirit in psychiatry are Sigmund Freud, with his deep commitment to understanding "mentally disordered" behavior and avoiding coercion, and Wilhelm Reich, with his passion to liberate man from his fetters, whether these be forged by his upbringing or by his political masters. The direction of this psychiatry is clear, though its movement is slow and halting: first, away from medicine and toward psychology; then, away from psychology and toward a study of man in society—that is to say, toward a study of the individual, with a past and a future and an inescapable moral commitment to himself and others.

When psychiatry is accepted as a discipline concerned with the study and control of personal conduct, it has no special relevance to medicine. I believe, therefore, that psychiatry should neither cloak itself in the mantle of medicine, nor use its semantic and social status scientistically. In the long run, it is as much in the interest of the medical profession as of the psychiatric profession and of the public to distinguish clearly between medical science and medical (psychiatric) scientism. Medicine is a natural science. Psychiatry is not; it is a moral science.

Accordingly, a possible—and, I believe, desirable—development of psychiatry would be to deepen the separation between itself and medicine. The result would be a non-medical—not an anti-medical!—discipline, equally open to physicians and non-physicians interested in the study of man and in psychotherapy.

What might be some of the practical consequences of such a change? At present, it is possible for a physician to be certified in Psychiatry or in Neurology; however, there is only one specialty Board for both. This is an historical anachronism. I suggest, first, a separate Board for Psychiatry; second, a similar type of professional certification for the psychotherapist; and third, equal recognition of the medical and of the non-medical psychotherapist.

Let us recall here that only in this century—and even then only incompletely—has psychiatry become a specialty separate from neurology and internal medicine. Freud and his early followers created a new profession—first a medical specialty, then a discipline outside the medical fold. But despite Freud's warning that psychoanalysis needed protection "from the doctors,"[23] the psychoanalytic counterrevolution overtook his movement. Today psychiatry, psychoanalysis, and psychotherapy are all ambiguous enterprises, precariously balanced on an invisible ledge between medicine and the social sciences, sometimes proudly claimed by both, sometimes angrily repudiated by both.

Although some of the theories of psychoanalysis may have been made to serve the aims of social engineering, its practice could not become wholly anti-individualistic. It is, therefore, to psychiatry proper, rather than to psychoanalysis, that we must look for the principal changes. I would consider it desirable if psychiatry would clearly separate, and then split away from, neurology and medicine. In a rudimentary and publicly unacknowledged way, such separation exists today between psychotherapy and medical practice. But it is not enough. Further changes in psychiatric practice are necessary.

The change that I consider most important is in the psychiatrist's social role and moral commitment. His social position vis-à-vis his client should be clearly defined: Does he represent the interests of the patient (as defined by the patient) or of others (the patient's family, society, and so forth)? Is his moral commitment to autonomy or heteronomy, to individualism or collectivism?[24]

[23] Freud, S.: "Letter to Pfister, November 25, 1928," in Meng, H. and Freud, E. L., eds., Psychoanalysis and Faith: The Letters of Sigmund Freud and Oskar Pfister, transl. by Eric Mosbacher (New York: Basic Books, 1963), p. 126.

[24] See Szasz, T. S.: "The moral dilemma of psychiatry." Amer. J. Psychiatry, 121:521–28 (Dec.), 1964.

In their extreme forms, these roles are often well enough recognized; but this does not prevent a particular psychiatrist from assuming one role one minute, and another the next. One role is that of the classic psychoanalyst, who is solely his patient's agent: he accepts payment from his client in return for a service that aims to promote the patient's interests. The other role is that of the "police" psychiatrist, who is solely the agent of the patient's adversary: he accepts payment from the police or the district attorney's office, in return for a service that aims to incriminate and injure the so-called patient.[25] Between these extremes is the hospital psychiatrist, who is supposed to care for involuntary patients and at the same time protect the community from them.

A separation of these roles is no longer difficult to imagine. It might result in a situation of the following kind: the psychiatric profession, like the legal profession, might remain a single discipline; its practitioners, however, would be split into two major categories, and perhaps several lesser ones. The distinction would be similar to that in the legal field between prosecution and defense. This division of functions would reflect the fact that the practicing psychiatrist is usually the agent of one party and the antagonist of another. I advocate a clear social recognition and professional codification of this situation. This would mean that just as a man charged with a crime would not consider retaining the district attorney to defend him, so a person "charged" with "mental illness" would not consider retaining a psychiatrist whose loyalty is pledged to parties with whom he is in conflict. The nature of the psychiatric profession and of psychiatric practice would thus be redefined.

Two types of psychiatrists would develop: "defense psychiatrists" (or, for short, D-psychiatrists), and "prosecuting psychiatrists" (or, for short, P-psychiatrists). Their functions are not new. What would be new is the consistent and publicly acknowledged performance of their respective roles. Let us review the essential features of each.

[25] See Szasz, T. S.: *Psychiatric Justice* (New York: Macmillan, 1965), especially Chap. 3.

VIII

The D-psychiatrist, like the defense attorney, is a private practitioner. He is sought out by his prospective clients, whom he is free to accept or reject, and who, in turn, are free to accept or reject him. Although some important aspects of such a professional relationship are controlled by the expert, its most important characteristics are (and, indeed, ought to be) controlled by the client: specifically, the client determines the ultimate purpose the professional help is to serve, and, as a rule, controls the initiation and termination of his relationship with the expert. This is rendered possible, and is at the same time symbolized, by the commercial character of the relationship; like the defense attorney, the D-psychiatrist is paid for his services by his clients, and his economic well being depends, in the last analysis, on delivering the service for which the clients contract. In short, the D-psychiatrist, like his legal counterpart, is an expert "for hire" by some parties—often to harm others: for example, the attorney Jones retains to sue Smith for damages tries not only to help Jones, but also to harm Smith. Similarly, the D-psychiatrist who accepts as his patient a man whose main problem is marital discord may "help" the husband, but "harm" the wife (or vice versa). Though this fact is common knowledge among psychiatrists, it is avoided as an embarrassing defect in psychiatry, rather than calmly acknowledged as a necessary part of a psychotherapeutic method whose aim is personal autonomy and dignity.

The prosecuting psychiatrist's role is also plain enough. But it is even less clearly articulated or accepted. Indeed, a description of this role is often considered defamatory of psychiatrists and of the psychiatric profession. This role is performed by a group of persons, who, like the district attorney, function mainly in institutional practice. The "clients" (if they can be called such) of the P-psychiatrist do not seek him out, nor is he free to accept or reject them. The clients are involuntary, and would, if left free, have nothing to do with him; this is obvious in the relationship of the criminal and the district attorney, and is equally true of the relationship of the involuntary mental patient and the psychiatrist. The P-psychiatrist enters into professional contact with his client by virtue of the power he has over him. He is paid not by his "client" but by an institution, usually an agency of the government. Furthermore, the P-psychiatrist's role is more narrowly defined than that of the D-psychiatrist. As the district attorney must, by and large, limit his work to prosecuting criminals, so the P-psychiatrist must, by and large, confine himself to protecting the interests of society from those of the "accused" mental patient.

The D-psychiatrist, like the attorney in private practice, is an independent professional. He may be hired for psychoanalysis, marital counseling, hypnosis, breaking a will, and so forth —just as his legal counterpart may be retained for defending a client from a criminal charge, suing for divorce, preparing a will, and so forth. In contrast, the P-psychiatrist, like the district attorney, is a professional employee, usually of the state. As such, he is a part of a complex bureaucratic organization, with all that this implies for his relations to his clients, whether they be voluntary or involuntary.

Considerations such as these point to intimate connections between economics and politics on the one hand, and psychiatry on the other. Clearly, the D-psychiatrist can exist only in capitalist countries, and his work will be valued to the extent that economic and personal freedom are valued; whereas the P-psychiatrist has a place in both capitalist and socialist countries, and his work will be valued to the extent that economic planning and the security of society are valued.

Should the future of psychiatry lie along the lines I have sketched—that is, progressively away from medicine and the natural sciences and toward politics and ethics—I venture to predict a further development. The separation of the work of the psychiatrist into the two large categories outlined above will be merely the beginning of a much more pervasive trend toward the precise delimitation and classification, not of psychiatric illnesses, but of psychiatric performances. The more the so-called mental patient will be restored to the fully human stature that is rightly his, the more will attempts to classify him —at least in ways we are now accustomed to—appear not only unnecessary, but harmful or even criminal. Having become a self-determining client, the mental patient will want to select psychiatric experts for specific tasks. For this, a classification of experts, not of clients, will be needed.

IX

As I discussed earlier,[26] classification—whether of plants or animals, medical or psychiatric patients, physicians or lawyers —always serves some practical, strategic purpose. What is the purpose of classifying a person as a psychiatric patient, and, specifically, as phobic, depressed, or schizophrenic?

The avowed aim of this kind of classification—and by this I mean the officially declared aim of the psychiatrists who engage in such categorization—is to identify the patient's "illness" so that it can be treated in the manner best suited to combat the specific affliction: in short, the overt aim of psychiatric classification is said to be the same as that of medical classification.

The actual aim of psychiatric classification—and by this I mean the aim of such categorization inferred from its actual consequences—is to degrade and socially segregate the individual identified as a mental patient; in short, the covert aim of psychiatric classification is social stigmatization and the creation of a class of justifiably persecuted scapegoats.

In regard to the alleged similarities between classifying a person as medically ill (for example, afflicted with peptic ulcer) and as psychiatrically ill (for example, afflicted with schizophrenia), we must not be misled by the fact that in both cases a diagnostic label (or at least something that looks like one) is attached to an individual. Although a person in search of medical care may, in the end, be diagnosed as suffering from a particular ailment, in his role as prospective patient he acts much like any client seeking expert assistance: that is, he forms

26 Szasz, T. S.: "Psychiatric classification as a strategy of personal constraint." This volume, pp. 190–217.

a concept of his need, and—in accordance with this judgment and his means to command the help he wants—he selects the expert whose service he wishes to enlist. When in need of medical assistance, some people thus go to the emergency room of a nearby hospital; some make an appointment with their physician; others travel to a famous medical center; while still others have a group of world-renowned specialists flown to their home. Additionally, the prospective patient may choose to consult a general practitioner rather than a specialist, or an osteopath, chiropractor, or faith healer rather than a qualified physician.

The individual beset with personal problems has a similar choice (provided that he has not yet been cast into the role of involuntary mental patient): he may seek help from a general practitioner, a clergyman, a lawyer, a social worker, a neurologist, an organic psychiatrist, or a psychoanalyst (the complete list is, of course, much longer). This list may seem to offer enough choice. Actually, it does not—and for several reasons. One is that the precise activities of the various "mental healers" are rarely defined by their practitioners and hence cannot be known to their clients; another is that there are usually no clear limits on what the experts are allowed to do, or what in fact they might do. Hence the clients are insufficiently protected from acts they deem to be against their best interests. One of these acts is invidious psychiatric labeling and involuntary mental hospitalization with consequent compulsory "treatment."

The involuntary psychiatric patient is in a radically different situation from the voluntary medical patient: whereas the latter can select his physician, can reject his physician's diagnosis (if he disagrees with it), and can sever his relationship with the diagnostician, the former can do none of these things. This imposition of a diagnostic label on an individual, without his consent and against his will, is one of the most important practical differences between medical and psychiatric diagnoses.

Because of these facts about the nature and consequences of the psychiatric diagnostic process, clients seeking help for problems in living will have genuine choices among alternative courses of action only after two requirements will have been met: first, the actual practices of various "mental healers" must be specified and made public; second, limits on these practices must be clearly defined and legally enforced.

X

If what I have said about the tactical character of the psychiatric diagnostic process is true, it follows that before we can have a radically different system of classification *in* psychiatry, we must have a radically different aim *for* psychiatry.

The Kraepelinian aim, never clearly abandoned (even by Freud), was to classify *patients*. Such a scheme makes sense only if we, the classifiers, intend to do something *to* the patients, the objects of classification: for example, if we wish to commit them or "treat" them.

However, there are many situations in modern psychiatry in which the psychiatrist need not have, and in fact does not have, such an aim. The private psychoanalytic, or psychotherapeutic, situation is the paradigm case: feeling distressed or troubled, a client seeks the aid of an expert to help him master his problems in living. The situation between such a client and his therapist is totally different from the one between a psychiatrist in a mental hospital and a person who is there against his will. Yet the private psychotherapeutic situation is not at all unusual: indeed, it is comparable to that between persons in various types of difficulties and the experts whose help they solicit.

Consider, for example, the person in trouble with the income tax authorities who consults a tax lawyer; or the person unable to get along with his wife who consults a divorce lawyer; or the person accused of a crime who consults a defense lawyer. Each of these lawyers has a problem, but that problem is not to classify his client in terms of guilt or innocence. Similarly, the psychiatrist consulted by a voluntary client has a problem, but, again, that problem is not to classify his client in terms of mental illness or health. What attorneys in these situations actually do will help us clarify what psychiatrists serving self-determining clients ought to do.

The attorney faced with a person seeking help for his problem with the Bureau of Internal Revenue need not classify his client as guilty or innocent of income tax evasion. That is a problem for the employees of the Bureau or for a jury. The lawyer's first task is to decide whether or not to accept the troubled person as his client. Once he accepts him, his task becomes more or less *defined by his client*: he must help the client achieve his goals, or, if that seems impossible, he must discuss with the client the advisability of modifying the goals. In the case of income tax difficulties, the client's goal will be to pay as little tax as possible while staying out of jail; he enlists the aid of an expert to help him select the strategies best suited to attain this goal, and pays him for this service.

The husband seeking a divorce, and his attorney, are in a similar situation. It would be unnecessary, and possibly ruinous, for the attorney to pass moral judgment on the husband: it is not his task to diagnose him as a good or bad husband, a suitable or unsuitable mate for his wife. This is not what his client is paying him to do. Should he persist in exercising such a "diagnostic" skill, he is likely to lose his client, and his practice as well. What, then, is his task? To help his client obtain a divorce on terms most advantageous for his client. If the attorney does not wish to perform this service, he is free to reject the husband as his client.

Let us reappraise the psychotherapist's role in this light. Why should he classify his patient as mentally sick or healthy, as hysterical or schizophrenic? He has no need to do so. First of all, the therapist must decide whether or not to accept the person seeking his services as his client. (The grounds for this decision are complicated and vary among therapists. This subject need not be discussed here.) Once he has decided, his task is not to classify the client (of what possible use could this be to the client?)—but rather to help him attain his goals. This requires a co-ordination of the goals and strategies of client and psychotherapist.

I maintain—and I hope this discussion has supported it—that psychiatrists need to classify persons as mental patients (in the traditional fashion or in accordance with some modification of this basic style) only if they wish to treat them as objects or things. This attitude or urge is not necessarily malevolent: mental patients are often treated as children or senseless bodies because they are considered unfit to care for themselves, and are therefore considered the wards of their families, society, or psychiatrists. In sum, if all adults (including so-called mental patients) are considered responsible individuals and the agents of their own destinies, then people who consult psychiatrists need not be classified psychiatrically.

However, people cannot conduct themselves as responsible individuals unless they live in a more or less manageable environment. Physically, this means that man cannot usually survive under conditions of extreme physical hardship—in the arctic or the desert. Sociopsychologically, it means that man (as person, not as organism) cannot usually survive under conditions of extreme psychosocial hardship—in the concentration camp or the mental hospital. Man's survival as person depends in large part on his opportunities to make informed choices. In order to make such choices, his social environment must be properly labeled. If, because of inadequate or misleading labeling, he cannot distinguish between rat poison and aspirin, he will be unable to care for his physical health; and if, because of inadequate or misleading labeling, he cannot distinguish among various experts whom he may consult for help with his personal problems, he will be unable to care for his so-called mental health.

Accordingly, to provide for the psychological needs of the responsible adult, we require a classification not of mental illnesses, but of expert services. Indeed, with the singular—and significant—exception of the mental health field, this type of classification prevails in all situations where clients must seek out and purchase expert services.

In the practice of law, for example, the objects of classification are not the attorney's clients, but the nature of his work. We thus have attorneys who specialize in corporation law, criminal law, divorce law, labor law, tax law, and so forth. Organized psychiatry is amazingly hostile to a similar division of labor among psychiatrists: the psychotherapist unwilling to use drugs or to commit patients is regarded not as a professional person exercising judgment over his own interest and competence, but as one who refuses to shoulder the onerous responsibilities of a messianic healing art.

This view signals a depressing and tragic situation. For it is a measure of the extent to which psychiatry has abandoned the liberal-rationalist values of science and the open society, and instead has committed itself to their counterrevolutionary antithesis, the illiberal and irrational values of scientism and the closed society.

XI

I have discussed the conflicting trends in psychiatry, both past and present. They are reflections of the waxing and waning of a basic thesis and its antithesis: of individualism and freedom as the great revolutionary ideas of Science and Mercantilism, and the equally great counterrevolutionary ideas of collectivism and order, the characteristic features of Scientism and Social Utopianism. Having reviewed, from this point of view, the recent history and present status of our discipline, what shall be our estimate of its future?

In forecasting the future, we must distinguish between short-term and long-term predictions. For the short term, our safest bet is to ride the trend: if the weather is hot today, expect it to be hot tomorrow. Applying this rule to psychiatry, we might expect a continuation of the present trend—that is, an extension of the scope and power of a collectivistic and scientistic psychiatry.

For the longer term, however, knowledge of the prevailing trend is of less value: the trend might continue, change direction, even reverse itself. Indeed, in social and political affairs, opposing trends often follow one another, in a spiraling dialectic of antagonistic ideologies and policies. It is idle, therefore, to speculate about the precise course of human events in the distant future. We should be satisfied with knowing the alternatives, one or another of which might prevail. J. P. Morgan's famous estimate of the future course of the stock market was, "It will fluctuate." Psychiatry, too, is likely to fluctuate, between the ideologies of individualism and collectivism, between protecting the citizen from the state and the state from the citizen. Which of these trends will prevail at any one time will depend partly on the cultural climate of the time, and partly on the intellectual and moral commitments of the individual psychiatrists whose daily work constitutes, in the last analysis, the practice of psychiatry.

INDEX